THE IMAGES OF MAN

BERNARD G. ROSENTHAL

Basic Books, Inc., Publishers

NEW YORK   LONDON

© 1971 by Bernard G. Rosenthal
Library of Congress Catalog Card Number: 79–135555
SBN 465–03200–1
Manufactured in the United States of America

TO JUDITH

and the creatures

from the wild lagoon,

No. 1 and No. 2

PREFACE

❧

This is a book on the future of psychology as it is on the future of man. For just as the current of the times moves to change institutions and behavior, so is psychology exploring new frontiers of knowledge about man and rediscovering, at the same time, neglected qualities in him. Perhaps it is these emerging institutions and social forces shaping these "new" dimensions of man that call for a new psychology, one divorced from the traditional, positivistic, mechanized, and unchanging concepts of human nature in imitation of those physical phenomena whose behavior it was presumed was also always the same. Or perhaps the openness of the times, the fatigue and failure of the old solutions, the emptiness of the once invigorating materialist values and objects has fostered a search for new human qualities with which to find new solutions for seemingly insoluble problems, for new types of human experiences to make life more meaningful and invigorating than it has become, and for new social practices and group processes to make institutional and collective life more reasonable and harmonious.

Out of the decline of this old order of behavior and institutions—and the search for a new one—has come an inevitable search for those basic endowments or principles out of which such an order may be found and which can, simultaneously, justify it. Such a trend is ongoing in psychology today, whether it occurs in humanistic psychology or is expressed in new trends in the traditional psychologies or in efforts to explore those aspects of men that heretofore have been little touched.

What distinguishes these new trends from those now preeminent in contemporary psychology are its humanistic orientations and its concern with so-called humanistic components of behavior. Indeed, such "new" forms of behavior and social arrangements whose precise "image" or pattern is not yet evident may be thought of as efforts to solve the exceedingly difficult problems of the lack of human fulfillment and harmony in

vii

modern society by the development of new levels of consciousness and of innovative problem-solving styles.

From these emerging forms of behavior and the value orientations that shape them may gradually be formed a new image of man. Just as the image of man of contemporary psychology reflects the present condition of man's behavior and the nature of the social institutions that have shaped it, so it is not impossible that a prospective "new" image of man will serve as a sanction, or "ideology," as I prefer to call it, for "new" or as yet unacknowledged forms of behavior and social arrangements that may eventually appear. Just as the studies and data of contemporary psychology indirectly legitimize contemporary modes of behavior and social arrangements (and the often unacknowledged value systems and cultural attitudes that underlie them, i.e., its image of man) so it is not impossible that a new ideology, possibly with substantial components of humanistic values, may in time give scientific sanction to presently emerging or reacknowledged areas of behavior through researches generated by its own view of man's nature.

It is here that the past may give us some guideposts to the nature of these future images as well as pointing to the vast potentialities of man that stand in contrast with the quite narrow segments of behavior now studied in contemporary psychology. For the past, particularly that of the West from the Greeks to the Renaissance, together with the images of man that have crystallized its rich diversity of behavior and values, will doubtless have connections with humanistic behaviors now again being acknowledged as worthy of study. And because of their effective integration of such humanistic qualities into a viable and durable mode of conduct and experience, these "historic" images may set guidelines, or even become models, for the future orientation of behavior and social arrangements now emerging in the Western world as well as for the direction of research into their nature. Further, by studying the Western past it will be possible to grasp the genuine nature of these qualities as they have functioned under actual conditions of life rather than in atypical atmospheres or in rare and fragmented episodes.

It is, however, with demonstrating the vast unexamined potentialities of modern man that this study is primarily concerned. For by ignoring this wide reservoir of human capacity, contemporary psychologists have narrowly restricted their scientific vision and scope of research into man's nature. If a study of the Western past heightens their awareness of this rich potentiality, it will ultimately be to the benefit of a more balanced and comprehensive psychological science. Not only would such an exploration point to human qualities that were once extensively found, but also to the ways in which their present, if only latent, existence could be scientifically demonstrated.

The images of man which capture and distill these potentialities reflect significant aspects of a society's behavior and social institutions and, in addition, are sometimes represented in ideologies which justify their particular, if covert, values and attitudes. Either directly through a formal ideology or more obliquely through particular ideas and cultural themes, these images will affect or permeate the psychology of a given period—presuming the existence of such a discipline at the time. Indeed, their spirit and values will often be directly expressed in a psychology's particular orientation and body of knowledge and, when opportune, will be supported by concepts and accumulations of data to give "scientific" credibility to its viewpoint. In this way, the psychology of a given period often serves to justify and sustain a society's prevailing image of man, and indirectly, the established behaviors and social institutions congruent with it.

Thus, significant areas in the psychology of a given society will reflect and even embody the orientations of its particular image of man. Specifically, it would do this in terms of the intellectual concepts or processes then prevalent and by the modes of proof then acceptable. In one society, these might take the form of enlightened essays and sensitive observations, in another of formal propositions and careful documentation, and in a third of clearly stated intuitions and naturalistic data. Such concepts and "proofs" would have the purpose of legitimizing significant aspects of the prevailing or ideal behavior of the society and its congruent image of man. Even in the most empirically oriented of societies, this purpose would, at least, be partially served, for however scientific the procedures and data of its own particular psychology, it might nevertheless have quite unconsciously selected certain areas or themes for its research interests or based its studies on only certain aspects of man's potentialities, leaving other vast areas quite unexamined.

It is with the object of throwing into prominence these crucial dimensions of man's neglected potentiality that this book is concerned. In doing so, possibly new links can be forged between the emerging images of man and the changing institutions of contemporary society, the exploration of his "humanistic" capacities now gaining momentum in psychology, and the wide range of his potentialities as they have been expressed in the Western past. In recognizing the rich human resources revealed in the course of this history—which have not yet been acknowledged in contemporary theory and research—it is not impossible that psychology's own image and consciousness of man will be enriched and extended, bringing it into truer balance with the full scope of human endowment.

I have a very great fund of indebtedness to acknowledge in the making of this book and do so conscious of the meagerness of words in this effort: To Gardner Murphy—who sustained my faith in it over so many years and, by doing so, also in the courageous Greek image I so admire, and whose help was so vital in the herculean task of finally bringing it to print—my debt is so great that nothing I might say here could adequately measure it; for his reading and rereading of the manuscript and for his innumerable fertile suggestions, whose frequent omission from the final version must be charged to me alone, my gratitude is immense. To Silvan Tomkins, for his continuous confidence and moral support of my efforts over the years. To Edoardo Weiss whose personal faith and wise and kind concern helped me to sustain my effort and fulfill the book's promise. These are a prominent few of my scholarly and spiritual debts.

Despite most difficult obstacles placed in the path of the book's completion by the nonhumanistic and inhibiting structure and atmosphere of the Illinois Institute of Technology, I am immensely grateful to Carol Barnes who, patiently, resolutely, and always with benignness and charm, typed and retyped the manuscript; to Belle Ellebrecht who indomitably supervised the final version through to typing completion; and to Professor Daisy Tagliacozzo, without whose intervention in the administrative machinery of IIT this book would not have been typed at all and who, in ways too numerable to mention, somewhat eased the rigidly oppressive burdens there in order to facilitate its completion.

Most of all, my spiritual and emotional debts are to my wife, Judith, and my children, Amy and Mark (the creatures of the wild lagoon), who are already represented in various of the book's humanistic images and to whom its dedication is but the smallest acknowledgment for the vast human riches they have given me.

BERNARD G. ROSENTHAL

Evanston, Illinois

CONTENTS

❦

THE
IMAGES OF
MAN

I

THE
RELATION BETWEEN
PSYCHOLOGY AND
THE AGE

❦

I

It is a truism in contemporary psychology that what a man sees in others is partially a reflection of himself. Not that this idea was not recognized and accepted before the present embellishments of depth psychology, and more recently positivistic psychology, have given it a scientific respectability. Indeed, in the past many writers advanced this idea and distinguished novelists of the last seventy-five years have dramatically documented it in their fictional works. So deeply has this concept become embedded in contemporary literature that, beginning with James Joyce's *Ulysses,* one of the common crafts of fiction has been the portrayal of the same individual or situation through the eyes of more than one of the main protagonists or as a reflection of the latters' changing moods.

If, with qualifications, modern psychology has accepted the tenet that perception of others and of events is in part an act of self-revelation of the individual, must it not also be partially true that a substantial part of its body of knowledge is similarly the self-revelation of the age that has provided the source materials for its collection? This idea, of course, is nothing more than the thesis of the sociology-of-knowledge school, but

3

in certain respects it has a unique significance for psychology. This may be so not only because the findings of contemporary psychology must be based on present-day individuals—and these are the materials of and, indeed, the age itself—but also because the criteria of evaluating them, the judgment of which issues are important for investigation, and even their conceptualization and conclusions are often based on the same forces that actuate the behavior and values of the individuals themselves. Whether or not the thesis of the sociology of knowledge (i.e., that the types of theoretical formulations and forms of knowledge prevailing in an area of intellectual discipline at any given historical period reflect the salient values and ideology of that period and can rarely transcend them) is more germane for psychology than for other fields is a moot question. There are substantial reasons for believing this to be true and particularly so in that area of psychology that has to do with human behavior at the molar level, i.e., personality, social psychology, perception, intelligence, etc. This is the case not only because the very materials out of which psychology is made are the individuals who constitute the age, but also because their observers and investigators, i.e., the psychologists themselves, are of the age too. And, indeed, to accurately comprehend their human materials, they must particularly participate or share in a goodly number of the age's values and behaviors.

Another compelling reason for this belief lies in the very nature of those areas of psychology that have to do with molar individual or social behavior. To comprehend this "nature" demands a uniquely human and empathic act of apperception, however abstracted or intellectualized this may ultimately become in theory or in research formulations, and this act must be based on certain prior assumptions of value, norms, and socialization provided by the society. It is very largely in this way that sympathetic rapport and communication can be achieved with the objects of psychological study (persons) with whom, in some degree, the psychologist's act of judgment and apperception must have some common base of understanding or identity. Hence this act with its potential power to "sense out" and "communicate with" some of the qualities of other persons embodies values and assumptions of the society from which it is largely derived and, further, shares in certain respects some of the features of the persons toward whom it is projected.

Healthy psychological development and normal acts of psychological judgment presuppose the satisfactory internalization of values of the society to some degree as a condition of healthy adjustment. Because most psychological work and research is done by individuals who have implicitly accepted the values of the society and whose development reveals

4

a degree of reasonably adequate tolerance or adjustment to it, one must conclude that the norms that are involved in this tolerance and adjustment and that permit psychologists to make prudent psychological judgments about individuals in their society must be drawn from the "spirit" and norms of that society itself. If they were not, then the evaluating psychologist would either (1) have not actively accepted the values of the society and, in part, not be in a position to judge or advise its members by its commonly held standards; or (2) be confused and in conflict about these societal values himself with consequent personal stress; or (3) openly reject these values and therefore not fully be in a position to sympathetically understand or facilitate psychological adjustment of others based on compliance or internalization of them. Indeed, the very nature of psychologically perceptive judgment requires an empathic and internal acceptance (at some level) of goals, value complexes, or norms of behavior that betray the values and "spirit" of the society or the age. These common value and behavioral assumptions may be adjustment, success, competition, getting along, striving, etc., but in whatever form they may be expressed (making a living, marriage, rearing of children, etc.), empathy with such values is a sine qua non for thorough psychological understanding. This is truer, doubtless, when the psychologist's role is not only understanding but also therapy, and, indeed, the two frequently become deeply intertwined.

It is also true that any act of psychic understanding must assume some affinity of spirit or commonality of values with the person or the processes assessed. To grasp the difficulties of individuals, to evaluate tests, to understand group behavior, and to measure intelligence, an implicit assumption must be that there are some shared values or types of mutual agreement regarding the processes, dynamics, and goals of the behavior in question. Indeed, to work insightfully in certain fields of intelligence, personality, or group behavior, an implicit comprehension or tolerance, if not acceptance, of the main societal values and norms interwoven with these psychological functions is required for purposes of assessment or even research. The measurement of intelligence or personality is premised on this status quo conception of assessment in terms that reflect the spirit of the society, and the successful "measurer" must either sympathetically or objectively accept these standards in order to complete his task successfully. In short, he must—if not empathically, then at least intellectually—concur in the accepted social standards and their related psychological capacities required for adjustment, which, indeed, are the only ones he can utilize if his own work as a psychologist is to be judged useful by these same standards. In fields involving explicit criteria of achievement, such as industrial, military, or vocational psychology, there is less difficulty in seeing the imperative of accepting prevailing societal values as the criteria of psychological truth. It is, however, in the traditional academic fields where the relation between value issues and the research orientations toward socially sanctioned and socially unacknowledged psychological processes is more obscure that a careful examination of all cultural, social, and moral attitudes must be made in order to see the interweaving between them and the type of psychological theory, research, and knowledge that emerges.

Not least important among the ways psychological work becomes a mirror for the spirit of the times is the compelling fact that the materials for psychological findings and theory are neither more nor less than the individuals of the culture. It is perfectly obvious, as a consequence, that the findings of psychology can be neither more nor less than what these individuals are. If they are shallow, the findings of psychology will reflect this together with the weight of scientific generalization; if their intelligence is mechanistic, the "laws" of psychology will identify intelligence with this type of mechanistic cognition. Not only do their capacities, attitudes, and values place restraining limits on the nature of psychological theory and knowledge but the investigations designed to describe and measure their psychological "reality" must be attuned to this "reality" and so inevitably reflect its limitations in breadth and emphasis.

The scientific description of this "psychological reality" is conventionally carried out at the present time on the basis of the frequency with which a "given" psychological datum occurs. This, in turn, becomes the source of appropriate scientific generalization. This procedure, also, has a practical economic basis, for the more subtle and less frequently found psychological qualities are more difficult and expensive to identify and not so profitable to exploit in applied and practical enterprises. Thus, they stand in contrast to the data or qualities most frequently observed, which, correlatively, have the largest economic or practical value in mass society and which, also, become the materials of evaluation in psychological work, the substance of much psychological testing or research, and the source of goodly amounts of theory. Thus, the most common features of the psychological character of an age, i.e., its most manifest characteristics or most easily ascertainable traits, become the basis for scientific results and generalizations.

This tendency is particularly augmented by the economic organization of contemporary society with its emphasis on mass production and consumption. To sustain this economy it is necessary to determine what the preferences of mass publics are—or to mold these preferences in prescribed directions—so that the large-scale production of goods and services will be facilitated. Because the success of large-scale economic enterprise will be much affected by the tastes and preferences of these mass publics, it is essential to ascertain their social and psychological characteristics in that, directly or indirectly, such qualities will determine what particular products will be consumed or what appeals must be made so that they will be purchased. Hence, by determining what mass publics will consume on the basis of their psychological dispositions, it may also be possible to ascertain which products will make a profit and which will not. Thus the preoccupation with the study of the highest frequencies of psychological traits and behavior (and thus of their lowest common denominators) is not unrelated to their function in maintaining the present economic system and in specifically facilitating the largest acquisitions of profit in the mass market of goods and services.

The foregoing economic and psychological patterns also dovetail nicely with one of the conspicuous features of the code of positivistic science. For the psychological characteristics that are presently studied have a ubiquity that is one of the conditions of admissibility to scientific generalization as well as a concreteness and manifestness (by virtue of their simplicity, recognizability, and measurability) that makes them easily statable in operational terms, amenable to positivistic research, and applicable to practical affairs. And this, in turn, provides an assurance of control and prediction that further qualifies the obtained findings as meeting the conditions of rigorous scientific admissibility.

If one were inclined to look for the economic and social values correlated with this concrete and quantitative approach, one might find them in the amassing of money or things as salient goals of modern society. One could argue that a search for scientific laws based on statistical frequencies of a superficial psychological order corresponds not only to an orientation underlying the accumulation of quantities of money or possessions but also is related to a cultural emphasis on popularity or, if preferred, on accumulations of social capital. All these factors have a remarkable congruence with the determination of the highest frequencies of traits and behaviors characteristic of the statistical, or "normative," orientation of contemporary psychology and reflect, in turn, the mass ideology of present society.

Indeed, the character of this statistical concept of "normality" is not unrelated to the inventorizing of such trait "frequencies" for the appraisal of an individual's behavior or to the appraising of a man's property and his other credits to determine a tangible denominator of his "worth" or "value." Note the economic origins or connotations of the latter two terms.

So it is that the determination of the greatest statistical occurrence of human qualities or behavior in society is consistent with a comparable appraisal of human "assets" in particular individuals when they present their psychological or monetary resources for approval *by* society. Such "frequency" implies, too, a concern not with the unique, actualizing, or self-determining characteristics of men but rather with the more practical, socially manifest, and economically expedient dimensions of behavior which also happen to be its most common denominators. Consistent with this orientation is the nature of contemporary mass markets (mass production and mass consumption) where the most successful products (popular and profitable) are those that appeal to the greatest possible number and hence to the most common social and psychological denominators of mass publics.

Similarly, commonly held characteristics or traits are appraised and esteemed, like all mass-produced materialistic objects, for their surface visibility, quantity, and concrete or practical values. If quantity, practicality, and concreteness are salient values in a materialistic and money-oriented society, it is clear that the most expedient, concrete, and visible psychological qualities will be those most desired by reason of their ease of identification and measurement (in accord with positivistic requirements), their facility for interpersonal meshing or congeniality (conformity) with the largest possible number of other persons (for purposes of "getting along" and "selling oneself"), and their psychological compatibility with a mass-production system based on the turning out of a large number of standardized products. For this process to be profitable requires, in the general population, the widest activation and prevalence of those types of personal characteristics that would be receptive to (i.e., a market for) these concrete, commonly distributed, and surface-attractive products.

Thus the façade, visibility, and socially enhancing qualities of objects produced by the economic system for profit becomes equivalent to the superficial roles, traits, or socially expedient "fronts" [1] that human beings acquire in order to become receptive to these produced objects and thereby to sustain this system. In this way, the human being becomes the counterpart of or synchronous with objects and the handmaiden, as well, of the economic system that produces them. It is these qualities—paralleled in things and in behavior—that become socially valued and the preeminent object of psychological study.

In an analogous fashion, the number of approved traits that are possessed by a person is related to the amount of money or things that he can amass; their surface or superficial quality, which is socially esteemed and positivistically appraised, coincides with the "impression" that possessions and money make as visible reasons for winning prestige and approval. The "impressions" (superficial appearances) and quantity of these produced objects—not their intrinsic character, i.e., their functional, aesthetic, or human value—and what they represent as accumulations of possessions and money (or status) have their counterparts in the social impressions, or "fronts," of individuals as if the real human and scientific issues were not the existential and deep-lying trait qualities or the inner spirit of an individual person but rather his surface features and social façades. In this sense, the human being emerges as a role-playing object or puppet who displays trait-qualities that "show," that sell themselves, or that socially conform to each situation. Measurement directed to these processes is, in effect, attuned either to the model of a social robot or to a "possessor" of traits (the counterpart of things) which constitute the social credits (the counterpart of money) to gain acceptance in society and to thereby achieve a culturally approved personal identity and sense of inner worth.

However unproved this analysis may be, what is noteworthy is that this type of traffic in "mass and superficial data" that is easily measurable does often lead to deceptive and shallow conclusions, to static descriptions or what Lewin[2] has called phenotypical analysis, and to a tacit impression, thereby, that the most frequently found qualities of a society mark its true identity. In a very restricted sense, of course, this is accurate, but in a more significant vein it tends to ignore other features, sometimes as prevalent as the more manifest ones but not so amenable to current types of measurement or as responsive to facile recognition. In short, there will be a tendency to emphasize the most obvious qualities by this methodological approach in preference to what are, at least, equally significant features and thereby ignore the more subtle, sensitive, or profound human qualities and particularly those of an existential, intangible, or inexpedient nature.

The essential point in all this is that man is limited by his own feelings, values, and cognitive structure in appraising himself and others unless he performs an act of judgment transcending the limitations of himself, his culture, and his age. Psychologically, this has been in part done for the individual by psychoanalysis. Here the discovery has been that man is a captive of his unconscious childhood feelings, and until he grasps or surmounts their significance his perception of the world and of others will be colored or distorted by unacknowledged experiences and feelings.

By understanding those attitudes within oneself that influence the way one looks at the world, one may rectify the impact that the past has on how the present is perceived.

It is the contention of the pages that follow that just as psychologists must transcend their own personal histories in order to understand themselves, other human beings, and the realities of the world about them, so must they transcend the ideology and social values of the present age if they are to achieve a more objective understanding of the nature of man. They must be aware that these value assumptions as well as the very materials they work with, i.e., contemporary human beings, seriously limit the concepts they can develop in the field of psychology and tend to restrict psychological theory and research to those aspects of man's potentialities that are most saliently emphasized or valued by present society. Indeed, so influential may these value assumptions be that not only conceptualization but also the methodology of investigation and the substantive research areas themselves become interpenetrated and conditioned by them. The result is that a picture of man, or, as some prefer to call it, "an image of man," is drawn that portrays more a model of contemporary man in modern American society (as seen through the eyes of the generally nondissenting scientific representative of that society—the American psychologist) than a model of what man's full stature and genuine aspect actually is. It is a picture limited in scope to the perspective that present-day psychologists have of some facets of man and distorts other features and dimensions that are equally and significantly present in him.

How can the value assumptions that limit and predesign the image of man that emerges from contemporary psychological investigation and thought be surmounted so that there can emerge a more accurate and fully rounded picture of his resources as well as a more effective method of studying them. This is the perplexing problem that has troubled social scientists for some time. Some say it is best done by anthropological study, and this approach has merit, particularly if systematically and carefully applied in detailed psychological research.[3] Though there have been several studies along this line, the vast majority of the attributes and potentials of men have not been so examined. Even were the preliminary efforts in this area to fully evolve, there would still remain serious questions regarding the application of this work to the particular conditions involved in the psychological study of Western civilized man. For the central issue here is not the extraordinary diversity of man's character and behavior as it has been shaped under different kinds of aboriginal conditions but rather the degree to which modern psychology has given a false picture of the particular variety of mankind it has laid claim to scientifically investigate most fully, i.e., Western man.

Another method for transcending contemporary cultural ideology is cross-cultural comparison, and it is to the credit of American psychology that it has, in recent years, taken cognizance of this approach.[4] The advantages of cross-cultural comparison between highly developed literate and civilized societies are very great. If, for substantial areas of behavior, rough constancies of technology, ethos, and institutions must be established between the comparison cultures before the results of such analyses have much meaning, this does not invalidate the results obtained for other, and more primary, behavior areas, such as mother-child relationships, nuclear family dynamics,[5, 6] etc.

Needless to say, there are legitimate diversities in the methodological approaches and standards of admissible knowledge between the psychologists of different Western nations. Indeed, American psychology does not greatly countenance the methods and conclusions of French psychology or even of certain varieties of phenomenological German psychology, which based, in part, on different cultural values are often deemed "unscientific" or inconsequential in many American psychological circles. Thus it is not only different human populations but also various conceptualizations of issues and techniques of investigation that may yield different results. Even substantially similar contemporary Western societies which have different values and ideologies may give rise to quite dissimilar psychological perspectives with accompanying differences in their theories, methods, and results.

One of the most useful and relevant ways to transcend the narrow perspective on the nature of man that may be integral to contemporary psychology is through the study of what man has been in the course of Western civilization. The fundamental assumption of such an undertaking is that there has been a basic continuity of cultural tradition from the Hellenic age to the present that has formed the essentials of a distinctive Western mode of life and that this line of development has a unique quality which has differentiated it from other civilizations and has given us those unique features and traits that have come to distinguish Western culture.

Through this line of development, originating in goodly degree with the ancient Greeks, there has been woven a continuous fabric in the last 2,500 years in which there are embodied significant and consistent human designs. The Greeks, for example, contributed greatly to our present tradition and values, but each succeeding age in the Western tradition also elaborated its own unique version of this contribution. It is the contention of this book that by the pertinent study of these historical periods, commencing with the Greeks, we will more clearly illumine many of the latent, or even atrophied, qualities of modern man and will more clearly grasp what man has been in the past and what his present potentialities might be. To that extent we will also understand that contemporary man and contemporary psychology, in mutual interdependence, have presented a different picture of man's nature than that set forth by previous Western historical periods. By studying this continuity of cultural and behavioral tradition, which began with the Greeks, and examining what it has emphasized at different periods of its development as compared with its present-day focus, it will be possible to obtain an overall survey of the several "pictures" or images of man that have emerged in the West.

It is, then, through history that an awareness may be had of how contemporary values have influenced our conception and study of man and through history, too, that we can get some broader notion of how man has behaved and how his character has varied. By this kind of perspective we will also be able to see how our very methods and techniques of psychological research are conditioned by the prevailing values of our age and, to that extent, blind us to other research possibilities or block the search for other dimensions of man's behavior. In this sense, just as the sensitive examination of one's personal history (e.g., psychoanalysis) corrects our assessment of ourselves and others by clarifying our distortions in perception and judgment, so cultural history—by revealing the values and ideologies of other societies, the types of human beings and patterning of their behavior within them, and the particular methods and standards for appraising these that each society developed—may show how many current psychological methods and concepts are affected by the unacknowledged biases and values of the contemporary psychologist's experiences in his own society, reflecting as they do, the values, ideologies, and psychological character of that society itself.

But why turn to Western history rather than Eastern or primitive cultures for illumination of these unrecognized aspects of man? To answer, once more, there is a continuity of feeling, ideology, and institutions in the West, originating largely with the Greeks and flowing to the present that make European (and American) personality, values, and social institutions understandable and recognizable to us. This continuity makes any deviations from these values and behaviors credible and unexceptional in that they neither appear particularly exotic nor require explanation by special complexes of cultural circumstances, as in the case of non-Western, simpler, or "primitive" societies. Hence, variation in cultural type, personality, and social behavior can be more sympathetically understood as falling within the realm of man's understood or plausible potentialities and less likely attributed to unique, aboriginal, and radical conditions or as representing an irrelevant or alien line of development outside of our contemporary tradition. Indeed, it is entirely possible that these Western variations in behavior, already acknowledged as falling in the range of man's reasonable capacity, may reveal themselves at any time and, indeed, often do so when looked for. Equally important is the consideration that the way we view present-day behaviors, and the particular behaviors we view, account for the neglect of other types of human experiences that have prevailed during previous periods of Western history. Moreover, it is not impossible that by changing orthodox ways of perceiving, investigating, and conceptualizing present-day behavior or by shifting the conditions under which it occurs, "new" experiences and characteristics may emerge that would be more similar to those that appeared at earlier stages of Western history than they are to contemporary behavior and traits.

Some of the contentions advanced here are neither unique in the sociology of knowledge nor even in the chronicles of psychology. It has been documented by many writers that there is a close connection between the *Zeitgeist* and the psychological work of any given historical period. Thus there was a relation between English associationism of the nineteenth century with its view of mind as a series of mechanical connections wired up through experience and the highly interconnected and "wired up" production procedures of the new industrialism with its mechanized techniques and rigid bureaucratic structure. Not only was this "spirit" manifest in the economy of the period but also in the rigid Victorian behavior and morality, in the rules of binding contracts, and in the conventions of "proper" relationships and transactions. In short, the organization of social and personal experience, like a well-run factory, was in many respects similar to the doctrine of mental elements organized properly through experience into a functioning machine. This ideology also reflected the development of Newtonian mechanics in the practical applications of nineteenth-century physics.

Much of Watson behaviorism, too, is an extension of the doctrine of man as a machine without consciousness or moral direction, and hence is a rather vivid psychological reflection of industrialized, depersonalized twentieth-century man. Such a species of man, operating as a human machine in a mass production society, is valued largely in the economic terms of labor costs and production profit and is minimally appreciated for the unique manifestations of his personality. Indeed, he is valued for

13

his embellished consumption of goods, his tooled conformity to the bourgeois values of society, and his capacity to be motivated and "conditioned" by money and other drives or lubricants in much the same way as any engine requires fuel and oil to function effectively. Here we have the expression of the ideal of man as a depersonalized machine: a model designed by the industrial system of the day for its laborers to emulate by responding to controlled external stimulation with a stipulated goods-producing and mechanical response.

Indeed, such a model was emulated in an impeccable, mechanized mode of psychological experimentation with humans and in the aggrandizement of the laboratory as the locus for the study of behavior. Everything reminiscent of authentic human experience was studiously avoided, particularly if it interfered with the laboratory capsule as a rigorously controlled machine. Anything that could make the S feel at home in this laboratory world, instigate in him value orientations to it, give him a sense of purposive action and of comforting or passionate orientation in it, or inform him of the authentic or human meaning of his experimental experience, was excluded. What remained, if not through deliberation, was a sense of a robot, Kafka-like atmosphere, artfully mechanized, without human aspect or cognizance, and without genuine meaning, purpose, or fulfillment. Further, such elements of human potentiality and satisfying human experience as laughter, friendly conversation, delight, recreation, genuine experience, and intimacy were removed. What was ordinarily retained was a dehumanized milieu surrounding a nonhuman task and performed by a S who was stripped of his ordinary human dispositions, orientations, and frames of reference when he entered. This, of course, willy-nilly, *was* a value system, which, indeed, informed and influenced the Ss in their view of the "experimental" experience and in their feelings, perceptions, cognitions, and other reactions to it.

The issue, then, is not that such a mechanized, depersonalized situation is not valuative, for it is intensely so, though in the model of a past physical science and of a depersonalized Kafka-like bureaucracy. Rather the issue is whether different kinds of such "valuative" laboratory and research situations (whether explicitly or unwittingly derived from certain predetermined psychological or social models) have differing effects on men and on their existential commitments, causing them to behave significantly differently in each such "valuative" scientific environment. Consequently, only by first acknowledging and then studying these different value systems—each as authentically and uniquely embodied in its own particular research milieu or setting as the present-day dehumanized, positivistic value orientations are in theirs—will it be possible to better assess the range of men's capacities and potentialities. Too, we will then be able to determine if, with such diverse "valuative scientific" situations —whether in or out of the laboratory—men will behave in conspicuously different ways, manifesting aspects and segments of themselves that they are neither capable of nor disposed to exhibit in the mechanically valuative scientific situations they presently are asked to confront.

It is only, then, in different value-oriented situations and environments (experimental, naturalistic, historical, etc.) that the full potentials of men can be realized and displayed. It is such milieux that can stimulate him to mobilize the full range of his often latent resources and response potentials and to which he can, depending on his own personal values and capacities, make a genuine commitment. The commitment he may make, existential or not, is informed and propelled in large measure by the experiential reality of the environment he confronts, and if this reality is mechanical or dehumanized, then substantially, too, will be the commitment—whether conscious or unconscious—of congruent behavior patterns. Thus the very presence of such a "valuative" environment or situation—be it mechanistic, humanistic, pragmatic, etc.—may evoke a "valuative" behavioral orientation that brings in train a related system of latent and overt traits, value moods, cognitive orientations, purposes, and feelings that influence the subjects' specific behavior and experience in every way.

Thus, in this view, the value orientation implicit in *any* psychological situation or experiment does influence the nature and hierarchy of the behavioral systems evoked. To demonstrate this, it would have to be shown that for each value or ideological system there is a related configuration of behavioral and and experiential characteristics or, at least, a parallel direction or system of organizing human behavior and feeling. This may simply mean a particular way of looking at a situation (i.e., congruent with a specific ideology or value position), determining the experiences one would like to have in it and then mobilizing the behaviors and feelings that are consonant with the experiences. It may mean, too, the activation of heretofore latent parallel qualities or the elevation of previously low-priority corollary behaviors and experiences to preeminent responsiveness. Further, each such value-ideological complex (mechanistic, humanistic, pragmatic, etc.), as embodied in the naturalistic or research milieu in which the S confronts it, will exert its influence on him either (1) through his conscious awareness and deliberate commitment to the "value mood" of the situation or (2) through unconscious counterpart responses induced through a sympathetic resonance with it.

In past work so little value had been placed on the notion of man as a knowing, self-directed, aware person that the most relevant areas for study were exactly those that were most mechanized, most depersonalized, and, in a sense, least human, namely the physiological and motor areas. Indeed, even learning—the apex of the behaviorist's interest—was virtually seen as a recircuiting process in which more efficient connections might be advantageously set up for the purpose of smoother functioning. The human machine was to respond in efficient mechanical fashion when the cues were presented, and hence it did not have to be concerned with such experiences as consciousness, ideals, self-awareness, purpose, or other existential themes.

To this "electrical circuiting" was added—in order to account for the energy and propulsion of the system—the notion of animal drive. This provided the source or fuel that instigated the charges that went around the various "conditioned" circuits. This notion, derived in part from nineteenth-century biology and permeated with Darwinian and evolutionary ideas, was the analog of the "crass" motives that drove the business and social world of that day: profit, ambition, self-aggrandizement, materialism, and all other propellants of a sprawling capitalism. Here, then, was the energy that drove the machine: as primitive and simplistic in its biological way as the conception of the "mechanically circuited" man was in its own physical-model way. Again analogously, these models had a remarkable correspondence to the great economic forces that drove the industrial machine system of the nineteenth and twentieth centuries.

Both models of these biological and physical forces were, as has been intimated, similar in their elementariness: Both had a brute and concretely physical character—the reduction of all facets, subtleties, values, and purposes of human experience to tangible, material, and positivistic orientations. The man of that period was seen as a sort of biological machine: an animal with greed, meanness, cunning; a biological specimen whose drives, however, were properly calibrated with machine-like efficiency or craft in their pursuit of survival-oriented goals—money, material things, etc. Such was the power of the biological-physical model that it changed the image and study of man from the complex, balanced, informed, and valuating organism it had once been in the past. As this "past" view was swept away, the only identities allowed (existential or other) for the psychologist and his subjects were shifted to this primitive, biological-mechanical model—so well sychronized with the values and temper of the society that informed and oriented these investigations. As a consequence, what was to be discovered by the use of these models could not be the human complexity that had previously strongly influenced the study of man. Rather it was to be in line with this "new" image

16

of man—and all the research findings would be consistent with this image because, in effect, the experimental and research situations were cast in its mold, not easily allowing an alternative perspective or a different behavioral repertory to become viable. The subject was compelled, if he had already not been correspondingly socialized, to fit his own orientation, identity, commitments, and reactions to this image. So what was obtained from this model—as usual—was what was put in.

Many more examples might be given of the relationship between a society and its psychological concepts, and in those systems of psychology that antedated its development as a scientific discipline this is strikingly evident. The relationships, for example, between Plato's theory of the soul and the stratified society of Athens, Thomas Hobbes's conception of the nature of man and the fierce struggle between Church and state for power during the seventeenth century, and the compelling emphasis during the nineteenth century on the instinctive, aggressive nature of man and the dog-eat-dog jungle of the economic system are all indicative of the significant relationships between various theories of man and the social milieux from which they derived. And the thrust of the work in the "sociology of knowledge"[7] goes even further in relating economic, sociological, and political knowledge to the power sources of a society and in seeing social or psychological conceptions as merely a rationalization of various economic or political forces struggling to obtain power from those sectors of society already possessing it or, conversely, as an apology for power by those who already possess control. In philosophy, Bertrand Russell[8] and John Dewey[9] have shown the close relationship between various viewpoints in metaphysics, ethics, epistemology, and other branches of philosophy and the prevailing social values or spirit of the period during which these viewpoints were preeminent.

For a moment it may be fruitful to examine such an atmosphere or value system as it applies to one orientation in contemporary psychology, namely reductionism. This doctrine, more popular in the recent past than now, is still important in such fields as learning, thinking, perception, and physiological psychology and, in various lesser degrees, pervades many other areas of psychology. Despite Mach's [10, 11] oft-repeated dicta that classes of scientific events are equally valid and that reductionism, in certain cases, has no special merit, the vigor of these reductionistic efforts have continued in the area of various complex psychological functions. It is not only that the system for such analyses was enormously effective in the physical sciences during the eighteenth and nineteenth centuries but also that there is a close similarity between this type of scientific orientation and an image of man that represents him as a complex machine, ever-manipulable, severely compartmentalized, and effectively separated from values, personal destiny, and conation. Such a view, consistent with the manipulation of several variables in a gigantic experimental design, not only fits into the idea of a well-ordered society of machine-men and machines (also reflecting the desire of industrialists for efficient and undisturbed production) but, by analyzing the nature of man into such separate and minute elements, leads to the easy conclusion that he is nothing but a conglomeration of "parts" or molecular constituents of a more complex apparatus that can be eventually reconstituted into a whole if the reductionistic analysis has been sufficiently detailed.

This reductionistic metaphysics suggests that such values as individuality, personal destiny, and moral purpose have little importance for such a human mechanism in such a machine-ordered society. Indeed, it does far more because it gives to the philosophy of depersonalization and mechanism a scientific respectability while undercutting the view of man as an actualizing, purposive being—a view that might conceivably contain notes of opposition to the values and social organization of the present status quo where it dovetails so nicely with the reductionist position.

Moreover, this position is based on materials (humans) that have been educated and socialized to this machine-like condition and, also, on a view of man that emphasizes and cultivates those automated aspects of him that contribute to the efficiency and preservation of the present social order. The inevitable result of this view is the difficulty of understanding man as an organic creature with purpose and potentiality who can change the conditions of his nature and his fate; such a position would involve concepts and categories of analysis in considerable conflict with many of those accepted today as well as being somewhat alien to the nature of contemporary man and the society that molds him.

The large inference from this analysis is that we must know an age's values, ideologies, or temper before we can safely interpret and understand the individuals living in it or before a psychology can be constructed out of it that is never more than a transposition of some of its ideologies or partisan values into the language and rituals of theories, experiments, test, scores, and "scientific" evidence. We may have formal systems galore, unlimited rigorous techniques, and extensive hypothetic deductive theorems, but we will have deceived ourselves, nevertheless, because we will have been practicing, in large part, "cultural rationalization" with the immensely respected scientific procedures of the day. We will have changed our studies, tailored our problems, fashioned our theorems and hypotheses, and cultivated our data to get, in a sense, what we have started out with—our value judgments, preconceptions, and self-interested feelings about the nature and spirit of contemporary society. Certainly the history of psychology as a discipline has already seen enormous amounts of this bias, though not without great contributions to knowledge within the confinements of the valuative scientific ideology of the day. Now the issue is how we can transcend these confinements if we hope to develop an authentic psychology of man rather than one linked only with present ideology or contemporary society.

The contention of this book is that we cannot transcend these confinements unless we know the values and ideology of that society and make corrections in our psychological systems for them once they have become part of our scientific consciousness. One way of doing this is to study various Western societies to understand how values and ideologies have historically changed—and with them man's behavior as well as the psychological explanations of it. By assessing the variation of "images" or "psychologies" of man in different societies—each in the main line of Western culture—one can form a more comprehensive notion of his psychological potentialities and hence judge with more proportion and accuracy the nature of contemporary ideologies and values, the behavior related to them, and the psychological concepts accounting for or rationalizing them.

To summarize, the assumptions of this approach are that the scope and variety of the psychological potentialities of Western man during his history have been roughly the same. However, various societies have emphasized or cultivated quite different potentialities during this history and have also had different ways of viewing and studying them. Therefore, to get a "realistic" picture of the nature of man it is insufficient to accept only the image portrayed in contemporary psychology, because it is based on contemporary society. This image presents only one perspective, which compared with other variants of the basic Western likeness ignores vast dimensions of what man's behavior and character has been and, by inference, what potentially it still might be today. This is what we neglect because of our culturally biased ways of looking at and studying this behavior, i.e., the contemporary scientific formulation and investigation of it. To rectify these conditions, the following steps are proposed: (1) Determine how man has functioned in certain psychological areas during various periods of Western history as compared with how psychological research pictures his behavior in these areas today. (2) Acknowledge the discrepant psychological pictures (if, in fact, they turn out to be so) between contemporary American man and his Western historical counterparts. (3) Reformulate those presently neglected historical or potential behaviors of man in relation to modern psychological methods and research.

The areas to be investigated in this manner are those of intelligence, group behavior, perception, and the ego. Very possibly others could be chosen with fruitful effect, and the fields of learning, thinking, clinical psychology, and much of social psychology fall within this prospect. It will be noted that these areas contain a good deal of "culturally" defined components of behavior, i.e., they are influenced, if not determined, by the social values and norms of a given society or historical period and, hence, can be scientifically defined, themselves, only by the ideology or values that the designated society used to approve their presence as "legitimate" disciplines in the field of science.

Much the same might be said for the functions of learning, thinking, etc. Indeed, in the case of learning, methods of education change so profoundly with the societies that form them that the actual theory, process, and experiences of learning (and teaching) become largely the handmaidens of society's values and goals. In such fields as visual or auditory sensation cultural factors do not directly enter into a substantial number of the actual phenomena themselves nor affect research perspectives and methods to as marked a degree. This is not only because these fields are less susceptible to the valuative and ideological influences of society but also because they are more inextricably interwoven with long-tested and established variables of the physical sciences. In.this respect they are more comparable to closed systems.

II

The problem that now confronts us is how a contemporary psychologist can understand and conceptualize the ideology, spirit, and mentality of a given past society so that he can make reasonably accurate descriptions and analyses of how the individuals and groups of that society behaved in the psychological areas under consideration. Not only would he have to know how this society functioned in general but he would have to reconstruct how the individuals in it would have behaved in these psychological areas had they been subjects of experiments or of careful natural-istic observation.

Essential to this undertaking is the assumption that an understanding of the culture can be achieved and that by means of historical reconstruc-tion and psychological intuition the patterns of behavior falling within the psychological areas of our concern can be rediscovered. From this reconstruction it would be possible to see how these once existing be-haviors compare with those found by contemporary psychologists in their present studies. If significant differences are then found in these psycho-logical areas between the historic societies and our contemporary one, they might be explained by any or all of the following reasons: (1) the absence of certain environmental conditions essential for the appearance of particular kinds of behavior; (2) the limitations of modern psychologi-cal theory, which is not attuned to certain types of behavior and hence makes no provisions for their discernment; (3) inadequacies in the assessment techniques of modern psychology, which are not responsive to these behaviors when they are discerned; (4) the preoccupation of modern psychology with certain "norms" or "averages" of individuals as well as with large numbers of persons (quantitative criteria), which obscures the uncovering of the more culturally latent and less typical behaviors, though these may be quite prevalent. If any of this is true, then the discovery of different behaviors in these past societies suggests the possibility of looking for them in contemporary society provided that (1) conditions could presently be established similar to certain of those that prevailed when these qualities formerly flourished; (2) the sensitivities of contemporary psychologists could be attuned to the existence of these qualities; (3) contemporary theory could properly conceptualize them and methodology could use adequate techniques for their determination; and (4) populations of subjects and appropriate conditions under which these qualities might emerge—differing from those employed at present—could be investigated.

The societies to be studied in connection with these issues are (1) the Greeks at the time of Solon, (2) the Middle Ages, and (3) the Italian Renaissance. To this will be added an analysis of contemporary American society in terms of the values, concepts, and research of modern psychol-ogy. Despite striking similarities in traditions between these past cultures and ours, substantial differences in behavior, values, and other psychologi-cal qualities exist, and many characteristics that were often prevalent or dominant in these cultures are not conspicuously evident in ours.

Because it is rather unlikely that such past dominant qualities have completely died out—indeed, many humanists, cultural historians, social

reformers, poets, and men of religion submit that they are alive today—
it is possible that our own contemporary values in science and psychology
have made us insensitive to them or have tended to treat them as non-
measurable and elusive. Conversely, if psychologists from another historical period (assuming they existed) were to have based their formulations
wholly on the materials and the orientation of the "science" of their own
age, their own analyses would have been as partial and inaccurate (with,
however, different qualities, perspectives, behaviors, and concepts emphasized or ignored) as our contemporary one.

With this orientation to what man has revealed his "human nature" to
be—its "unfolding" in the course of Western history—we may see the
possibilities for an authentically realistic psychology. Only within such a
breadth of behavioral possibilities can we rigorously assess what we have
overemphasized and neglected in our contemporary work, how much
more investigation is needed here and how much there, and how distorted
or bland, narrow or weak our perspective and concepts might be. It is
for these reasons that the behavior of man displayed by various societies
of the West represents a first approximation of the framework within
which a realistic and comprehensive psychology of any age must be
evaluated and built.

Not for a moment does this mean that other cultural traditions—
Mideastern, Eastern, etc.—cannot also add to our picture. Indeed, they
represent possibilities heretofore little examined in the West both philo-
sophically or scientifically, which eventually must be explored to define
the total scope of man's endowment.

Whatever the source of the concepts of what the nature of man is, it
should now be clear that unless one uses some broad basis for theorizing
and research the dangers of scientific provincialism become very immi-
nent because of the inevitable tendency to proceed, in any given society,
on the basis of its dominant values and to carry on investigations only
within the framework of what the society sanctions and ignores. The purpose of the present exploration of a portion of Western history, then, is
only to clarify our vision of certain neglected areas of human behavior
and to give us an enriched appreciation of what these areas include. If
this exploration adds but a faint trail to the many and fertile paths of
knowledge that must be traveled before the image of man emerges clearly
in all its intricate richness, it may, nevertheless, have made us a bit more
reluctant to depart for the monotonously similar and limited vistas that
many of the swift and efficient superhighways of scientific psychology
now offer.

III

Athenian Greece, the Italian Renaissance, and the high Middle Ages were the historical periods selected for this exploration because, to repeat: (1) They all are a significant part of the Western tradition and have contributed essential unique ingredients to the substance and values of contemporary life and, to that extent, to the human phenomena that contemporary psychology attempts to analyze and understand. (2) Each society or culture complex was a relatively individual cultural constellation with a central system of values on which enormous historical research has been lavished and which can be fairly well understood. (3) Each society brought to fruition certain values and qualities of men that, though perhaps found to a degree in contemporary societies, certainly do not enjoy the prominence that they had in their originating cultures. (4) Each society represented a different development of the spectra of human potentialities so that understanding them enables us to grasp how variable Western man has been, and how the assumptions of one culture can be openly denied in another or deprecated by omission in a third. Thus it will be seen how qualities or behaviors we think today to be deviant and rare were, in another period, the day-to-day texture of experience for the peoples involved. (5) These "obscured" qualities, then, indicate human potentials that may be made viable again or point to the kinds of conditions and environments under which they may more profusely flourish. (6) Finally, these societies or cultural complexes threw up behaviors not only manifestly different from those that modern psychology has "scientifically" legitimized and studied as being within its proper domain but also those that represent a more humanistic and, in some respects, a higher standard of excellence of behavior. It is in this regard that contemporary psychology with its emphasis on the most commonly distributed behaviors and psychological traits prevalent in a mechanistic, practical, and adjustment-oriented mass society neglects a whole reservoir of other qualities. In contrast to this, we will see that our selected cultures emphasized qualities of humanistic and nonpractical character that contemporary psychology too often perceives as uncommon or deviant, as too remote or elusive for study, and, in fact, frequently rejects as neither conforming to nor measurable by the predetermined prototypes of its positivist methodologies.

23

IV

How do we come to understand a "past" cultural complex with its myriad social and psychological aspects? The methods of cultural history have been refined and developed so that together with archeological materials, artistic works, and other cultural products a rather accurate reconstruction can be made of the life, social experiences, and values of a past Western society. This is not the place to discuss the validity of these methods, adequacy of research, or authenticity of conclusions. It is sufficient to say that history, both as art and science, has developed quite exacting methods of validating its inferences and deductions, and in many respects its proofs and documentation are as credible as those of several areas of scientific psychology. The materials vary, it is true, but within the context of evidence the proofs are as rigorous as in many of the other disciplines of the science of man. Through autobiographies composed during the designated historical period, through written records of events (current histories, diaries, newspaper reports, ecological and population records), through cultural products (art, philosophy, science, technology, general knowledge, material culture), through records of other intellectual activities (ideas, educational methods, debates, books), through reports of commercial and business activity, and through records of political activities (government organizations and processes, political history, public participation, political processes and discussions), very adequate reconstructions of a society may be made. Indeed, in many respects there is little more reason to doubt the resultant picture of these societies as there is to doubt the results of confirmed psychological experiments or the reality of the battle of Waterloo.*

* In many respects historical evidence is equivalent to that obtained from clinical case study work, from careful observations of individual behavior, and from experimental reports of subjects' responses and feelings in various test situations. Further, if social and personal reactions to one pattern of social and cultural stimuli were to differ from social and personal reactions to a quite different pattern of these stimuli, this may be considered analogous, if not identical, with response differences of subjects to different classes of experimental variables. Too, these cultural milieux are, in a sense, historically established natural experimental situations where approximately similar social stimuli are repeated during a period of time. Through the examination of individual and group responses to these stimuli, a certain rough similarity to the scientific analysis of data based on reactions to recurring constant experimental stimuli might be plausibly conceived and, on the basis of which, the data of the former can be given, if not the same precise credibility as a laboratory experiment, nonetheless a substantial degree of confidence approximating it.

The method of presenting these cultures will be as follows: After a brief description of the given cultural complex, a careful attempt will be made to imagine how a psychologist living during that period (assuming such "scholars" existed then) would analyze four categories of behavior of his culture that are also treated in modern psychology, namely, intelligence, perception, group behavior, and the ego. This analysis would be based on all the relevant cultural behavior of which this historic "hypothetical" psychologist might be aware just as a modern psychologist would have knowledge of comparable areas of behavior in his own culture. Fundamental to this analysis would be the empathic reconstruction of the historic culture's spirit or atmosphere—a process comparable to one which a modern psychologist would employ in sympathetically understanding another human being, another contemporary culture, or, for that matter, almost any human experience. The analysis of the four psychological areas of the past culture would then be compared with a parallel analysis of modern man made by contemporary psychologists, as it has been represented in current psychological theory and research. If the comparisons revealed important differences, they would be attributed to discrepancies in behavior and experience between the two cultures and/or to the failure of modern psychology to acknowledge and investigate various dimensions of behavior in contemporary man. After an enumeration of these "neglected" dimensions has been made, an effort will be undertaken to remedy these "deficiencies" in the four psychological areas by proposing experiments, studies, and theoretical innovations that may correct the presumed limitations in contemporary experience, perspective, and procedure.

The rectification proposed here will be formulated in terms of researches that can be carried out within the standards of modern scientific credibility. In order to properly treat these "new dimensions" of behavior, a radical change in the methodology of research may be required in some instances. Or, in others, it may mean the necessity of questioning an established rigid methodology (which has already yielded a body of facts) in favor of a more unorthodox one that may yield valuable information on other aspects of a problem. Such revision shows no disrespect to traditional method but simply suggests it is most valid for obtaining a certain segment of truth and must now be expanded or superseded if other segments are to be discovered. If orthodox methodology must be superseded in the search for such "new" segments, a careful effort will be made to demonstrate why the pursuit of such "traditional" methods is irrelevant and, indeed, "unscientific" in discovering such "new" facts, and thus is no scientific method at all. By contrast, the "new" proposed method, however "unscientific" it appears from the conventional view-point, may, in truth, be the only scientific (effective) way to achieve the expansion of psychological vistas and the undiscovered facts encompassed by them.

There is at least one point in the logical chain of this discussion that may be questioned. This is the contention that from the materials of the past society its hypothetical psychologist (or his twentieth-century alter ego) could come to cogent conclusions about the behavior of its members in the psychological areas under consideration. Though there is a readily available accumulation of more or less systematic historical studies of these past cultures, there were, in fact, no contemporary scientific psychological studies made of their members. How, then, can any reliable conclusions be drawn from these cultures about the psychological areas with which we are concerned? Though it is impossible to get as rigorously accurate a picture of them as of comparable behaviors in present-day society, the available historical materials, nevertheless, enable scholars to make a rather adequate reconstruction based on numerous original sources. Then there are quite adequate psychological descriptions of individuals and groups—not, of course, using technical concepts but, nonetheless, fairly amenable to translation into such terms. Further, there are innumerable autobiographies, diaries, contemporary histories, letters, biographies, journals, etc. in which these behaviors are described in detail by eyewitnesses and others. Inferences from such data are comparable to those made in modern case history technique, to appraisals or diagnoses made in group psychology, and to certain studies of intelligence. Indeed, a great deal of modern clinical work is based on similar naturalistic and observational accounts. In addition, these behaviors were conscientiously described by competent scholars of that period, e.g., historians, economists, etc. Either they were quite wrong—or their accounts ought to be accepted with only the normal amount of scholarly skepticism.

If sensitive observation and ingenious experiment can demonstrate the general existence of these behaviors in present-day culture, this will be additional evidence for their importance in the scientific understanding of man. If their uncommonness at present merely means methodology or theory is not alert to them, it will be the purpose of the studies proposed here to remedy this condition. If, however, their nonoccurrence does not mean lack of methodological appropriateness or limitations in theory and psychological sensitivity, then we will have to concede that their rarity is owing to something other than not correctly investigating psychological potentialities that we have presumed might be realized in the modern world.

V

It should be made clear that the effort of this work is not directed to explain all aspects of the societies it deals with. Such a task is not only vastly complex, involving large numbers of contradictory elements and gross variations in behavioral norms and social institutions but would, in fact, be a diversion from its main purpose.

For the primary concern of the descriptions of these cultures is to distill their most general aspirations and value patterns as embodied in those who expressed them most clearly or as seen in a general, if not completely actualized, behavioral model. Such patterns were not universally present but their very existence as ideals and their full realization in a small but significant number of individuals demonstrated that they could be attainable or at least serve as influential models for others to attempt to emulate. Indeed, each of these behavioral models was, in a varying degree of dilution or contamination and in one fashion or another, copied by a substantial number of members of the society. Even when only evident in truncated or adulterated form, its component features pointed to a broader behavioral ideal which, honored more in the breach than in the observance, made evident its power by the amount of lip service that was paid to it. And if only hypocritically followed or violently opposed, these behaviors nevertheless became a model for men's conduct and experience—a standard that was either explicitly sanctioned and followed or taken as the central reference point for their rejection and for the effort toward the cogent development of a contravening position. So powerful, then, if only by implication and tacit recognition were these models that they often became the orienting point by which men tried to create a new system of behavior by overthrowing the one that these "ideal" norms represented.

The behavioral model or values of each of the societies to be subsequently described represents the single most coherent experiential, behavioral, and value orientation that the culture embodied. Thus, it symbolizes a magnetic pole of induction by which many types of behavior were influenced in their patterning so that they took on varying aspects of this central model. Necessarily, all cultures have basic contradictions and extensive diversities, but many of these may be fairly consistently affected by such a general model even if it is only a system of values or an inexplicit "ideal" mode of conduct and experience. Further, all cultures have unique, indigenous dimensions (biological, material, technical, etc.) as well as different subcultures, contracultures, and autonomous forces, but various aspects of all these may still be oriented to such an ideal pattern. It is this configurational model—permeating in varying degree even independent biological, social, and cultural forces—that is pertinent to the viewpoint advanced here. To the extent that various elements of the society turned, at one level or another, to such values or behavioral ideals as points of reference and aspiration and to the extent that other autonomous cultural and biological patterns were in some way affected by them, the wider relevance of these model influences is supported.

Thus, in some societies it was materialism and a pragmatic orientation that affected the perceptual, group, cognitive, and ego processes—or other psychological functions—of its members. In other societies, these processes may have expressed themselves differently because their particular behavioral models or aspirations were "romantic" or "humanistic." In addition, societies exhibit behaviors of a universal or transcultural nature that may or may not be affected by these configurations. It must also be recognized that some societies are more coherent in embodying and extending the influence of these ideals to numerous modes of behavior while in others this influence is restricted to only a few areas. There will also be variation in the degree to which different groups or social classes of the society evidence these model behaviors.

These "ideal" patterns may be most clearly expressed in certain minority groups of society—elite groups, upper classes, etc.—which represent desirable standards of behavior and experience for the society as a whole. Whether the remaining sectors of a society honor these patterns in frequent conduct, only by occasional behavior, only as aspirations to be hopefully achieved, or mostly in verbal expression, the fact is that these models exercise an ineluctable influence on the behavior of a large number of a society's members. Of course, many other cultural forces are present—particularly in those groups that do not predominantly embody these values, cannot honor them fully, acquiesce to them only opportunistically, or, because of poverty or repression, are so removed from the preeminent ethos or spirit of the society that they cannot be exposed to the effects that these models may have. But even in those groups where these "ideal" patterns are more attacked than emulated, there may even be some degree of lip service or small conformity that betrays their power. Indeed, sometimes when these models were openly transgressed or repudiated, it signified a reaction formation to a denied wish—and so reflected the frustration and discouragement that often came with harboring too long the often disguised and put-off hope that when one's position would be more advantageous or the time more propitious, one would be able to exercise these "ideal" model behaviors for oneself.

VI

The first society chosen for presentation here is that of Greece at the time of Solon. In the reconstruction of the values, ideology, and psychology that follows, a thorough documentation of all aspects of Greek culture during Solon's time will not be attempted. What will be emphasized are those salient values—most typical of that society and most frequently accepted by Greek scholars—that have bearing on the main propositions of this essay. No attempt will be made to specify historical events or to cite particular political or social institutions and movements but rather to set forth the quality of the Greek way of life, its values, its temper, the psychology of its people, and what that psychology has to teach contemporary psychologists about the nature of man. Descriptions of and assertions about the mentality of the Greeks will be made as generalizations that have been attested to by substantial documentation. Because this is not an essentially historical work and because the extent of such documentary evidence is vast, no attempt will be made to marshall this evidence here. Though, in a few respects, some variation or minor deviations from such generalizations might be conceded, it is to be remembered that the object of these descriptions is simply to reproduce the general value orientation, spirit, and patterning of these cultures from the works of acknowledged authorities and on the basis of accepted reconstructions.

REFERENCES

1. Goffman, Erving. *The Presentation of Self in Everyday Life*. Garden City: Doubleday, 1959.
2. Lewin, Kurt. *A Dynamic Theory of Personality*, 1st ed. New York: McGraw-Hill, 1935.
3. Klineberg, Otto. *Social Psychology*, rev. ed. New York: Holt, Rinehart & Winston, 1954.

4. Lesser, Gerald, and Kandel, Denise. "Cross-Cultural Research: Advantages and Problems," *The Human Context*, I, no. 4 (1969), 347–376.
5. Murdock, George Peter. *Social Structure*. New York: Macmillan, 1949.
6. Stephens, William U. *The Oedipus Complex: Cross Cultural Evidence*. Glencoe, Ill.: Free Press of Glencoe, 1962.
7. Mannheim, Karl. *Ideology and Utopia*. New York: Harcourt, Brace, 1936.
8. Russell, Bertrand. *A History of Western Philosophy*. New York: Simon & Schuster, 1945.
9. Dewey, John. *The Quest for Certainty*. New York: G. P. Putnam's Sons, 1960.
10. Mach, Ernst. *Contributions to the Analysis of Sensation*. 1886.
11. Mach, Ernst. *Errkentis und Irrtum*. 1905.

GENERAL REFERENCES

Asch, Solomon E. "Effects of Group Pressure Upon the Modification and Distortion of Judgments," in H. Guetzkow, ed., *Groups, Leadership and Men*. Pittsburgh: Carnegie Press, 1951.

Barnes, Harry Elmer, with David, Henry. *The History of Western Civilization*. New York: Harcourt, Brace, 1935.

Boring, E. G. *A History of Experimental Psychology*, rev. ed. New York: Appleton-Century, 1950.

Dewey, John. *The Quest for Certainty*. New York: G. P. Putnam's Sons, 1960.

Emerson, Ralph Waldo. *Complete Works*. Boston, Mass.: Houghton Mifflin, 1883–1898.

Goodman, Paul. *Growing Up Absurd*. New York: Random House, 1960.

Hayes, C. J. H. *Political and Cultural History of Europe*. New York: Macmillan, 1932–1936.

Hobbes, Thomas. *The Leviathan*. New York: Dutton, 1914.

Krutch, Joseph. *Human Nature and the Human Condition*. New York: Random House, 1959.

Lewin, Kurt. *A Dynamic Theory of Personality*, 1st ed. New York: McGraw-Hill, 1935.

Lewin, Kurt. *Studies in Topological and Vector Psychology*. Iowa City: University of Iowa Press, 1940.

Lewin, L., Lippett, R., and White, R. K. "Patterns of Aggressive Behavior in Experimentally Created Social Climates," *Journal of Social Psychology*, X (1939), pp. 271–299.

Mannheim, Karl. *Ideology and Utopia*. New York: Harcourt, Brace, 1936.

Mumford, Lewis. *The Condition of Man*. New York: Harcourt, Brace, 1944.

Murdock, George Peter. *Social Structure*. New York: Macmillan, 1949.

Murphy, Gardner. *Historical Introduction to Modern Psychology*, rev. ed. New York: Harcourt, Brace, 1949.

Orwell, George. *Nineteen Eighty-Four*. New York: Harcourt, Brace, 1949.

Randall, John Herman. *The Making of the Modern Mind*. Boston: Houghton Mifflin, 1940.

Robinson, James Harvey. *The Mind in the Making*. New York: Harper, c. 1921.

Russell Bertrand. *A History of Western Philosophy*. New York: Simon & Schuster, 1945.

2
THE GREEKS
❧

What are the chief features of the Greek mentality and spirit? Those that immediately concern us are:

1. Humanism or the belief in the value and significance of man as the salient measure of life. Man's experience and its richness is the justification of life as well as its purpose. The cultivation of man, his capacities for happiness, his talents and sensibilities are worthy of the highest effort, and it is toward the maximal development of these ends—which distinctively identify man—that this effort must be directed.

2. Excellence in all qualities is the guiding principle in life. This excellence is both mental and physical, both moral and spiritual. The Greeks felt that an integral facet of humanism was the optimal development of one's potentialities. In athletics, this meant that grace, symmetry, coordination, physical courage, skill, strength, resolution, and bravery were to be aspired to. In the case of the intellect and spirit, it was logic, reason, sensitivity, philosophical balance and detachment, integrity, contemplative capacity, argumentative and dialectic skill, and similar qualities that were to be assiduously cultivated. The premise of this pursuit of excellence was that only through the perfection of human capacity and function could the proper end of life be achieved, i.e., excellence was a self-contained end of life because it gave its possessor the realization and exercise of all his constituent talents and functions. Thus happiness resulted from the aspiration to and practice of excellence. Also, because it was intended to cover a broad spectrum of human endowment, the practice of excellence provided a full-bodied fulfillment of much of the impulses, talents, and penchants of men.

3. Intrinsic to humanistic excellence was the search for the realization of the individual's destiny or unique personal fulfillment and fate. This striving and quest gave rise to exhilaration, excited delight in doing and making, generated the engagement of vast personal energy in activities of

purpose and significance, and, not infrequently, brought a glimpse of perfection, which, if never attainable, could, nevertheless, be constantly pursued.

4. The Greek concept of humanistic excellence was also reflected in the obligation on the citizen to serve the Athenian body politic in many roles, ranging from participation in the arts to vocal and dynamic citizenship to service in war. Thus the human personality was given full play for development of its manifold dimensions, and this varied and rich development was thought to be the apotheosis of the good and happy life because it brought into vital functioning a vast potentiality of men. Such stimulation and heightening of activity was the equivalent of being alive and of giving free reign to all proclivities for the fullest realization of one's being.

5. The ideal of multifaceted development is particularly clear in the cultivation of all aspects of intelligence. This capacity is viewed not alone as "careful intelligence," "shrewd intelligence," or "analytic intelligence," but equally as "aesthetic intelligence," "spiritual intelligence," "human sensibility," "political intelligence," and "reflective theoretical intelligence." To these must be added the use of imaginative gifts, artistic talents, and spiritual and religious resources as functions integral to and, at times, preeminently characteristic of the intellectual life.

6. One of the more interesting qualities of Greek mentality was the emphasis on the purity of scientific contemplation and search. The purpose of science was not a practical one for the Greeks; it was primarily to explain the reasons or causes for events. For this reason, as many have suggested, they were the first pure scientists, because they were preoccupied with explanation or understanding for its own sake to the exclusion of ulterior purposes. This purity of intellectual search, this uncontaminated delight in curiosity and freedom of the mind—devoid of the inhibitions and digressions of practical ends—and this pursuit of truth for its own sake were all passions that not only involved the full exercise of the mind but also those fundamental attitudes of questioning of assumptions, free speculation, and authentic intellectual skepticism that are integral to the pursuit of truth. This free, unfettered mind—questioning everything, taking nothing for granted, and yet uninhibited and unrestricted in its capacity for theory, explanation, and vision—was one of the great triumphs of Greek civilization and was the foundation of a tradition that, if somewhat contaminated, is nonetheless very strong today.

7. One of the most distinctive earmarks of the Greek genius was its unfettered individualism, at once a source of great achievement and of cumulative deterioration of the Greek city-state. Individualism of this sort

connoted the most extreme development of personal conviction and re-source in their broad many-sided aspect as well as the courage to pride-fully stand alone for such conviction and resource irrespective of the consequences. The Greek defiance of fate—*hubris*—claimed its origin here and from this source, too, came the urgency of men to achieve excellence in all avenues—to ape the gods—as well as the complementary belief that but for some fundamental flaw, supreme felicity and the highest avenues to perfection might be attained. At the same time, this flaw spurred men even more, by the effort to remedy its discredit, to attain god-like status and yet to be compassionate with the inevitable failure and accompanying tragedy of this quest. In contrast to the contemporary cult of success via popularity and conformity, the Greek conviction was that only through the exercise of the best and most distinctive qualities in oneself might excellence and godliness be reached, and compassion was at the ready to be extended when immutable failure ended this striv-ing. Nonetheless, the belief that man did have the capacity to achieve supreme felicity and excellence by using his best traits was prominent, and if failure was inevitable or if there was an excessive amount of such striving, it was because men aspired to ape the gods for whom, reassur-ingly, adversity was also inevitable.

Some consequences of this form of individualism included a profound courage of conviction, a respect for excellence and indomitable will, and a willingness to stand by one's beliefs to the bitter end as the authentic and assured way to achieve self-respect and personal fulfillment. Courage in word and deed, worship of excellence, and acceptance of the inevita-bility of failure and tragedy were the values distilled from this outlook. The defiance of public opinion, when and if necessary, was only a wholly natural result of these same beliefs.

8. Sustaining at all times the Greek belief in excellence, activity, and versatility was their faith in the gods, who, in a world of conflict, tempest, and uncertainty, incarnated and gave renewed worth to human quality. The gods were super- or hypermen with all the virtues and defects there-with, but because of their power and endowments mortal men could take encouragement from them when fortitude in belief and courage in deed were required. In crisis, the Greeks could appeal to virtue, honor, integ-rity, or similar values as sanctioning their conduct and, with the convic-tion that such values were those of the gods, could achieve such security and strength in personal action as is rarely found among persons who when alone must rely exclusively on their self-evolved values and identi-fications. At the same time, when tragedy came, when life was dour, when frustrations impeded movement, the gods might be appealed to for ex-

planations or understanding; thus solace for one's sadness and standards for judging undeserved adversity were constantly available. Defiance of these standards and this code usually resulted in catastrophe whereas conformity to or internalization of it was a great source of strength. With such sentiments, life was not so lonely a struggle as might be true for a people who valued individuality and excellence as much as the Greeks and, as a result, the need to depend on others was diminished. Further, the hardships of life could be attributed to malevolent gods or to defiance of some time-sanctified god-ordained value.

And because man could, in fact, never achieve the god-like state and because the emulation of it, *hubris,* was doomed to failure, tragedy and compassion were organically assimilated to each other and failure in great enterprises, with accompanying sadness, was accepted as a normal event. Men would persistently strive for the highest apex of excellence, for the self-fulfillment and felicity it brought, and for the identity with the gods that it conferred. Thus the hero became vastly important in Greek life and literature and was revered because he pursued this preordained path of tragedy and failure, which, nevertheless, brought to him the intoxicating vision of approaching a god-like state and the vast exhilaration of almost achieving ultimate personal fulfillment. And if failure and tragedy were inevitable, they neither debased nor dishonored the individual. Indeed, the very best of men, just because of this magnificent striving, were often the great failures, and compassion with this inexorable tragedy further encouraged and freed men to make the effort to fulfill themselves through this quest and not to be defeated by insufficiency of material reward or popular approval. Hence, great failure was understandable, acceptable, and nothing to be ashamed of. And this meant, too, that one important basis for personal insecurity did not significantly exist.

9. One of the great traditions that the Greeks originated—political democracy—had in fact a somewhat different stress among them than its heirs have given it. In the Greek city-state there was a direct, immediate relationship between citizen and government that was sustained by the franchise and by the required public participation of the citizen in the body politic.* A vital and active concern with the processes and details of governing, politics, and the state was intrinsic to this participation, which was the highest order of social responsibility and which composed the core of community life. The resulting integration of state and citizen led to an alert, vigorous consciousness of political and community life, a vital response to its shifting moods and events, and an invigorating interest in what might be accomplished or what policies could be executed. This

* Substantial portions of this discussion do not apply to women and slaves who were denied participation in numerous areas and institutions of Greek society.

vital responsibility, in turn, led to a more acute delight and heightened feeling in life and a more dynamic sense of personal destiny owing, not in small part, to the conviction that events, in some degree, could be under one's control. The additional experience of vital participation in all activity, which stimulated this exhilarating sense of life as well as delight, health, and the invigoration of mental functions, also created an awareness and concern with all facets of the political life in which one moved. This vital interest, thence, gave the necessary identity and cohesiveness to the body politic and so balanced, to some degree, the centripetal vigorous individualism. The sentiment of community participation directed the concern for and activity in community matters that constrained the somewhat anarchic and individualistic forces in social life, cemented a sense of community with the institution of the city-state, and channeled individual zest and talent into community functions. And, thus, excellence was directed to group ends, cohesive community values were assimilated to a degree, and a sense of personal influence over events was provided that enhanced vitality and confidence and nurtured a type of participation that endowed life with an exhilaration and gave it meaning and direction.

By giving each citizen this chance to participate, the community was, at the same time, extended and welded into a more vigorous whole whose well-being, contingent on the contributions of talent and energy of its citizens, accounted for the stimulation of as vast a diversity of ability as a dynamic and excellent society can exploit for its further advancement. So it was that each citizen, if able enough, might exercise these abilities in an almost infinite variety of ways and, too, would, at some time in his mature life, be offered heavy and vital community responsibility. All this decreased apathy, provided incentives for personal and social improvement, stimulated the most provident and variegated capacities, and contributed to the sense of community awareness that controls excessive individualism.

10. To these high points of the Greek experience must be added the important moderating factor of the balance between passion and intellect, the notion of sensitive control or, as it is commonly known, the "golden mean." Whether realistically attainable or not, this ideal had an enormous influence on the Greeks, certainly on their art and literature and noticeably on their science, politics, and thought. Whether stemming from the exaggeration of a certain intensity or passion in Greek life and the correlative desire to control it, or from the more reasoned deliberation that excess in any modality is dangerous or eventually desensitivizing and that moderation ensures continued pleasure by guarding against jaded sensation, despair, bitterness, or exhaustion, this value exerted a not incon-

siderable influence. Valuable, too, was the consideration that moderation assures available energy for other pursuits and, by facilitating a more balanced enjoyment of versatile experience, it persuades a more or less dispassionate view of which needs should be satisfied. Such an orientation enhances the possibility of a greater span and enrichment of feeling and experience rather than channeling all energy into one outlet or activity. It continually renews the possibility of enjoyment of work and experience by allowing the play of human emotion to be engaged with them while, by disengaging each channel of experience or activity from these same emotions at various other times, enabling the different senses and functions to be refreshed for renewed or more vital experiences. Also, the continual enrichment of various modalities of pleasure, work, and sensation would play into one another with the healthy vitality that results from such stimulating contrast while the potentiality for feeling and other functional responses would suffer no numbing and dullness through disuse. For a number of these reasons, balance became an ideal in Greek life—a compensating power against the strong passions and intensities of feeling. Its influence was evident in the Greek capacity for detached contemplation, the development of those interests in science and philosophy that have esteemed the Greeks in these areas, the balanced regimen of physical and intellectual work that marked the Greek aristocracy, and the manifold development of personal qualities that ensured the enrichment and vitality of man's endowment. With this balance could come the judiciousness of wisdom and the calm consideration of problems as well as the development of numerous mental faculties. All were enriched by the modalities of feeling and the resulting integration led to a calm and reasoned perspective that assigned to the intellect a priority of sorts, but never at the expense of the curiosities, sensations, and impulses that could awaken and heighten its powers and direct its course. One form of this integration sanctioned an objective and dispassionate view of phenomena —a view necessary to the development of pure mathematics and science. Though not always carried out in practice, such values as these often enough led to pride in the intellect, to diversity of talent, to vitality in experience, to a rich sense of well-being, and to the feeling of a rounded and full development that emerges when many functions and capacities are being exercised. With the greater interpenetration of these modalities of experience and ability came intellect's infusion with feeling and a greater richness of both mind and experience. Other fruits of this psychological process were that shifts could be made from one area of interest to another without all effort and energy being directed to specialized areas alone; it was possible to be detached from experience while engaging in

36

it, a process that derived, in part, from this lack of overinvestment in any specific area and from a confidence emanating from a wide and satisfactory variety of other experiences; a broader and more extensive view of life was evoked because of the greater diversity of experience obtained from it; a skepticism was cultivated in regard to any single paramount viewpoint, involvement, or specialization and thus dogmatic extremes were less frequently maintained. Such skepticism, too, led to critical self-examination of what was known and then, often, to a sense of tentativeness about the ultimate certainties of knowledge or the meaning and vital matters of life.

So the two-faced but complementary Greek image is seen in one view as picturing verisimilitude, dispassion, richness of experience, and pleasure in the search for truth and in the other as depicting the ultimate tragedy and incompleteness of life as well as doubt regarding the prospect of attaining truth. To these views must be added the interpenetrations of sensation, feeling, and thought, which made thinking not inevitably a simple, mechanical, neatly differentiated process but transposed it into a function that ferreted out life's recesses, visualized new possibilities and explanations, probed for depths of insight and understanding, and, in general, proved to be a much more complex and mysterious process than is presently congenial to admit. Though "complexity" can lead to seeing too many facets of a problem, particularly for simple rules of scientific function and procedure, it also leads to constant enrichment and deepening of problems and to humility regarding their ultimate resolution. It may also lead to the humanization of knowledge in relation to values, human purposes, and morals. If there is an objective examination of phenomena, then objective questions and solutions should emerge, but if, in addition, questions are asked, as they were by the Greeks, in terms of man's condition and human values, then such inquiries become indispensable for the expansion of human wisdom, even if resistant to neat, ready answers.

11. Many of these foregoing viewpoints are eloquently manifested in the artistic expressions of Greek life. Without entering into controversial issues of the relation of art to psychology and society either as an expression of individual or cultural aspirations and frustrations or as a wish-fulfilling compensatory reaction to a society's established patterns, the fact remains that a type of balance was achieved between passion and intellect in Greek art and architecture that has been the wonder of all succeeding ages. Its triumph was the capture of the essence of the idealized or "pure" act (actually the abstraction of an act): the exquisite moment at which the beginning of the act ends and the apogee has not yet been

reached—a sort of "preparation for action" that does not reveal the completed action—in short, the distillation of that ideally perfect moment in an act when it is neither germinating nor perishing. The complete or almost complete lack of self-consciousness in such an act stems from a detached absorption in the immanent "action" itself which, in abstract, is the essence of an act—an essence in which the act is caught in its purest form. It is as if no effort or involvement in calculation about, or aesthetic termination of, the act were involved; such is the empathic response to it that, in the purity and capture of its quintessential moment, dissolves both the act's inception and end. Such an artistic conception can hardly be carried out except when there is capacity for absorption in the act alone, a delight in its perfection, and the necessary ease and detachment that is capable of giving it dispassionate presentation (often confused with coldness or intellectualization). The impression of coldness paradoxically results both from the artist's presumed objective scrutiny of the act without the personal overinvolvement and passion characteristic of the art of other historical periods and from the idealization of it by crystallizing and intensifying the moment that is its essence. To achieve this aesthetic response requires a capacity for sensitive feeling without striving or violent passion, a delight in the act alone with one's complete energy allocated to it, an absorption in it without exhaustion, and a detachment without coldness. It is this balance of passion and reason, of absorptive interest without distortion, of the capacity to treat emotion reflectively from a dispassionate distance while still enjoying it, and the feeling of being completely in the act and absorbed by it that demands a fluidity of emotion that simultaneously evokes the capacity to reflect easily, to see the spirit of the act itself, and to capture this spirit without organic distortion or to intellectualize it without disturbing passion. This humanistic fusion of reason and feeling which infused Greek life with so much that is admirable led to the association of organic purpose with intellectual activity and emotional experience, and thus to the balance of feeling and thought. There resulted a dispassionate but great capacity to enjoy action unselfconsciously and to make it the delight of life while arranging emotions in proper balance so that satiation, exhaustion, and distortion would only minimally affect the realization of the ideal of symmetry and elegance of action.

With this general characterization of some of the main themes of classic Greek experience, we must now determine—hypothecating a psychologist to be living at the time who would not have disagreed with the foregoing description of Greek culture—what his appraisal of the Greeks would be in those areas of behavior selected for study here. Each of these areas will now be considered as this hypothetical psychologist might have observed and discussed them and then will be compared with analogous behavioral areas discussed by contemporary American psychologists. Then, if appropriate, proposals will be made for the expansion of contemporary American psychology on the basis of the grounds previously presented.

Intelligence

Our hypothetical psychologist would be concerned with the following features of intelligence based on the foregoing analysis of Greek society:

1. The capacity for imagination. The ability to accept suggestions and elaborate on them, to develop new themes, and to see new possibilities was fundamental to Greek thought. To speculate freely, carrying thought and idea as far as the mind and spirit could soar, was a distinguishing mark of Greek mentation. The role of the psychologist would be to devise test items and problems measuring this kind of speculative flight and freedom in association. Imagination of this nature would be measured in fields ranging from the poetical to the mathematical and would be of different forms: associating verbally, broad speculative ideas, new intellectual contrivances, etc. Boldness in conception, questioning conventional assumptions with novel alternatives, and wide speculative capacity would all be part of the imaginative process that the Greeks would unquestionably assess as essential to intelligence.

2. To this act of bold imagination and unfettered speculation, the Greek conception of intelligence added diversity and flexibility of intellectual movement, i.e., the capacity to range over a broad realm of facts, issues, and problems with great agility and deftness. Included, also, would be the ability to bring information from diverse fields to bear on the one being considered so that a more complex and rich effect was produced. Rapidity in ranging over many areas and variety and richness in conception were aspects of this broad intellectual activity. Related also was the facility in bringing ideas or issues from quite disparate fields to bear on a problem, as from philosophy or poetry to a political issue. Flexible riposte in disputation and the rapid and smooth flow of logical argument were other facets of this ability. Involved here was the notion that intelligence embodies coping quickly with situations, restructuring them through visualizing manifold possibilities, and selecting from these the worthiest

alternatives. This aspect of intelligence would be measured by the fluidity with which a position is developed, the rapid analysis of weak points in other alternative positions on the basis of a broad perspective, and the analysis of this perspective, in turn, from an even more generalized frame of reference. Smoothness of the flow of ideas and proposals, constant questioning and examining of assumptions from other frames of reference, and the capacity to bring many different themes to bear on a single area while quickly penetrating to the significant core of the problem would be some of the distinctive features of Greek intelligence that our hypothetical psychologist would have had to gauge.

3. Related to the foregoing is the concept of balance in Greek intellectual activity. It will be remembered that the Greeks judged the diversity of mind and its capacity for reflection as an indication of excellence. Overspecialization, in the Greek view, did not fit a man to be an excellent human being, an excellent citizen, or even aid in the proper development of his own capacities. Rather it indicated constriction of the mind, the suffocating of intellectual potential, the failure of mental functions to interpenetrate and fertilize each other, and the undermining of the humanistic dimension of the intellect which was responsible for some of the delight and wisdom in men's lives. Thus in achieving intellectual balance, the Greeks included not only special fields but such aspects of intelligence as intuition, imagination, speculation, fluidity of thought, and richness of conception from which a humanistic intellectual balance would emanate. Because the overdevelopment of one function was humanistically "bad," the salient goal was to maintain proportion among all of them both in theory and practice. At one time speculation, at another rigorous logic, at another breadth of comprehension, at another agility in disputation, all in addition to the fusion and interplay between them: such was the rounded regimen of the Greek mind.

4. To a considerable degree, the Greeks placed emphasis on that peculiar amalgam of imagination, *Gestalt* perception, feeling, and implicit logic that, for lack of a better term, has been called intuition. The flashes of insight—whether before or after preparation, the rapid movement of mind—without explicit intermediary logical steps from premise or assumption to resolution, the immediate penetration—not at all by laborious proof—to the heart of a problem are all encompassed in this process. Indeed, such mental activity frequently goes on, even in societies of the highest intellectual rigor, but it is customarily controlled or suppressed for fear of embarrassment or disguised with highly ritualized, cautious, and detailed steps of reasoning. The crucial operation is the flash of connection—the passing over interminable boundaries of seemingly

obvious, inconsequential, but distracting barriers—and the assimilation of the crucial connections in a comprehensive resolution. Much of this has been the subject of discussion in contemporary psychology.[1] The elevation of thought and ideation to this level of intuition functioned in every modality of Greek life and thought. Indeed, as the complexity of an issue multiplies, as it is imbued with more "human" elements, and as more factors are introduced, this process of intuition more readily comes to the fore. Therefore it is most important to assess this capacity for making imaginative leaps, for seeing new orientations without the aid of suggestions, and for identifying the crucial point out of a medley of stimuli or a chaos of material.

Part of this intuitive process is the flash of insight that transfigures perception. Sometimes this occurs with little objective information, sometimes after a profound relaxation of the cognitive functions or some kind of hibernation, and sometimes without any predetermined direction. This type of imaginative intuition—often creative in its ramifications—is marked by boldness in ideation and the courage to make cognitive and logical leaps, but is not satisfied with narrow, ritualistic, piecemeal thought. Also this type of cognition has a profound emotional component —a fact that will be considered later.

5. For the Greeks, intelligence also encompassed the consideration of moral and humanistic matters. The solution of a problem would ideally be tempered with "wisdom," with evaluation of the purpose of a proposed action, its relation to other ramifying or associated actions, and its moral significance in general. Thus an act, resolution, or decision could be considered as intelligent only when these other factors were included as part of the problem and its solution. There was, then, the integration of the unique, narrow, sometimes shrewd or clever solution of a problem with such factors as the purpose, meaning, and "good" it served. Thus many items in modern IQ tests would be considered as "unintelligent" and certainly "unwise" by the Greeks in that the purport, end, or value of the "correct" solutions to their questions or the activities embodied in these test items would be questioned by them. Hence, broader considerations would have to be weighed along with the narrower problem posed by these items before a "correct" or "intelligent" answer could be genuinely given. This kind of humanistic approach would influence every deployment of cleverness, shrewdness, canniness, and even the "clever" type of originality so much admired at present, and would furthermore place the appraisal of intelligence on a broader, purposive, moral, and consequences-involved basis. It was for these reasons that the Greeks were so free in speculative thought, in the balanced play of intellect, in detached, un-

bridled curiosity and were not at all excellent in the overpractical orientations that require the uses of the mind for some specific pragmatic purpose. Humanistic, purposive, and moral considerations, therefore, constantly defined and directed the uses of intelligence, freeing it, at times, for the most liberated and pliable reflections, at other times for questioning implicit assumptions, and, at still others, for provoking uninhibited imaginative play. The inevitable result was a more profound use of cleverness for problem-solving and for questioning the purposes of problems or tasks rather than for blindly following to an expedient solution the implicit values and other "given" premises laid down in the presented problem. The permeation of intelligence with such humanistic and purposive factors made it not only a sensitive and profound instrument for the resolution of human problems but an unfettered process for the satisfaction of wide curiosities.

6. This fundamental examination of the assumptions and purposes of problems also revealed itself in the distinguished speculative quality of the Greek mind. The freedom of the speculative mental act lay in its not having a specific, practical problem to solve nor requiring a commensurate channeling of mental energy to a specific goal. It rather lay in the freedom to organically integrate impulse and cognition so that the intellect was not driven by the immediacy of practical problems and, accordingly, was not limited by the shallowness and speed that such problems often require. This kind of speculative freedom lay in examining the assumptions of all problems and eventually in devising a more profound and significant resolution of them. The freedom of choice and idea implicit in this process and the fluidity of the use of information and resource from all fields allowed the mind to meander where it would and, in this manner (if not contaminated by practical purpose, immediate striving for success, and compelling drives to attain an artificial or externally set goal), it voyaged hopefully to find what the Greeks thought to be of the largest importance for the intellectual life: truth and wisdom. Because of the lack of restriction owing to rigid purposes or practical goals, the mind might wander at will to satisfy the impulses of curiosity and to raise issues not previously posed or standardized. Thus the Greeks explored an enormous number of areas, utilizing those powers of intuition and curiosity that are so often richly rewarding in the quest for truth. Speculation became a basic mode of Greek intellectual life and overshadowed the empiricism that later ages made their scientific *pièce de resistance*. The free movement of the mind as it unimpededly took in whatever was available, using its total resources to resolve an issue (and without contamination because of the pressures of the moment, practical efficiency, or machine-like models of cognition),

and, accordingly, startling in its original discoveries was one of the great contributions that Greek thought made to its intellectual descendents.

7. Related to the deemphasis of practical solutions as the primary goal in the thinking process was the deescalation of those orientations that limited in time and place the scope and diversity of speculation, constricted cognition to a specific mode or problem, and required solutions of a concrete or immediate kind. Such influences reduce the thinking process to a type of canny shrewdness whose purposes are the accumulation of things and the manipulation of things or people and whose processes are those of detached problem-solving. In this view, all emotion is ideally left out of thinking except for the cold canny pursuit of a given, tangible, pragmatic objective.

In contrast, the Greeks vitally utilized emotion in the thinking process, not disassociating the two but pervading thought with humanistic feeling and making it responsive, also, to tendencies such as aesthetic delight and uninhibited curiosity. Perhaps the disassociation from or subordination of these feelings to "cold detached" thinking makes the latter more ingenious or intricate and gives it a clever quality in practical matters that "humanistic types" of thought may not have. On the other hand, the free availability of affect at certain stages of the thinking process may foster richness and inventiveness in the emergence of ideas, giving them movement and emphasizing their potentiality through the zest and versatility dispensed by the emotions of adventure, delight, and aesthetic sensibility. As a result, new eruptions of ideas may occur as the emotional-ideational current continues, providing different perspectives of the same phenomenon as it flows from one feeling and idea to another, adding various emotional-cognitive textures to stimulate different associations and inventions, and giving breadth and richness to ideas and insights. Perhaps it is for these reasons that a practical problem in a limited time period cannot generate those fertile conceptions that unrestricted time and free emotional and intellectual exploration are more capable of doing. It must be clear that overstrict attention to immediate or practical objectives tends to restrict emotional and cognitive play and thus the variety, richness, and scope of intellectual production. It is precisely this freedom to let ideas emerge and develop as they will plus a complementary diversity of emotions that, together, stimulate additional reflections and ideas in link with those already conceived and shed a rich character over the entire product. The indulgence in speculation means the free play of curiosity, a keen desire to unearth knowledge, a delight in intellectual elegance and balance, and the interaction of idea with idea which is attended by the interplay of related emotion. Consequently there is further enriching and multiplying fertilization among ideas and, too, there is often more demand of exact logic than, at the time, it is capable of giving. Of importance is the balance of emotions in this ideational process for exclusive development along one line drives an idea to narrowness and diminishing returns and fuels all psychic energy into one cognitive channel. The shifting of energy from psychic area to psychic area, one function or capacity taking over when the other is waning or has made its contribution, gives richness and variety to experience and ideation and is the basis for balance and complementariness in cognition. In this view, ideas have a many-faceted character, one aspect playing against another, or there is a relay and tandem effect in which manifold ideational possibilities are explored to their full. As each emotion or aspect of ideation plays its part and finishes, another enters, giving rise to the inexhaustible play of rich ideas characteristic of the best of Greek thought.

Hence, all emotion had an enormous role in Greek thinking. Further, wisdom and feeling for justice constantly impinged on the modes of Greek thought giving them an immediate human texture or relevance. It is this valuative aspect of Greek thought that must be deeply considered in our contemporary measurement of intelligence, just as the hypothetical Greek psychologist would have appraised it in classic Greek society.

CRITICAL EVALUATION OF CONTEMPORARY TESTS

These, then, are some of the neglected dimensions of intelligence in contemporary American psychology that the classic Greeks, by contrast, evidenced so clearly. Perhaps most seriously neglected among current concepts and methods of intelligence measurement are the attributes of intuition and imagination as previously discussed. Indeed, what is typically found in current conceptualizations of intelligence and intelligence tests are theories and measures of shrewd cleverness, cunning, the ability to embrace and grasp the cultural status quo, definitions of conventional situations and experiences, and the capacity to solve practical problems in the most expeditious way or to proceed in step-by-step fashion to achieve immediate, tangible solutions. Arithmetic problems of a business variety and derived mostly from the profit and loss values of current society, vocabulary learned on an additive, mechanical basis, practical problems to be resolved economically, concretely, or expediently, and rote knowledge—these are the modalities in which intelligence is generally assessed at present. Not that these modalities are in themselves unimportant or, indeed, measures of certain aspects of intelligence. But they omit what, from the Greek view, accounted for the unique "higher" mental capacity of men and for much of what they have achieved intellectually in the past as well as the present. Thus they reflect a dangerously narrow view of man's intelligence and its attendant functions.

The Greek view would further hold that those components of intelligence that are most universally common in contemporary mass culture are made the criteria of intelligence and intelligence testing. These are the types of intelligence that have mostly to do with economic and social survival or adjustment (learning about the society, its cultural content, and the rules of the social system) and that rarely transcend their own cultural or cognitive premises and conditions or rarely suggest solutions to problems at a different level of assumption than that sanctioned by the intellectual status quo. These types of intelligence are usually confined to capacities for "knowing the ropes" and are illustrated in the kinds of test questions that ask about problems of profit and loss or concrete, practical matters and that demand rapid solutions to problems dealing with material things or money. This orientation, in turn, leads to the appraisal of intelligence in its more clever and shrewd aspects which are not dissimilar from the contrivances of a canny, crafty, and singleminded rat in an unimaginative but intricate maze. Indeed, test items are cleverly worded and craftily put together to elicit the clever, shrewd, and tricky answers that are inevitably equated with intelligence. Speed, rather than depth—both a value and an economic essential of our society—too often obstructs appraisal of the assumptions of the test questions and their value context by the testee, inhibits understanding of the larger significance of such items, and so sanctions tacit and unthinking acceptance of the values and norms of the culture. These conditions are analogous to a situation confronted by rats placed in a maze that has seemingly restricted choices which they accept only because the limitations of their imaginations prevent them from seeing the obscured but realizable alternative possibilities. Hence, they must behave in accordance with such an ostensibly (but not actually) circumscribed maze design (equivalent to the values of the culture or the premises of tests) if they are to be rewarded (succeed).

As to more time being made available for answering test questions, as to different orientations or hints being presented to the S which might induce doubts about the values and implicit purposes of the test items, and as to the available or suggested possibility to him that quite different solutions might be put forth than the "standard" ones—such proposals for the modification of testing procedure evoke little sympathy. In fact, "correct" answers to questions are standardized or scored by reference to common norms so that the uncommon or unique response may be marked down as wrong by many examiners, while the "pedestrian" or average answer is appraised as the "intelligent" or proper one. Further, the pressures of the test situation induce a psychological "set" that makes for responses analogous to those stemming from the "set" or conditions of business, where some "thing," result, or asset must come out of the factory, office, or laboratory irrespective of its human value, functional utility, or capacity to be beneficial. Indeed, the quality and level of required "solutions" is often far more similar to that of a robot, a rat in a maze, or a computer cognizing the world than that of a human being with such qualities as alert curiosity and lively thoughtfulness. Another earmark of these solutions is their "elementary" level of cognition of the world, a cognition in substantial degree oriented to "animal" survival: how to find one's way around the world, not imaginatively but by learning the "lay of the land" and the techniques of survival, including those of lifemanship, gamesmanship, and profit-making. Whatever "intelligence" is assessed, therefore, represents shrewd, shallow, and manipulative mental functions devoid of exploration of the premises and valuative orientations of the test questions, which, in turn, are oriented to elicit superficially clever, quick, and conventional responses representing the values of acquisitiveness, security, or social status. With, however, more generous allotment of time for testees to draw on their resources and to cultivate their thoughts, there might be greater likelihood of obtaining more reflective, probing responses that would challenge the premises and values of the test questions.

In many cases these ritualized and standardized test items reflect the "mass" culture of materialistic goals, economic gain, and achievement or success orientation and thus duplicate the world in which the psychologist himself lives. Indeed, it is the world that he must deal with in order to survive in much the same way as his Ss deal with intelligence test questions. Thus he often uses the same intellective processes that characterize the members of the "mass culture" and that also are incorporated in the psychological tests he devises. These test items also reflect the culture in their preoccupation with materialistic purposes and hard-headed cognition, numerical (and hence monetary) manipulations, quantities of accumulations (whether of money or of words), and rapidity in producing results or answering questions (related to speed in "bargaining" or negotiation and to expeditiousness in seizing the "main chance" in business).

Equally interesting is the relation between the significance of intelligence tests and children's abilities. It must never be forgotten that these questionnaires of information and problem-solving skill had, at first, the very practical purpose of excluding from certain school grades specified unqualified children.[2] The main underlying issue in all this was appraisal of the capacity of the very young to acquire the simple rudiments of culture as it was transmitted in the educational system, in this case a French culture that inevitably emphasized a characteristic French rationality: speed of comprehension and response, logic, lucidity of thought, and accumulation of concrete facts—in brief, a type of intelligence peculiar to a given culturally valued view of the functions of education and the mind. Different cultural or valuative views of these functions might very well produce different kinds of intelligence tests involving quite dissimilar modes of problem-solving and cognition which in these views would be judged as "intelligence" but in other views would not.

Also, it should be noted that current intelligence tests reflect a policy of "separating out" the inadequate capacity for learning relatively simple materials or appropriately responding to certain primary, cultural "know-how" problems rather than of differentiating abilities of higher order mental processes. Thus they largely appraise the "lower levels" of abilities but hardly embrace the broader and more complex range of intellect or the more sensitive and free dimensions of cognition. Such tests doubtless can be discriminating in excluding those who do not possess aptness for the mastery of shrewd, sensible, and business-like mental activities so essential for survival in this culture. To all this, again, must be added the preoccupation with vocabulary (related to the verbally manipulative and exhibitionistic aspects of advertising and to the selling of goods, services, or oneself to others in business and social transactions), the importance of practical and concrete information, and the concern with speed of response. Not that these are not important features of the intellective process, but the exclusive preoccupation with them creates a superficial and limiting view of this process and gives no perspective on its much broader scope. The talents assessed by current intelligence tests produce shallow, shrewd answers in place of thoughtful ones, constrict the boundaries of speculative thought, generate immediate, obvious, and practical solutions rather than penetrating and perceptive ones, and compel acceptance of the implicit values and norms of the test items and test situation. As a result, those involved in these situations are subtly influenced to accommodate to its values and hence subordinate whatever potential richness of thought they may have to the "proper," "correct," and meager responses that get approved. The cultural or societal values of the test which are, in effect, practiced in both test and nontest situations are also the recipe for the mental abilities essential for adjustment to the marketplace as well as the cognitive model of what comprises "intelligence" or "brightness" in the culture. Those passed by these tests have shown they are qualified candidates for the world of the marketplace and business or have the capacities for achieving sophistication in that world. Certainly they have not demonstrated that they are committed to or have the resource for such dimensions of intelligence as imagination, wisdom, intuition, and contemplation—all of which have much less to do with practical and business ends. The result is that only certain qualities of intelligence are assessed and these, in general, are consonant with the prevailing "establishment" philosophy of education and with the policy of selecting those individuals for advancement in the culture who are most responsive to the further development of these qualities. Hence "testing" becomes a technique of socialization of the young by rewarding the commitment to certain intellectual abilities or skills rather than others. Consequently the less practical and the more imaginative or original aspects of intelligence—those which have not so much to do with the capacity to learn about the marketplace but more with speculative power beyond a "survival-oriented" level of cognition, with the capacity to question premises and assumptions or to transcend mere cleverness or shrewdness, and with the ability to use the values and norms of the culture with flexibility and imagination—are hardly examined or measured. It is preoccupation with the mental processes necessary for adjustment and survival in this culture and with the methods by which these processes are learned (methods that convert human materials, too often, into human machines) that has hindered American psychologists from assessing the aforementioned dimensions of intelligence. Such a preoccupation has often been self-defeating because it has diminished the role that these broader aspects of intelligence might play in the educative process and in the culture in general. The emphasis on education of mass publics—on molding "all" in the pattern of the prevalent economic and cultural values so that the greatest number may be processed most expeditiously in their survival-oriented and economically exigent abilities and stamped with the commonest denominators of desires and motives—so that they better fit into the system of standardized mass production and consumption further increases the power of the marketplace in evoking the swift, canny, and shrewd talents of men. In this process the other values and capacities of men may be lost, and even those intellectual resources (imagination, intuition, etc.) that might transform this human machine so that it might effectively deal with and adjust to new conditions—and so better survive—are disregarded in the contemporary testing process.

RECTIFICATION

The characteristics of Greek intelligence which may be latent in contemporary individuals or, indeed, might be clearly evident if only properly

assessed are intuition, imagination, depth of thought, speculative freedom, capacity to question assumptions, fluidity of thought and its interpenetration with feeling, boldness of thought, constant probing and the
refusal to accept superficial or simple solutions, constant attempts to
reformulate ideas, and the capacity to be "open" to new values, ideas, and
approaches.

We have seen that contemporary psychology rarely takes into consideration these intellectual traits and so neglects them in mental tests as well as
in studies of the general population. If one were to depart from the preoccupation with the practical, speedy, and shrewd facets of intelligence
involved in middle-class survival and security and now almost exclusively
measured in contemporary tests, and emphasize other variables of intelligence, what sort of tests would be constructed? Where would our hypothetical Greek psychologist, possessed of knowledge of modern "testing"
techniques, look in order to appraise these other variables?

The following suggestions apply to such other variables and the related
methods for their assessment:

1. Imagination. The capacity to take any theme and further develop,
refine, or complicate it. What would be looked for in the S's response
would be the complication of thought, the boldness of speculation, the
interweaving of several types of material, the development and richness
of the theme, and the details and variety of characterization or description.

The following proposals are designed to assess this intelligence factor:
(1) Present a simple story incident, theme, or situation which the S
would have to develop and give substance to. (2) Request the S to concoct a story with some common elemental theme, e.g., boy meets girl, the
tragedy of life, the loss of ideals. (3) The S would be asked to tell a story
about a great painting or a cartoon. (4) An explanation for some happening or event would be asked for, e.g., a historical phenomenon, an episode
in a person's life, or a political event; (4a) The S would be asked for his
own conception of the cause or the theoretical explanation of a designated event in one or more of the following areas: the physical or life
sciences, ordinary human experience, international affairs, and crime
detection. A specified number of relevant facts would be presented to him
pertaining to such an event or phenomenon about whose explanation he
would know little or nothing. He would then be asked to concoct the best
explanation from the presented facts. (5) New solutions would be requested for various riddles, slogans, or tricks that would be presented to
the S. (6) Various types of practical problems would be presented
(mechanical, spatial, economic, personal survival) and different ideas for
their solution would be elicited. Also, the S would be required to formu-

49

late plans and procedures for specific new products, for certain social programs for mankind, for an advertising campaign, for an artistic design, or for some carpentry construction. (7) Another test would be to require the S to compose sentences or longer texts, starting with merely a few words strung together. He would be urged to make his composition as imaginative as possible. (8) Some discordant or paradoxical facts and experiences would be presented, and the S would be urged to give as speculative an explanation as possible, however extravagant it might appear. This "free speculation" also would apply to the previous item.

None of the above tests would be administered impersonally or coldly but rather in an atmosphere of relaxation and in a context that would facilitate the desired imaginative responses. Thus the S would be under no pressures of time or urgency for success and would not be precipitated abruptly into an "examination" situation but rather slowly be drawn into it.

2. Intuition. This component comprises the immediate perception of a relationship, apprehension of the crucial factor in an explanation, sensitivity to the basic dimensions of a person or a situation and recognition of how to proceed in the case of the latter. Intuition implies both a passive sensing of the situation and an active apprehension of the proper direction to take. The passive aspects derive from the empathic relationship to the object and its quasi-internalization; the active component from the imaginative act of psychic movement wherein the relevant factors can be acknowledged and their proper proportion established by a type of fantasy or prospection; or, put in another way, the recording and mental dramatizing of all these components in various projected future resolutions. Intuition may also involve seeing beyond surface impressions to a more profound design or can encompass the glimpse of a hidden meaning that the facts rarely hint at but that, nonetheless, may be apprehended in a vague and ineffable way.

How can this function be assessed? The following proposals are made: (1) Poetry. Read to or have the S himself read poems and ask for their meaning or whatever illumination they may have given him. (2) Do the same for recondite, ambiguous, or mystical texts. (3) Present odd sequences of numbers which may vary from simple to very complex order, but without preordained relationships, and ask him to derive any patterns he can from them. (4) After a scene or event is described, ask the S what additions would best fit into the specific context that was presented or into further passages that he might add. Give the S a choice of words and phrases or request his extemporaneous insertions and additions. (5) Riddles and Chinese puzzles are presented for solution. (6)Epigrams, precepts, wise sayings, and fables are presented for interpretation. (7) A "problem" situation is described in detail, and the S is asked to solve it: how to escape from a jail; how to get out of a forest one is lost in; how to make a big coup in a business deal or choose the right business venture for a future "sensational" success; how to solve a given detective mystery. (8) The S is to be asked to describe the characteristics of people. Characterizations would be made from their presented portraits or photographs. (9) Character descriptions of individuals are to be requested on the basis of a presented account of their overt behavior, i.e., only of what they did. (10) From a list of personally descriptive separate words the S is to be required to write a personality evaluation of an individual. By changing or omitting a few trait words in such descriptions an opportunity would be provided for any new character analysis that the S might be disposed to make. This would be especially relevant to appraising his intuitive flexibility. The same could be done for the descriptions of overt behavior (acts) in the previous item. (11) Arithmetic problems requiring flashes of insight for solution—not step-by-step logic—are presented to the S. (12) Detective mysteries with additional variations of material are presented for solution, i.e., more complex conditions are added to the initial presented "case" after the S presents his solution to it. Again, this is relevant to the S's intuitive flexibility. (13) Explanations for certain phenomena are requested from the S: why are there so many uniformed officials in Italy? Why did some particular American president take a given action? Why are there proportionately more women in the Eastern than the Western states? Explain a specific individual's behavior.

3. Depth of thought. Proposals for appraisal of this factor are: (1) The S would be asked to make a detailed analysis of the character of an individual as inferred from his portrait by a great painter, such as Titian, Rembrandt, Holbein, or to give an explanation of the forces—aesthetic, social, psychological, symbolic, or dramatic—in some other dramatic painting. (2) Interpretation of passages from works of poetry, philosophy, and religion would be requested, the S being encouraged to go as far and as deep as he can in his probings. (3) After reading a problem play or having its outline presented to him, the S would be asked to give an explanation of its various themes, its development, and its ultimate meaning. (4) The S would read an essay and be given the opportunity to develop its themes and ideas, to present criticisms, or to otherwise discuss his reflections and original conceptions. (5) The S would be presented with the propositions or premises of a philosophical viewpoint, would be asked to question them, and then to present an alternative approach. (6) The S would be presented with an idea or theme in a special field (his

own) or in some other area of which he has knowledge. He would then be required to go into these presented issues as deeply as possible, bringing all his information, ideas, wisdom, and imagination to bear on them. (7) Themes and values in morality and ethics would be presented to the S, especially those of general importance: the relations between individuals, conformity, the values of life, the morality of contemporary society, etc. The S would be asked to reflect on and discuss these subjects as deeply and elaborately as he can. (8) Maxims, gems of thought, wise and profound extracts would be presented to the S for interpretation and development. (9) The S would be presented with aphorisms of earthy practical common sense and then would be asked to probe the assumptions underlying them, the extent to which these maxims may be applied, and his contradictions or reservations regarding them. (10) The S would be asked to give advice on what to do in various personal and social situations including the understanding and treatment of particular individuals. Various situations would be described and his counsel would be solicited on practical problems, on the sympathetic understanding of other persons, or on crucial decisions affecting the course of their lives. The S would be encouraged to question all implicit values and assumptions of these presented situations in his suggested advice, i.e., conventional morals or traditional ways of behaving.

What this component of intelligence calls for is the extension of the mind to examine concealed values or unexamined assumptions as, in the questioning of certain assumptions in physics by Einstein or as in poetic questioning about the experiences and values of life. Such questioning about the implicit values in contemporary IQ test items, for example, would take the following forms: "Why should the boy want to run fast?" "Why should he change money at the highest rates?" "Why does the man do the job in this way? Are there not other and better ways to do it? In fact, why should he want to do the job at all?" It is such questioning and resolution through more comprehensive and profound alternative solutions—be it in puzzles, values of life, more general theories in science or philosophy, and more basic ways of doing things—that is involved in this factor of depth of thought.

4. Speculative freedom. This factor accounted for the ability among the Greeks to go as far with data or experience as the mind could reach (1) in the development of intellectual concepts and vision, (2) in transcending traditional values and ideas, and (3) in the capacity to take nothing for granted and to reverse conventional conclusions. Included, also, was the fresh reexamination of feelings, actions, and ideas. Consequently, there was a seeking out of novel possibilities, a searching for and playing with

new conceptual and aesthetic permutations, and vigorous explorations in imagination and perception.

Proposals for the measurements of this factor are: (1) Ask the S to compose a most incredible story or narrative. Its theme may or may not be suggested to him. (2) Present some kind of problem—a detective mystery, a riddle, an espionage case, a political or human relations difficulty—and ask the S to contrive the most speculative kinds of solutions. Present some pedestrian occurrence or event—an argument, an accident, the finding of a wallet—and ask that it be accounted for in the most uninhibitedly speculative way. (3) Allow the S to freely proliferate ideas and suggestions for advertisements for some products, slogans for different causes, plots for stories, titles for literary works, etc. (4) Ask the S to imagine what life would be like on other planets (under certain specified conditions) or what man's life would be like on earth under different specified social, economic, technological, or physical conditions. (5) Present a sequence of national or international political events and allow the S to speculate on their widest and most far-reaching ramifications; or ask him to make a future projection of these events; (6) Ask the S to compose an uninhibited adventure or Western story, a science fiction narrative, a fable, a fairy tale, or a horror story—all as imaginatively as possible. (7) Present the most absurd series of facts, scientific or other, in direct contradiction to experience or to current theories and ask the S for as many uninhibited explanations—however fantastic—as he can make of them. (8) Ask S to manipulate a specific story so as to reverse its plot or to otherwise change it about so that its values, conclusions, and mood are in opposition to the original. A specific poem, play, novel, or short story could be used for this. (9) Ask the S: "Can you imagine what would happen if our present-day values were reversed in actual practice, e.g., if children were to run things and adults became the dependent wards; if altruistic love became primary and personal selfishness were almost eliminated; if men were to assume the psychological qualities of women, and vice versa; if people were unreservedly sincere or trusted each other completely; if we always followed and lived by the best ideas in every area of life and work." The S would be asked to imagine the consequences of these hypothetical conditions in various fields and for life in general. (10) Ask the S to compose a language with sounds or words derived from the same "vocal core" as English: onomatopoeic or comparable sounds could be used or a "neologistic" equivalent of English words and sentences might be asked for. Fantasy languages expressing experiences, sensations, or moods also ought to be elicited. (11) Ask the S: "Assume colors were interchanged (by name, hue, or pattern) or people saw colors but not forms (or the reverse), then what kind of color (or form) schemes would one have for different kinds of rooms, buildings, churches, etc.?"

5. Fluidity of thought. This factor constitutes the rapid succession of ideas, the sequencing of cognitive perception after perception, the freedom of association of concepts, the pursuit of ideas with many facets in such a way that one facet does not overwhelm or oppress others, and the carrying through of a conception as far as it will go while balancing it by contrast with ideas of some other dimension. It involves, too, the mobilization of relevant associations to an idea, its connections with other fields, and the conjoining of varied and even seemingly remote materials to this idea or theme. The resultant effect is to see this idea from many perspectives and in a very rich context by linking it with other meaningful materials rather than maintaining the limited view of a single idea with its ensuing ossification, tenuousness, or exhaustion.

Proposals for the assessment of this factor are: (1) A simple problem (arithmetic, social, mystery, factual, etc.) is presented that has several alternative solutions. The number of such solutions the S suggests or works out would be the pertinent "answers" for this test. (2) A theme is suggested to the S. The examiner is interested in the number of variations and complications of it that are elicited or adumbrated. (3) An ambiguous topic is presented for discussion: an issue in international affairs, the purpose of life, mysticism in man, etc. The number of different areas, varied materials, and insights or intuitions that are woven into the S's discussion is appraised. (4) Epigrams, maxims, fables, allegories, and parables are presented. The number of different meanings or possible explanations that the S produces are assessed. (5) A business problem either of simplicity or complexity is described. The number, versatility, and multifaceted quality of the alternative proposals the S makes for its resolution is evaluated. (6) The different types, levels, and richness of the S's cognitive responses to poetry, ideas, stories, paintings, music, architectural structures, scenes of nature, etc. are appraised. (7) A philosophical passage is presented. The different meanings, varied assumptions and several implications that it arouses in the S are evaluated. (8) A social situation is portrayed in words or pictures. The S's capacity to see it from varied dramatic, psychological, moral, or social angles, to interpret it from the viewpoint of each character involved, and to offer different types of resolution of it is appraised. (9) Data from a scientific discovery or experiment, from historical or economic research, or from some geographical, sociological, or economic findings are presented. The S must determine how such data fit into different domains of theory and knowledge, what implications are involved for the specific area under consideration and for more remote areas, and the general ramifications of such data in regard to people, life, and the future. (10) A political situation is described with all pertinent facts. The S is required to make all the possible analyses he can and to project all possible strategies for different specified goals. (11) The S is required to report his different levels of intuition and perception of ambiguous portraits or of verbal descriptions of complex persons. (12) A description of an individual's character and appearance—or of only certain aspects of it—is presented. The S is then asked how this person would fit into or behave in various, specified situations. (13) The S is asked to show how different moralities may be either valuable or an impediment to different people in different situations. Specific moralities as well as specific individuals and situations are described and the S is asked to explain which morality is best for which circumstance or individual and to indicate, too, its drawbacks. (14) A painting or a universal literary theme is presented: The S's capacity to change from aesthetic to historical to dramatic and other orientations in response to these stimuli is appraised.

6. Integration of feeling and intellect. This factor entails the infusion of thought with different emotional qualities so that some form of balanced integration is achieved. The resulting interpenetration of feeling and intellect is simultaneously evidenced in the capacity for emotional involvement in a problem or topic, in the ability to consider it with some detachment, and in the infusion of the reflective process with such emotional and value factors as virtue, aesthetic orientation, zest, honesty of purpose and elegance.

Proposed tests for this factor are: (1) Essays on logic and feeling or on law and compassion would be presented. An analysis would be made of the manner in which the S would develop his discussion or reach a resolution of the issues involved in these essays that would deal with various aspects of the integration of feeling and intellect. Materials chosen for presentation might vary in the degree to which they embody such integration, e.g., optimally possessing it, minimally possessing it, or exhibiting only one of its dimensions (intellect or emotion). (2) Perceptual objects representing pure form or pure "feeling" would be presented. The S would be required to find "emotional" values in the pure form stimuli (geometric art, abstract designs, or certain kinds of "'mathematical" music) and to find formal dimensions in purely "emotional" productions, such as color-dominated art, impressionistic paintings, wild free associations, tautophonic sounds, clouds, disorganized narratives, manic or schizophrenic speech and drawings, disjointed materials in a room or landscape, etc. (3) Purely formal or intellectual problems would be presented requiring the driest, most logical procedures: geometric problems, financial problems, and legal problems. The S's responses would be examined for evidence of feelings, such as aesthetic delight, enthusiasm, wit, affective purpose, or other emotional components. Conversely, emotional issues as embodied in personal relations, poetry, impressionistic music and art, children's behavior, mass manias, individual and collective hysterias, and moral and political controversies would be presented and the S asked to organize and analyze such materials into a logical chain of propositions of a rational order. (4) Emotional problems of a personal, marital, valuative, or political nature would be presented as they were embodied in the "raw data" or "primary source" form of the "emotional dimension" (passion, controversy, stream of consciousness, sequence of experiential events, etc.). A complete record of facts, chronicle, discussion, or experience would be presented and the S asked to distill their rational and logical quality. Also, formal intellectual issues (e.g., military, financial, or scientific decisions and business or technical problems) would be presented to see if the S would take into account their emotional facets. (5) It would be vital to assess the capacity to take the most profound emotional problems (e.g., life and death, war and peace, individuality and conformity, humanism vs. the machine) as presented in concrete, detailed emotional experiences, occurrences, and personal events and to dissect such "raw" material into a rational and logical order. (6) Also appraised should be the capacity—when stimulated by pleasant, exciting, sad, indifferent, or tragic events or materials—to respond by emotion (compassion, crying, laughter, sadness, delight, etc.) while remaining capable of making an objective evaluation of these stimuli by means of logical and technical analysis, factual knowledge, or rational understanding. Conversely, intellectual materials when presented might evoke primarily cognitive responses in the S, but his capacity to simultaneously experience aesthetic, moral, compassionate, and other emotional reactions should be appraised whether the stimuli be geometric figures, scientific problems, cold legal briefs, etc. (7) In all these materials (formal and intellectual, on the one hand, and emotional on the other) the S's capacity to shift from one of these orientations to the other should be appraised. Finding "emotional" aspects in intellectual material which, in turn, leads to deeper and different "feeling" experiences and thence to further and more profound intellectual insight and response (all of this being a kind of leapfrogging mental interaction, often digressive or parenthetic) are the processes to be appraised. The stimulus materials presented to the S should vary in the amount of intellectual or emotional components they possess—ranging from equality of both to high of one and low of the other, and vice versa.

7. Wisdom. This factor may be considered to be the realistic projected judgment of a course of events together with the reasonably accurate appraisal of the best course of action to follow regarding them in order to achieve the most beneficial results. As such, wisdom requires awareness of the nature of a situation as well as insight into the character and needs of individuals participating in it, and then weighs these factors in terms of projected future developments and repercussions. It thus comprises a nice balance of practical, human, and social considerations and requires the broadest possible perspective if the maximal good of the individual, group, or society is to be achieved. Such a dimension of intelligence would subordinate immediate economic gratifications to long-term ends, might make the immediate issues of one's present status secondary to long-run honor or achievement, and, in general, would see issues, ends, and values in the longest possible view. Suggestions for assessing this quality are: (1) The S is asked "What is the best thing to do now: make a great deal of money despite attendant pressures, drives, and anxieties or not try so hard, make considerably less money, and have peace of mind?" As part of his answer, the S would have to project the economic, psychological, and social consequences of the choice of each of these options and develop the reasons for his final selection. (2) The S is presented with a general or very specific issue involving the following terms: He may complete a big economic transaction with enormous profit that, however, necessitates antagonizing many people including close friends and that also risks an increasing callousness of his own feelings and conscience as well as the loss of his warmth and sensibility. Alternatively, he may not make this deal, resulting in a train of quite different consequences. The detailed reasons for the S's choice and his appraisal of the consequences stemming from each of these alternative courses of action would be called for. (3) The S is presented with this choice: a career that will fairly immediately yield economic success and social status vs. the search for an occupation that will be deeply gratifying and significant but not necessarily yield economic or status rewards. Again, the S is asked for the projected consequences of each option and the reasons for his choice. (4) The following job "options" are offered to the S: an uncertain position as head of a frantic enterprise or a much lower-paying, lower-status job which, however, offers economic security and tranquility in connection with it. The S is asked to give reasons for his choice, the projected consequence for each option, and, in addition, to indicate the choice that he thinks would be made by various particular types of individuals. (5) The S is asked to determine whether a committee-type or an individual executive procedure is better for the wisest decision-making in various types of

situations. These may be political situations; situations calling for speed and maximal efficiency; situations involving emergency or urgent circumstances; situations involving complex personal relationships or other factors in one's personal life such as delicate feelings, integrity, health, work, and even death; situations involving small groups, corporate bodies, and military units; circumstances involving negotiations and conflicts. (6) The S is confronted with the choice of taking a long-run risk or of proceeding in a conventional manner in any one of a number of situations that are described to him. In addition, a variety of types of persons who would be protagonists in each of those situations is also described, the S being required to make this choice for each one of them, taking into account their character and the nature of the situation. Such situations might be in business, politics, science, or interpersonal affairs. The S would be required to give the reasons for his own choice in each case and for each of the hypothetical protagonists considered. (7) The S is presented with the following options: to follow his own desires, impulses, talents, purposes, and beliefs even at the expense of a break with others (friends, colleagues, membership or reference groups, or parents) or to conventionally proceed in his life, mechanically copying his group's or family's values and thus permitting their purposes to predominate over his own. These options would be conveyed through detailed descriptions of concrete events and episodes in the following areas: career, status, choice of university, selection of friends, choice of marriage partner, choice of manners, conduct or morals, deference to authority, and membership in various groups. The S would be asked to spell out the reasons for the choice he would make in each instance. (8) The S is presented with the choice of either pursuing a path that would be of deep personal significance and fulfillment for himself, however uncertain its prospects of success and reward, or of following a conventional path that would bring certain success and acceptance. Issues and situations comprising the objects of his decision would lie in the areas of marriage, justice, politics, honor, or career. He would be asked to make a choice of the presented alternatives and give his reasons. (9) The following choice is presented to the S: do something easy and simple that produces only limited results or, in the same area, do something that is complicated and requires much effort but has the potential of very rich and significant results. The "areas" to which this choice would be directed are: a job, a research study, a large enterprise, construction of a house, etc. The S would also be required to make the wisest possible choice of these options for a variety of types of individuals whose character, values, and personal situation would be described to him. (10) Another series of items would require decisions involving choices in the following areas: alternative driving maneuvers while motoring in heavy traffic; route planning decisions for an automobile trip; job choices; specific behavior alternatives in office politics, in interpersonal relations on the job, and in problems intrinsic to the "work" aspects of the job itself; selection of an area, apartment, or house in which to live; available alternatives involved in the financing of a house, in furnishing it, and in selecting various features of it in conjunction with one's budget and various personal needs; planning the time budget of one's day in relation to various tasks, leisure, and rest that must be apportioned; choices involved in planning and executing a shopping trip including the time and money to be allotted for purchases, the selection of stores, and the wisdom of making many price comparisons in relation to available shopping time. Another group of items would require the S to select from various presented options a sequence of acts to be executed in a minimum time and by the most reasonable method. These would include alternative presented ways of doing administrative chores, repair jobs, and of organizing tasks for a group. The S would also be confronted with budgeting an income for family and personal needs, recreations, and luxuries, the budget to be drawn up by the S for different types of persons whose personalities and background situations would be described. The S would be asked to select and plan an optimal vacation—from among several alternatives—for a variety of different types of persons. He also would be asked to choose recreations such as theater, music, art, dance, or television for himself and various other types of persons for their different moods and for various occasions.

As part of the preceding questions, the S would be asked to explain the reasons for his choices which would, in each case or issue, be made from a large number of presented alternatives. In addition, the choices could also be made under specified conditions, such as poverty, wealth, relaxation, pressure, happiness, and sadness.

Perception

The Greek view of perception will be primarily derived from the nature of Greek art. As expressed in the classic period of Greek culture, it had the properties of balance, idealization of emotion and of the human figure, and delicacy in the integration of feeling with intellect. As reflected in

59

Greek sculpture, its features were tranquility of sensation and feeling, serene but not intellectual detachment toward the artistic object and the experience it evoked, and accessibility to the essence of this experience without disturbing it through the intrusion of personal passions. The full experience of the undiluted emotional elements of the art work as embodied in the idealization and stylization of its form and content accounts for the viewer's intensity and purity of feeling while simultaneously compelling that psychic distance that prevents emotion from drowning cognition. This intriguing mixture of aloofness and intensity of experience in the realms of both the intellect and emotion is a unique feature of Greek sculpture. The slow permeation of feeling through the viewer and, simultaneously, his calm, aloof perspective of it made for a kind of emotional-intellectual experience in him. The constant interplay between this affect and this intellectuality was one of the most dynamic aspects of the Greek perceptual experience calling, as it did, for a fluctuation of perceptual orientation: absorption in the intensity of feeling oscillating with detachment from it. This latter aloofness also engendered an additional dimension to this experience: a constancy of feeling which, owing to the psychic detachment, took on a coolness and a duration that strong emotion could not possess. Shifting to and fro between these perceptual points of view refreshed emotion through rest and contrast, for too much intensity tended to exhaust it while the detachment permitted the "objective" perceptual component to be part of the ongoing aesthetic experience.

This idealization of emotion by visualizing it through the eyes of the intellect, then, gave rise to awareness of a protracted process, which while appearing static in fact evoked emotion. The intellectual perspective accounted for a detachment that gave the illusion that the process might continue endlessly so that the aesthetic experience left the impression of an eternal verity or "idea." Thus it was neither that feeling was exhausted nor that the art work incorporated an "idea" that was excessively intellectual or structured which would have merely made an essay of it. All this is aptly conveyed by Keats's idea of "something eternally happening," [3] which also describes an experience or process that is "becoming" or emerging but before it has reached its culmination. If a completed act is represented, the perceptual response will be similar to abstract intellectual activity. If, however, the depicted act is at its beginning (and before its apex after which exhaustion occurs) then the potential of its fulfillment is still in the imagination and it still has the full prospect of growing and ramifying as the cognitive and emotional interplay develops. The perceptual action appears to be constantly in process of "becoming," an ambiguity allowing for much imaginative play in the spectator as well as evoking the feeling that the artistic action is infinite in that only its continuance, and not its end, is experienced or foreseen. This adds to the growing intensity of the experience while permitting further oscillation of perceptual orientation so that the aesthetic perceptual experience is viewed as an indefinitely continuing process that, in turn, is responsible for its components of detachment, serenity, and abstractness. It is this balance of—and to and fro shifting from—emotion to intellect, this idealization without coldness, this richness of imaginative intensity without exhaustion, this capacity to evoke intense feeling by exciting exceptional perceptual and emotional possibilities but without excluding the idea of the finished act or of detachment that makes the Greek artistic experience so extraordinary. Fluidity and balance of idea and emotion so that coldness and fatigue do not occur, suggestion of only the incipient nature of the completed act, allowing the spectator the fullest play to complete it in himself while permitting his detachment from it and from its oscillating perceptual elements prior to its culminating aesthetic point—all this excites an extraordinary interplay of feeling and intellect.

CRITICAL EVALUATION OF AMERICAN STUDIES

From the Greek perspective, the omissions and allied defects of current perceptual studies in American psychology are serious. First, these studies are very often carefully controlled laboratory experiments which limit, channel, or denude the perceptions that might be evoked under freer conditions. The results, therefore, are consonant with these present-day experimental operations insofar as the flow, freedom of sensation and emotion, and interplay between intellect and feeling of the Greek perceptual process cannot be generated in a research environment that regiments perceptual freedom and forces the responses of the S into a narrow mold, thereby paralyzing the vital Greek exchange between feeling and intellect. The S is aware of the expected and sanctioned perceptual response just as, when completing a form or answering a teacher's question, he knows what is "correct."

But perhaps it is the selection process that is as much responsible for the results obtained in present studies: the choice, most often, of those Ss who are deferential and conformist or simply those who, in return for being paid, happily defer to the ineffable imperatives of the experimental atmosphere. (A not parenthetical issue is whether those not selected as subjects or those rejecting selection differ significantly from the "selected" as regards conformity, fear, etc. Indeed, what experimental results would be obtained if persons who were freer, more courageous, less "polite" or proper, and more independent or disrespectful of "authority" were to be used as subjects?)

Even in experimental situations where "new" experiences and stimuli are presented under uncertain or ambiguous conditions, conventional responses continue to be made though the experimental stimuli were adequate to have excited a broader, richer spectrum of reaction. Contributing to this tendency is the presence of complex experimental apparatus and observation screens which, by frightening or overawing the S, provoke a "regression" to simpler, less expressive, more conforming, and thus more concrete responses—an effect not diminished by the authoritarian directions and prescriptions delivered and symbolized by the E as the agent of science. Compounding these effects is the emphasis in American work on "reality" dimensions of perception, such as accuracy, concreteness, judgment of space or depth, and the influences of the American cultural milieu itself (both in and out of the experimental situation): materialistic, realistic, concrete, "knowing the score," and exploiting this "know-how" and "reality orientation" to win, acquire, adjust, or get ahead. This commitment to such manipulative, motor, adjustment-oriented, and executive values is then extended by means of corollary experimental methods to studies of profoundly different perceptual values, problems, or processes even though these methods are not germane to the authentic nature of the psychological phenomena that the latter require for proper investigation.

By contrast, the manifold nature of the perceptual act to be examined here represents a peculiarly Grecian combination of qualities: the fluidity and ease of balance, the hint of fulfillment in the incipient stage of the perceptual experience, the movement from mood to mood fused by an underlying continuity, the reach for the eternal, and the genius for fully involving the spectator and achieving a completed experience.

In American perceptual work there is a substantial neglect of studies dealing with the salient features of Greek perception. Thus, for reasons already cited (instrumentation, the laboratory, and the E's authoritarianism) plus factors such as the lack of relaxation of the S, his inability to substantially fulfill his full perceptual potential in the research environment, and the pressure of the experimental situation to segment and regiment perceptual experience by focusing on only one component of each perceptual stimulus, there occurs a fragmentation or deterioration of the organic perceptual response. Moreover, the mood of tranquility and receptivity which evokes rich perceptual responses and sensitive facets of feeling to design, color, and other stimulus properties is neither present in the perceptual experience nor in the perceptual environments characteristically investigated by American psychologists. Thus the Greek heritage and potential for perception are all substantially fragmented in such situations.

If such potential perceptual experiences have not been already obliterated by the life histories of Americans, then American psychological research assures their nonappearance by restricting perceptual experience to those components required for action, manipulation, or survival and to those concrete, mechanical, or "reality-oriented" perceptions that are intrinsic to industrial society and to a preeminently materialistic outlook on life. The perceptual component par excellence for such an outlook is the cognitive one, for it is most congruent with an empirical, manipulative, scientific, "know-how" orientation to the world. Thus American psychology makes of perception a phenomenon molded to a mechanistic, materialistic, and survival-oriented image of man. Whether these efforts are owing to the conception that perception consists of such mechanistic or materialistic elements and, in addition, reflects the importance of the role of primitivization and instinct in the unconscious process or whether they are a calculated attempt to reduce and organize the total perceptual gamut to a very few manipulable and somewhat dehumanized dimensions in the hope of achieving a certain operational and mathematical clarity on the model of the more successful and fashionable positivistic disciplines is not easy to determine. The conversion of the total organic perceptual response into only one of its components—cognition—reflects an overcontrolled, overrationalized effort analogous to the rational ordering of principles and operations that go into the functioning of a machine or to the organized procedures of a mass production system. It is of course perfectly proper to use rational and positivistic procedures to test hypotheses about perception, but whether formulating these issues in mechanical, reductionistic, and cognitive terms does any more than ensure conditions that give rise to only congruent perceptions is a different and important matter.

American perceptual studies, then, tend to artificially separate the specific, concrete, cognitive components in perception from the emotional, valuative, and aesthetic ones as well as from the organic context in which all perceptual components are embedded. These studies further tend to divert organic, many-faceted perceptual responses into the cognitive channel or, alternatively, restrict or abort them except for their cognitive components. Hence, this component becomes disproportionate in mirroring the nature of the perceptual process in present studies, because the other perceptual components have only the smallest chance of revealing their importance inasmuch as they are frozen, ignored, or channeled into cognitive or manipulative perceptual modes. As a result, these latter are exaggerated, with accompanying rigidity, and a wider and more varied perceptual range does not emerge. Depth or fluidity of perception can hardly be realized under these conditions, and if emphasis either in research design or in proficiency of perceptual functions is strengthened in such areas as cognitive analysis, reality manipulation, and practical problem-solving, it is too often to the detriment of the aesthetic, organic, and other many-faceted perceptual components.

In the other major dimension of perception studied, i.e., unmodulated emotion, a parallel orientation is present. In studies of the effects of strong or primitive feeling on perception (pain, anxiety, frustration, and certain instinctual affects) there is a division between feeling and cognition issuing in the exaggeration or distortion of the one and the unbalancing or weakening of the other. While revealing the power of emotion, such designs foster the destruction of the integration of the salient emotive-cognitive complex in the organic perceptual act or stress one to the diminution of the other. The methodology consonant with such psychological atomism and reductionism fails to give a balanced view of what occurs in integrated perception or of what perceptions could emerge in designs of freer latitude which would be carried out under more natural, full-bodied conditions.

Speed of presentation and response, too, is often emphasized in these experiments—a condition that provokes blatant, rough, or unproportioned affects, sharpens perceptual responses, and truncates their outcome in quick quasijudgments and reactions, thereby impeding the emergence of full-bodied integrative perceptions. From these experiments, the more obvious, rough, and sensational perceptions emanate, abetted by the character of the test stimuli and, in some cases, by the subject population employed. It cannot be surprising, then, that the prospects for more subtle or balancing dimensions of perception to come forth, including the intuitive, aesthetic, and richly organic, are less than excellent.

Preoccupation with Freudian dynamics is also a strong mark of modern perceptual studies. Experiments are designed to make "depth" factors preeminent and thereon cognitive, empirical, and other modifying variables are often diminished in importance in these studies. This is the other side of the perceptual coin, nakedly and radically revealed, but the organic nexus that integrates and interrelates this face with its cognitive opposite is ignored. Is it a case of scientific and/or ideological compensation: the extreme emphasis on intellectual, "respectable," concrete, empirical, logical, conscious, and rational dimensions of perception necessitating balance by an equal emphasis on the "disreputable" instinctual, impractical, unconscious, irrational elements? Whatever else, it reflects the spirit of the age: the disassociation of intellectual, rational, and practical mentality from emotion, sensibility, or animalistic passion as well as the emphasis on the corollary methodology of a disassociated atomistic, reductionistic, and discrete type of analysis.

RECTIFICATION

According to the Greek view, the rectification of these conditions would require strong emphasis on the fluidity, detachment, incipience, empathy, and the natural organic unity or cohesion of the perceptual act. To implement such an orientation, the following proposals are offered:

1. Studies in this area should place high priority on ensuring the S's relaxation, on the exclusion or concealment of apparatus that he might be aware of, on giving him a generous amount of time to adjust to the experimental situation and, if he so desires, to reflect on the experiment itself and on his prospective responses in it. He should be given, in many studies, a sense of relaxation approaching that of home-like ease and his perceptual responses should be allowed to germinate and grow over a period of time. Desirable sets such as "flexibility of mood" might be induced by appropriate music, by pleasant conversation on some interesting but undisturbing subject, by carrying out the experiment in a relaxing but "psychologically enriched or warm" room, and by having a good friend of the S play the role of the experimenter. All this is designed to induce the fluidity of mood that is conducive to a plastic and many-faceted perceptual response to the stimulus object.

2. To achieve flexibility of mood and the constant movement that marked Greek perception, it may be necessary to train the Ss in sensitivity of perceptual movement as well as in the varied modes and levels of perceptual response. This could be done by using ambiguous pictures, shifting designs, or illustrated lectures about the proper orientation to great Greek art, by constant variation in presented visual stimuli, and by showing the different levels and modalities of a perceptual object to the S in such a way that he can appreciate and fully respond to each of them separately in preparation for an integrated response when they are organically and naturally embodied in a single perceptual stimulus.

3. Serenity and detachment of mood, requisite for the Ss in these experiments, can be cultivated through: experiences obtained by viewing appropriate art objects in tranquil museum settings; repeatedly experiencing situations that have a serene and balanced quality; relaxed and pleasant experiences involving contemplation of objects, landscapes, and

rooms; tranquil conversations or colloquies, quiet meditation, rest, and idleness; restful music or movies. An experimental setting comparable to the serene and harmonious atmosphere of Greek temples would be of great importance for evoking the mood and attitudes these experiments require, and furnishing the experimental room itself to induce a similarly tranquil and balanced mood would be helpful. Selecting readings of Greek literature, philosophy, and poetry as well as having the S engage in various of the above activities immediately preceding the experiment would be other useful approaches.

4. Cultivation of sensibility that is responsive to the nature of the Greek aesthetic experience can be achieved by orienting the S to and having him actually practice the Grecian aesthetic response or by having him empathically observe others engaged in it. What is required for the refinement of this sensibility is delicate training in lightness of mood, supple responsiveness, capacity to feel deeply but empathically, and the unimpaired freedom of primitive impulse. The last excepted, this complex of feelings might also be evoked by deeply experiencing the sentiments and mood of certain kinds of poetry and music, by experiencing certain kinds of agile, sensitive, emotionally supple discussions and interpersonal relationships, and by protracted training in plastic, empathic, unencumbered reaction to sounds, colors, landscapes, panoramas, houses, rooms, and other kinds of objects or environments.

5. Intuition and "response to incipience" are such delicate segments of Grecian perception that a simple training scheme alone would not ensure their activation. Intuition could be nurtured, partly, by relaxation and freedom from tension. It might also be cultivated by training and practice in assessing and understanding other individuals, through psychologically insightful reading of novels, by the sensitivity attained through sophisticated orientation and practice in judging social situations, through the experience of poetic feeling coming from observing nature, through participation in sensitivity training seminars and Esalen-type experiences, through the sound and rhythm of language or appropriate poetry readings, and through all sorts of delicate and fragile sensibilities or moods. This kind of intuition also might flower in conversations in which precise logic and "hard realism" are soft-pedaled and where fantasy, uninhibited feeling, and gay interpersonal feeling are the main ingredients. Specific direction, training, and practice in acting on feeling and impulse and in subordinating empiricism, practicality, and concreteness might also stimulate its arousal. When appropriate, some of these suggestions could be carried out just before the S begins the experiment. Indeed, even an easy, relaxed preexperimental setting may help in getting the desired effect.

66

6. Other suggestions that may prove useful for exploring this perceptual component are plentiful use of chiaroscuro in the stimulus objects (shadow, subtle shadings, etc.) together with blurred, sensitive, and intricate forms; "aesthetic" free association in naturalistic "artistic" situations; intuitive discussion of works of art and art experience; listening to certain kinds of music; using an E who is intuitive, sensitive, and capable of projecting such an atmospheric mood; decorating rooms conducive to this desired mood; and stationing persons of high intuitive sensibility in the preexperimental and/or experimental room. Such persons may exemplify or proliferate the desired attitudes and mood by means of their discussions, model behavior, interaction, etc. Still other devices that might evoke these perceptual reactions include constant reexamination of the same stimulus object under circumstances of increasingly greater relaxation; increasing the depth of feeling and acuteness of sensibility through moods of heightened consciousness or through increased accessibility to the unconscious, whether these conditions be reached in repose, artistic excitement, intense emotionality, under hypnosis, or by the use of drugs; presenting the same test object in various "intuitive" surroundings, e.g., specific colors in settings of shadowy mist and haze, object-connoting words in different poetic contexts, rigid forms in flexible and suggestive configurations, etc.

"Response to incipience" is unquestionably difficult to demonstrate in the perceptual process. In its activation, many of the dimensions of sensibility and feeling previously discussed are essential. To these should be added an extraordinary delicacy of feeling and sensitivity, best attained either by possession of a special capacity for artistic sensibility or profound training in it or by proper use of psychedelic drugs. To a somewhat different degree this exceptional sensitivity may be achieved by "assimilating" the atmosphere of situations whose distinctive characteristics are freshness of outlook, novelty of experience, openness of mind, ease of spontaneous feeling and interpretation, and a protean youthful spirit. If possible the inculcation of empathic response, capacity for openness to new experience, and freedom of feeling and expression would be part of this essential orientation process.

Specific techniques designed to facilitate the emergence of "response to incipience" are free associations on all manner of themes, subjects, fancies, or objects; stimulating uninhibited responses to the merest "beginnings," semblances, or "hints" of any perceptual subject, e.g., the first line of a poem, a few sketch lines of a drawing, an unopened flower, or the first buds of spring; studying the natural growth of a phenomenon or of a living process; giving the S an empathic appreciation of the delicacy of a raindrop, an image from a poem, a fleeting expression on a person's face.

In addition, the preexperimental and experimental rooms should be full of budding and blooming greenery and various other hints of spring; the E ought to have a vital and youthful style; the experimental directions should emphasize a subtle, unfolding process, one of quiet vigor and growth—in short, a potentiality or "becomingness" quite opposite from that of conventional, static directions. During the experiment itself, similar hints of growth or emergence ought to be made, whether through sounds or music that are reminiscent of spring or through signs of animal and plant growth. Other possibilities for exploration would be abundant evidence in preexperimental or experimental rooms of structural or architectural designs with stress on the emergence of qualities and impressions; gradation of colors on the periphery of objects (e.g., red-orange subtly shading to red, a vivid red with the indication of changing to a blue, or the hints of a shift in the intensity of a color) should be worked into the decorative scheme of the research rooms; the beginnings of an actual structure (house, museum, etc.) could be shown; the primordial design or mass from which a human form could emerge would be presented to the Ss (e.g., sculptural forms such as Michelangelo's figures in Florence, pictorial drawings such as Goya's works in Madrid, or intimations of human figures in suggestively arranged materials with or without various bodily parts). Also, static objects (leaves, rigid human forms, etc.) could be shown and their subtle or dynamic transformations and "emergences" could be demonstrated by their constituent moving parts, shifting lights, changing perspectives and angles, internal movements, or mobile backgrounds. Other suggestions include a changing landscape as the background of a specific color; a burgeoning, shift, or "emergent growth" in the background of a specific form; a painting or design of which the frame or background conveys the maximum mood or suggestion of growth; adaptation of the ambiguous paintings of Tcheletchew or other "fuzzily" ambiguous works for perceptual studies with particular reference to their depictions of figures within figures, forms growing within forms, colors emerging from colors—and all, when appropriate, presented to the S within an environment of shifting lights, phantasmagoric forms, and moving shadows. In respect to color, impressionist or postexpressionist works would be especially valuable, and cubist and op art designs would be useful for the investigation of forms in connection with this perceptual dimension.

Additional methods to facilitate the exploration of some of these Grecian perceptual experiences must also be considered.

1. Proper subject selection is an important aid to these studies. Artists, sensitive persons, and intuitive women might more often have perceptual responses of the desired kind. By contrast, at least to the early and mid-1960's college students (on whom most perceptual research is based) may not, because they are more often tense, concrete, or conformist and have less sensitive feeling, intuition, and subtlety of perception than the aforementioned types of persons. Also, the pressures to conform, in the college group, to the precise specifications and rituals of the experiment and to accept the "typical student" role are so formidable that the resulting tension and supineness of these situations cause any subtle, delicate, and "deep" perceptual responses even if previously present, to be pre-empted or lost. Further, the lack of time (as an experimental variable) and patience to sensitively appreciate or take delight in delicate perceptual experience, the emphasis on success striving (the effort to obtain more of the E's approval than the other Ss do), and on "realistic" concrete perceptions of test stimuli compel a rather crude and indelicate judgment of the presented experimental materials. And caught up in a whirlwind of other campus activities, by and large oriented to an extroverted model of experience, it is no wonder that the characteristic perceptions of the student Ss will be of a conventional, practical, and surface type.

If college students must be used, however, then those judged high in feelings of delicacy, sensitivity, and aesthetic responsiveness should be selected. Similarly, girls should be chosen over boys, introverts over extroverts, rebels over conformists, and the intelligent over the dull. If possible, however, those selected should be mature, sensitive adults, artists, or others of great delicacy of feeling, and individuals not susceptible to influences of conformity, ritual, and authoritarianism. Artists who have been trained in aspects of the perceptual processes under consideration here would be particularly interesting to use as subjects: cubist and op artists for the study of emerging forms; impressionists and post-impressionist artists for studies of "shifting" color; and students or lovers of Greek art for explorations into various aspects of the Greek aesthetic experience. Europeans with deep humanistic values and a strong cultural background, individuals who have cultivated tastes and artistic interests, humanistic scholars and patrons or others allied to the humanities, and those who rebel against patterns of conforming mores and feelings would all be desirable subjects for these studies.

Efforts to increase the relaxation and sensitivity of these already "select" subjects should be made during the preexperimental period, whether by means of alcohol, drugs, the dance, certain physical exercises, or appropriate modes of social interaction. Another facilitating possibility would be to duplicate as closely as possible, in the atmosphere of the experiment, the original psychological conditions under which the foregoing types of Greek perception took place.

2. Naturalistic settings for these experiments might also prove valuable. Carrying out such studies in the home, in comfortable surroundings, or in environments of elegance and delight might facilitate the "desired" responses. Rooms decorated to achieve the atmosphere of Grecian temples and other decorative schemes that would evoke detachment while permitting the engagement of the full spectra of aesthetic sensitivities would be excellent. Creating a preexperimental and experimental psychological atmosphere that is highly pleasant and "sensitive" and also offering extended time for the S's feelings, mood, sensibilities, and perceptions to gestate and emerge (without even the barest hint of "pressure," reward, rivalry, or approval) would be of great help. The elimination of any trace of a "scientific" or "laboratory" atmosphere is essential. Similar precautions must be observed while securing the S's participation in the study and when directly introducing him to the experiment itself.

3. Other research ramifications would include study of perceptual responses to a specific stimulus over an extended time period to determine the extent of their diversity and mutability. Under such conditions, significantly different aspects of perception may emerge. Subtle orientation to the various aspects of the stimulus, (e.g., color, form, content, abstraction) might facilitate such diverse perceptions, though idle revery, relaxed contemplation, or attentive concentration may have the same effect. Revery may be particularly valuable in a naturalistic situation as would free association. The deleterious effects of commerce, business activity, achievement or success orientation, and other practical, "driving" preoccupations on such "mutable and multifaceted" perceptions should also be experimentally or otherwise demonstrated.

4. Training in the shifting modalities and varied facets of perceptions would also be worthwhile. The capacity to momentarily transform ambiguous figures or other sensory stimuli into complex, evolving, and fluid perceptions might be achieved through proper training and through stimulation of free play of the emotions during the actual experimental period. Pertinent methods to this end would be (1) the encouragement and support of "desired" responses as they occur, (2) demonstration of the "desired" responses by "model" subjects, and (3) the presentation of the perceptual object in different ways and perspectives so that the S acquires a feeling for the fluidity and richness of perceptual experience.

70

Here, the use of abstract or abstract expressionist works of art and constructions from op art would be valuable.

5. Manipulating the specific components of a percept should be attempted. Thus, shifting the focus or way of looking at a somewhat ambiguous "form" aspect of a stimulus may determine whether it is seen as a sex object, as another concrete object, or as an abstract design. The same for color: Studying a color either intensively, delicately (empathically), or casually will determine the resulting perception. Changing the milieu of the experiment (Grecian, conformist, cognitive, or uninhibited) and transforming the role and behavior of the E (to an artist, a pragmatic realist, a zestful libertine, etc.) in harmony with the perceptual orientation needed for a given component would be interesting. Even enclosing the stimulus in a frame and varying its decorative setting (e.g., furniture, varieties of lighting, design of surrounding fabrics or hangings) should be studied.

Also, presenting a stimulus object (e.g., a color) with preliminary orientation only to visual values, to tactual values, or to psychological values should be explored. Forms, too, should be presented with separate orientations to structural qualities, geometric aspects, psychological values, or discrete details. Simply exposing a form for various, prolonged lengths of time accompanied, on each such occasion, by differing perceptual attitudes (intensive, delicate, etc.) of the S toward it should also be tried.

The effect of slight or subtle changes in the experimental environment should be examined. What is the influence on the perceptual response of releasing the aroma of perfume, of an attractive woman or man momentarily entering the experimental room, of a musical phrase, of raucous noise, of whispering, and of snatches of amusing or somber talk? Placing next to the stimulus another object high in the sensory modality that the former is deficient in is worth exploring (e.g., placing fur next to a stimulus lacking in tactual values). Evoking salient memories and nostalgic moods (by presenting "reminders" of past events) are additional things to try when test objects are presented to the S. Juxtaposition of contrasting or contrapuntal stimuli may be especially evocative of certain latencies in perception. Examples of this include presenting a specific "pure" form to the S when a color is the primary stimulus object; when a sexual symbol is the primary stimulus object, then either a repressive, a spiritual, a prosaic, or another primary-drive "representing" figure would be presented; if a practical, prosaic figure is the test stimulus, a cubist or subtle geometrical design would be introduced. Depending on just such preexperimental orientations and experimental methods as have been described in the foregoing discussion as well as on the sensibilities and types of the selected subjects, it is possible that hidden and latent perceptual modalities, usually subordinated to the reigning conventional or sanctioned perceptual responses, may be liberated.

Group Behavior

The Greek conception of society had as its goal the creation of a group experience that would foster individual richness and excellence of character as well as energetic qualities of community commitment and participation. Excellence of mind and effective participation in government were the desirable criteria of citizenship and, through political expression and activity, it was thought vitality and balance could be achieved in the political body. The exercise of one's talents in governmental or political activity was a guiding principle for the good life of the community. This, too, required a balance of freedom and order: an atmosphere stimulating the best talents of all citizens as well as inciting the efforts of the best individuals to substantially contribute their energies to the body politic while fulfilling their own private obligations. This issue was conceptually solved by the recognition that simultaneously through individualistic activities and community participation an acute awareness of the tribulations of unbridled license could be obtained while, at the same time, fulfillment of personal capacity in part could be achieved by involvement in the affairs of the community. Also, only with such participation could there be developed loyalty to a body politic that went beyond individual self-interest, so that the political irresponsibility and apathy associated with the latter would be counterbalanced and contained. Further, political life was thought to require the highest level of abilities and so called for the best of men. Hence the optimal utilization of ability could be achieved through the participation of citizens in the body politic, thus stimulating their talents to the utmost as well as fostering social cooperation, mutual responsibility, and adjustment. In the involvement of the self in political activity, an appreciation was cultivated of the free exercise of the talent, opinion, and speech of others with a proportionately greater conviction in such freedom for oneself. With such views on the mutual advantages and potential stimulation that freedom could offer, less control over individual activity and freedom was required, especially as men knew the bounties and hazards of freedom and the dangers of extending it beyond judicious limits. The fact is that recall from public office could be added to the confidence in freedom in a context of public responsibility. And the smallness of the Greek city-state was of advantage, too, because it made possible the careful scrutiny of operations in the body politic and energized an alert and responsive communications network within the constituency and between citizens and officials that cannot be implemented in larger political groupings.

In summary, the values of Greek political and group life were: (1) the maximal individual freedom and self-realization that is commensurate with the good of the community; (2) the maximal participation of men in the political realm for the fulfillment of their personal, political, and social talents as well as for society's welfare; (3) through one's participation in society, through mutual respect, and through the realization that the freedom of other citizens is a condition for one's own, less stringent requirements were necessary for discipline, military control, and policing of behavior; (4) through this participation and its accompanying scrutiny of others, greater confidence in group and political activity developed, the sense of community responsibility grew and with it the conviction that the ordinary citizen could influence events and actions of the body politic.

The implications of these values for group and individual activity were vast. They meant confidence in personal convictions and dedication to their pursuit. They meant that the lowest common denominator of values or understanding was not to be the criteria of group approval but that high specified standards were to be honored. They did not mean the attenuation of integrity or belief through the pressures and exigencies of compromise because, to the contrary, every encouragement was given to excellence in thought, behavior, and talent. Indeed, by deemphasizing social acceptance or "getting along," pressures leading to the compromise of conviction, feeling, or individuality in the interest of conformity were substantially diminished in effectiveness. If groups did not fulfill the purposes their constituents desired, they withdrew, joined or formed others, or remained apart. Issues were fought through to the end without sugar-coated bromides of adulteration, or truncating compromise. As individualism was so highly prized, there was no necessity for submerging the ego into the morass of group commonality or for playing the cat and mouse game of permitting one's genuine ideas to show only when confident of not arousing group disapproval. These independent convictions were encouraged by a sense of control and responsibility for one's destiny and the community's respect for personal autonomy. As a result, leaders were evaluated as arbiters of issues or as initiators of ideas—and hence, for what they stood or what they were rather than as sycophantic followers of mass sentiment. Thus, independence, courage, and the capacity to defy group sentiment and persevere in one's own convictions became esteemed qualities. At the same time, respect for the free expression of others and the integrity of their views prevailed in contrast to a disposition to reject or castigate individuals and viewpoints because of their deviation from a leveling group consensus or norm.

These qualities, including the obligation to be vigorous in the advocacy of their views, ultimately derived from the free cultural climate of Greece with its emphasis on individuality, excellence, participation, and the fulfillment of human potentiality. Contrast this with substantial areas of group experience in contemporary America where, as has been documented extensively,[4] the group and its members are insecure, lonely, and frightened, where the lowest common denominator of value and cognition often becomes the group norm, and where compromise with integrity is a recurrent experience. These features are too often allied with fear of the courage of one's convictions and with suspicion of freedom of thought and individualistic excellence so that respect for dissent, assertion of one's views, and affirmative individuality become diminished. Neglected, as a consequence, in the topography of American group research are studies on dedicated and idealistic groups, on courage of convictions, on the affirmation of individuality and uncompromising integrity, and on the salutary effects of the free expression of one's viewpoints. The emphasis in research has rather been on the huddling together of group members, on rigid, machine-like role behavior, on conformity, and on the fear of independence or individuality as these reactions have been induced when the group depreciates, isolates, or otherwise punishes its individualistic or deviant members, by the derogation of dissent in the group, and by the very nature of a conformist, superficially egalitarian group atmosphere.

Certain crucial issues and latent potentialities of group life have not been adequately looked into because of this orientation. Among these are: (1) The behavior of the courageous individual who is buttressed by conviction, passion, or dedicated values and goals. This may be studied both in the case of individual behavior in the group and in the case of an entire group supported by passion and purpose. (2) The group's potential respect for intelligence, for intellectual honesty, and for similar qualities with which they are in sympathy might militate against crucial compromise of their principles and major concessions to inferior goals and procedures. In such groups, the desire for objective and excellent solutions to problems might prevent such practices as adulteration of the high purposes or the task of the group for the sake of intragroup harmony and personal acceptance, or the favoring of collective group mentality and standards at the expense of individual excellence. (3) In groups where there is greater respect for the integrity of the individual on the basis of his unique qualities of personality, there may be greater personal autonomy and freedom. As a result, group members will be judged more objectively for their contributions, and more deviation and variation will be permitted both for oneself and others in group activity. Active search for such groups whether they are found among certain social elites, in protected environments, or are identified with specific ideologies and goals must be furthered.

However, the most serious deficiencies in contemporary group research are found in the realm of small-group experimentation. In this area, the lesson of Greek experience would be to relate all contemporary small-group experiments to their immediate, full, and authentic connections with the ongoing and antecedent condition of human "reality" of which they are but an artificial part. Put another way, when a subject participates in a group experiment he participates as a human being with the full complement of the characteristic feelings, perceptions, and responses that he habitually brings to any situation, experimental or other. This human complement of reactions often significantly and unpredictably influences the specified and hypothetical variables the experiment is presumed to control and assess, frequently distorting or nullifying them and thus preventing accurate scientific interpretation.

Another important characteristic of present group research is that its experimental procedures and conditions encourage anxiety, insecurity, estrangement, hostility, and isolation of group members and its research results reflect these conditions.[5] Such effects are achieved by a variety of procedures: the manner of soliciting subjects, the physical and psychological conditions of the experiment itself, the actual testing procedures—all these combine to create an atmosphere that encourages anxiety, lowers standards of performance, abets mediocrity, and promotes those dimensions of group life so frequently found in contemporary America. Group conformity is one of these dimensions and experimental data bearing on it too often reflect an experimental atmosphere created, not by the designated research variables, but quite inadvertently or unconsciously by the methods and procedures ancillary to setting up the variables to be investigated. The consequence is that those qualities of group life found in classic Greece and in some atypical contemporary experiences of American groups, are neither acknowledged nor assessed in present research. Over-anxious concern about the opinions of other group members, fear of personal independence or conviction, diminished care for truth, and preoccupation with personal success or social approval are some features of the group atmosphere in which present research is conducted. Indeed, there is often tacit acquiescence during the experiment of the group members with the E's unspoken values or purposes which, often being those of expected cooperation with the experimental directions and other varieties of compliance, tend to reinforce similar conforming influences of the experimental milieu. Indeed, a most intriguing problem involves the processes by which the S detects these unstated goals and values of the E as well as his own implicit wish to carry them out while, simultaneously and sometimes at cross purposes, he is subject to the stated directions and influences of the experiment itself.[6] A third source of influence is the social and economic pressures the experimental situation has placed him under: the need to succeed in order to get paid, the necessity of getting along with the E and other group members, and the various pressures to act "properly." A fourth set of variables may be the S's own awareness of "acting" a role on lines defined by the aforementioned factors or on other ones of his own. To the extent that these paravariables are analyzed indispensable material will be uncovered for the proper interpretation of results from these studies.

This "group atmosphere" complex of anxiety, reaction to anxiety by conformity, robot-like submission to the E's instructions but also reaction against them by a vague struggle for independence are all characteristic of the aforementioned type of experimental group situations as they subtly reflect and engender various themes of contemporary society such as the sense of "aloneness" of the individual and the pressure to conform and produce the desired behavior or results. The S is aware of some of the experimenter's needs or values and unknowingly, perhaps, tries to satisfy them by conforming to the societal values that the E (by formulating his research design in the manner he has) often unknowingly injects into the experimental situation. The result is a complex interplay between the societal or "experimental atmosphere" influences, on the one hand, and the specified, rigorous variables the E ostensibly is scientifically and independently appraising, on the other. In one study more emphasis, unknowingly, may be given to the unacknowledged or unspecified influences of status, conformity, fear, or alienation and in another less, so that the differences in obtained results might be attributable to the difference in such emphases rather than to differences between the specified experimental variables themselves. When one adds to the influence of such

factors the effects of varying laboratory conditions and minute dissimilari-
ties in research procedure, accurate explanation of research results becomes almost impossible.

CRITICAL EVALUATION AND RECTIFICATION

With the Greek example of group experience in mind, how can rectification of these deficiencies be achieved? (1) By translating those conditions of group life responsible for the group experience of the Greeks—as
well as of their contemporary, natural group counterparts—into hypotheses, experimental variables, experimental milieux, and criteria for the
selection of subjects, it may be possible to produce types of group experience and phenomena, rarely studied now, which are consonant with those
of the Greeks; (2) by a realistic analysis of group experience as found in
natural life conditions and in grasping the implications of this analysis
for "meaningful" and realistic group research; (3) by making a particular
effort to find or create in group experience those conditions making for
dedication, freedom, purpose, and individual independence.

These studies may be carried out on several fronts. Their object would
be to determine the conditions under which such "Greek-like" group
experiences occur and the frequency of their occurrence. The following
suggestions are directed to this end.

Natural groups that are characterized by (1) a significant tradition
(aristocratic, noble, old family), (2) some type of professional or work
integrity (skilled craftsmanship or the search for truth as in scientific and
scholarly work), or (3) a high purpose of dedicated belief should be
sought out and studied. Investigations of these groups should be undertaken regarding their conditions of interaction, group members' satisfactions, cohesion, freedom, and capacity to pursue ideas wherever they lead
without the restraints imposed by vested interests or personal status.
Studies should be made of the relation between the professional, traditional, and idealistic value commitments of groups and their capacity to
have strong convictions and to be free in opinion and action. Thus one
might find that groups dedicated to values of intellectual honesty and
freedom or those with older, well-established traditions of truth might
have greater courage and integrity in pursuing their ideas and courses of
action than those of not so strongly marked emphasis in these respects.

Studies also should be made of the group behavior of members distinguished by strong, individual values (as distinct from their group
values) compared with those who are much less secure in these respects.

One may speculate that with greater security in individual value commitments there may be increased tolerance of freedom and greater capacity for exploration of new vistas, providing these forms of security are not identical with smugness, narrowness, and obfuscation. Excluding these latter contingencies, such security may endow those possessing it with additional adventurousness and alacrity in group enterprises when the latter are of a purposeful, dynamic nature or when such individuals experience delight and vitality in life. When, however, such security is of a different kind or is not associated with dynamic groups or with personal vitality, then the result may be passivity, complacency, or conformity for both group and individual. In contrast, personal insecurity, particularly in youth, may lead to an anxious conformity but also to eagerness, responsiveness, courage, and exhilaration. For these reasons, older organizations may be more stultified or more oriented to excessively prudent and vested ways, while younger groups, in a society that values novelty and success, may emphasize more varied or original approaches and purposes. These speculations should be tested by studying such "younger," "older," "secure," and "insecure" types of groups and individuals though it is essential that the group's purposes, traditions, and statuses must be fully considered before a valid analysis can be made.

Further suggestions for studies of natural groups, both historically and currently, are (1) a study of the integrity and dedication of youth groups in certain social classes or at certain historical times, e.g., the idealism of youth in nineteenth-century tsarist Russia or in Germany before the revolutions of 1848 and the idealism of American youth in World War I or of various youth groups in the present-day world; (2) studies of atypical courage or pursuit of truth or freedom in groups not usually exhibiting these traits. Certain events or crises may induce such unusual behaviors just as they do, at times, in the lives of individuals. At such periods (national survival, armed conflict or other types of collective crisis) unexpected heroic courage, self-sacrifice, or steadfast endurance may be displayed; or, on the contrary, unanticipated collapse, despair, or passivity may then occur. Which of these behaviors at such times are found more often in groups with high member participation in their activities? Which groups emphasize freedom, independence, and strong societal commitments or, conversely, do not possess these qualities? In general, are the conditions for "heroic group behavior" a high purpose or cause, sustained group commitment, critical external pressures, or some other characteristic? Here, a full historical appraisal would be valuable.

To determine the social psychological conditions for the presence of the aforementioned "affirmative" group qualities (courage, integrity, respect for honesty and intelligence, maintenance of high standards, and tolerance for deviation) the following group variables should be studied: identification with a high social or community value, vital participation in the group life by all group members, and openness and freedom of expression in group proceedings. Such conditions may be found among the following: certain groups of scientists, intellectuals, and other types of associations of men of integrity and high purpose; dedicated youthful groups with some dynamic social and artistic purpose; certain political groups of high idealism; groups providing "tenured" security but with traditions of tolerance, free expression, and openness of mind; groups permitting rich and varied use of individual talent such as those small organizations requiring their employees to fill multiple roles; small communities with established mutual trust where participation in varied community roles, functions, and offices is open to all.

In addition, an historical survey should be made of the occurrence of these affirmative group qualities both in the United States and Europe. They might be found more frequently, e.g., during the latter half of eighteenth- and early nineteenth-century America, among aristocratic classes of eighteenth-century England and France (during the Enlightenment), or in varied other groups at different historical periods. Correlations should be computed between the frequency of these traits in such historic or contemporary groups, the economic and social characteristics of the groups themselves, and the periods in which they flourished.

When it comes to group experimentation, however, another approach is required. If we are right in thinking that the general cultural milieu and the experimenter's values are among the crucial factors in determining the experimental results, then a change in these values and milieu might be at least as instrumental in obtaining different findings as would modifying the stipulated experimental variables. Hence, a chief obligation of current group research must be to acknowledge that group members are antecedently participants in a larger natural group (culture and society) before they enter the laboratory and accept the experimenter's directions. Such preexperimental group identification and membership may be the most significant determinant of their experimental group behavior and, together with the "controlled" experimental variables, may account for all of it. Antecedent group membership and identification imply an internalized set of values or dispositions drawn from such group associations, and often these give evidence of being the suspiciousness, anxiety, rivalry, and deference that are endemic to present-day natural groups. The experiment itself, as something of a mysterious situation, is often judged as a challenge, threat, or imponderable and reciprocally evokes certain forms of fear, anxiety, aggressiveness, uncertainty, or alertness in the subjects. Also, payment for their participation may influence their group behavior in directions similar to those of the experimenter's values or wishes.

The "mysterious" experimental situation—as the S anticipates it—is more often a trial, a test, an exhibition, or an intriguing, uncertain adventure rather than an organic and meaningful experience for his life. Such "tests" or mysterious entertainments are perhaps associated by him with other experiences of being a psychological subject and so may predispose him to the self-consciousness of being a "guinea pig," which in turn may greatly influence his experimental behavior—whether toward greater defensiveness, anxiety, conformity with the E's wishes, psychological paralysis, uninvolved "role-playing," or even a special kind of protest. The S may see the experiment as a "big show," a chance to impress someone, an "exhibition" of himself and his personal fears, disguises, and trepidations, or a trivial sport of no personal significance rather than as an occasion for authentic, serious group behavior. In this perspective, a fairly common portrait of the S's psychology in the group would be: wary and suspicious, afraid of being independent but wanting approval from the E, sensitive to aspects of his own behavior that might invite the E's rejection, and yet suspicious, frightened, and perhaps resentful of the E's manipulations of the group situation and of himself as one of the "guinea pigs" in it, attempting to gain approval from the group (which may, in fact, be a surrogate for the father figure E) and yet suspicious of it because the group serves as a substitute for his suspicions of the E as well as a rival for his approval. One result of this syndrome is that the S relates to the group according to the formula of the "lonely crowd" mentality, the group, to some extent, substituting for the E, and by this formula the previously indicated ambivalences are focused. Conformity to the group can be now seen as a reaction formation to suspiciousness and rivalry with other group members which, in turn, may be a displacement from dependency and resentment of the E as the authoritarian manipulator.

Naturally, other fundamental preexperimental values and feelings influence actual experimental group behavior: the desire to psychologically learn something about oneself as human being, a healthy curiosity to participate in an experiment as an adventure and for information, a desire to associate with others, and similar satisfying experiences. These factors, as those previously mentioned, are also intrinsic to the S's preexperimental social affiliations and values and, to that extent, too, may be more important than the "experimental variables" themselves in determining the group behavior of the S. Hence, it is essential to design studies that demonstrate how a change in these preexperimental conditions or "culture" will substantially affect the obtained results of present research irrespective of the experimental variables employed. The Greek group experience was described as one such type of preexperimental "cultural" condition whose effective implementation at the appropriate point in present group research procedure might profoundly influence obtained findings. The following discussion presents proposals for types of preexperimental and experimental conditions or variables modeled in varying degrees on the nature of the Greek group experience.

Group experiments should be made an organic part of the life experience of the Ss and pose genuine and vital issues to them. Rather than groups working under artificial, contrived, or meaninglessly rewarding and punishing conditions and on trivial, pointless topics, they should be presented with vital problems of realistic significance which can excite authentic delight, disappointment, frustration, and challenge. The study and manipulation of natural groups in their real-life settings would be an obvious way to cultivate such experiences, and if the evoked behaviors and values were those of intelligence, vigorous member participation, integrity, and courage, an approximation, if remote, to the nature of the Greek group experience would have been made. Either by selecting groups that already embody these values or by modifying the modus operandi of other groups toward this Grecian norm, some of the requirements for the desired milieu might be achieved. Indeed, there are some reports of such successful modifications, though not of the Greek type, which represent opposition to the values of the larger culture. Relevant here are the studies of Coch and French,[7] Lewin,[8] and numerous others that demonstrated that distribution of responsibility among individuals and subgroups was related to improvement in morale and productivity as well as to the increased fulfillment of the ability of individual group members. More studies that emphasize this sort of mutually responsible participation are needed: e.g., in labor unions, cooperative associations, dedicated scientific establishments, projects of high purpose, great departments in great universities, groups with vigorous member participation and high social goals such as the Israeli kibbutz, small decentralized industries where autonomous subgroup authority exists, or other natural groups where integrity, vital participation, and mission are high. Also valuable might be efforts to persuade group members to accept certain values and purposes: inspiring them with ideals of community and participation and fostering in them appreciation of the values of integrity, intelligence, self-expression, and quality of contribution.

In general, then, the approach recommended here is to implement these Grecian-like group values in various groups and to assess their comparative effect on the involvement, effectiveness, courage, and standards of excellence of the groups concerned. Such efforts should be made in open-minded and "dedicated" groups where the oppressive or rigid organization and conforming behavior of the larger culture are not so paramount. However, studies should also be carried out on groups varying to the degree that the suspiciousness and conformity of the larger culture in fact enter into their group processes. It may be that "idealistic" innovative, "young" or youthful, or mutually supportive groups will exhibit a greater effect when these Greek value variables are "experimentally" introduced into their transactions than will bureaucratized, overorganized groups that may show no effect at all, or even a reverse one. Similar studies should be carried out on groups that vary to the degree that they embody these Greek values. Examples of the various types of groups to be so studied are depersonalized or bureaucratic groups (factories, large business and government organizations); groups devoid of strong moral principles (advertising, public relations); groups in which the participation and involvement of personnel occurs at all levels of operation (certain small businesses and labor unions); groups with high principles or standards and "open-minded" groups (certain scientific, intellectual, or "dedicated" groups and some aristocratic cliques).

To implement these value variables in existing groups for research purposes the following suggestions are made: Motivations of members would be increased through maximum and versatile participation and responsibility, through decentralizing and delegating responsibility, through encouraging shared distribution of the group's functions and roles, and through vigorously emphasizing the highest purposes toward which the group is capable of being committed. Further, a program for encouraging honesty, integrity, and intelligence would be instituted by rewarding or supporting members who display these qualities, by exhorting their emulation by others, by the use of honestly persuasive techniques such as the patient discussion of the pros and cons of a proposed new policy or procedure, by appropriate uses of role-playing, and by certain inspirational appeals.

Many research issues are raised by such a program. Antecedently, of course, there is the problem that current studies are preoccupied with the static nature of group experience—a research orientation that, in fact, creates the conditions and, thereon, the phenomena from which much of the results and conclusions currently found on structure, cliques, and process are derived. Such an approach reflects a status quo perspective on group experience: stabilizing and freezing it under experimentally regulated conditions consonant with an eighteenth-century model of physical science in which the determination of facts depended on regulated (usually by experiment) and orderly (rigid, neat, specifications and machine-like controls) measurement of a static, clockwork universe. Such an approach, too, reflects or is congruent with modern bureaucratic social organization and especially with the orderly, controlled, conformist-demanding behavioral processes required in mass production, whether of products or services, and the efficient, set, cost-accounting practices that oversee and synchronize them.

But under more dynamic or evolving natural group conditions, unthought-of aspects of group structure can well appear: Cliques may vary, the interaction process may be transformed, roles might shift, and even reaction to conventional experimental variables can be surprisingly different. In present studies, group experience is largely frozen or caught, as in a photo, at one brief point of a much broader historic time continuum (this point frequently being an artificially contrived laboratory one), and often it is only from the natural and evolving sequence of such photos (a group in normal development or in other dynamic movement) that an accurate estimate of group behavior can be obtained. Indeed, it is the time-evolving character of group experience that betrays the obscured but potential qualities of the group and, thus, what is available in it for change and new development. For this reason, group crises of a natural and organic kind are enormously valuable for the study of group life (laboratory group crises are too artificial), and in such crises these latent, unexamined qualities can be most insightfully assessed provided that specified new conditions, educative influences, and novel social stimuli are simultaneously introduced into the group. The nature and degree of group reaction to such stimuli during such crises can indicate the power these latent qualities and dynamics have in group behavior, and so can yield evidence bearing on the validity of some of the aforementioned ideas.

Other methods for the improvement of studies in the group laboratory would deemphasize the suspicion, conformity, and deference now endemic to such researches. Using the model of Greek group experience, an atmosphere of independence and courage as well as of honest, intelligent leadership and meaningful group goals vitally connected with the Ss' lives must be created antecedent to or in the actual experimental situation. To dissipate the traditional "negative atmosphere" of purposelessness and anonymity, the experiment, as a human experience, must be part of some significant group purpose or enterprise and of some vital organic interest to the group members. Greater independence must be achieved—from the E and from the Kafka-like "castle" atmosphere of typical small-group experimentation—and perhaps not paying the Ss for their participation (a procedure that often induces dependency, obligation, desire to please, and even resentment of this very desire by the Ss) should be examined for its potential in facilitating such independence. The impact of going to a laboratory for the "group experiment" may incite the feeling of being manipulated or of being a "guinea pig" in a research project and so aggravate the suspicions of coming to a strange place where omniscient scientists presumably perform mysterious operations on human beings. All this neither relaxes the S nor facilitates his natural spontaneous interaction with others.

Thus it may be better not to have group studies carried out in clearly identifiable laboratory or "experimental" environments but rather in natural and realistically appropriate places, e.g., dormitories, homes, clubs. Moreover, the role of the E must be reconsidered as authoritarian (or authoritatively permissive) as well as the Ss' often ambivalent perception of him. To what degree does his role and behavior determine the "atmosphere" of the group and to what extent do the Ss extend their perception of this role and, accordingly, their behavior to the group itself? Does the E's not infrequent behavior of aloofness but intimacy, direction but yet indirection, and his "image" of being both a manipulator and a "nice guy" mold the conditions responsible for the "lonely crowd" groupings of the laboratory? If he took a different role: tore away the mystery and obscurity from the experiment, deviated from his omniscient position in the "castle-like" situation, or became genuinely congenial and helpful, the group milieu might be significantly different and, correspondingly, so might the experimental results.

How to induce such an atmosphere of openness, relaxation, nonmanipulation, and lack of suspiciousness deserves the fullest study so that the group atmosphere that breeds anxiety, dependency, conflict, and doubt may be dissipated. Proposals to this end include the following: Experiments should not be conducted in the kind of laboratory atmosphere that suggests a "guinea pig" approach to the Ss, which excessively encourages the rivalry of group members or deference to the E, and which induces a sort of role-playing self-consciousness that shifts the substance and dynamics of the group behavior to a different level than that occurring under natural conditions. When students, student groups, or other natural groups are the subjects of experiments, the natural environment or day-to-day surroundings of such subjects should be used. Greater psychological security for the Ss may be achieved by downgrading the invidious evaluation of their own activities, and by creating situations in which they have had experience or feel self-assurance and to which they can become emotionally and intellectually deeply committed. All this would diminish suspicion, the inclination to please the E, and other aspects of the "lonely crowd" mentality.

Also, by the greater use of established, "affirmative" groups in actual experiments or of individuals with "Grecian-type" value commitments, a rough approximation may be made to the conditions of independence and freedom that marked the Greek experience. Thus, groups with dedicated purposes and those with high and open-minded standards should be the subject of experiments and compared with groups of low or mediocre standards and those whose goals are expedient, ritualistic, bureaucratic, or exclusively self-aggrandizing. Similar studies could be made of individuals, in groups, who vary in courage, independence, freedom, and the strength of their value commitments. A distinction should be made between groups whose security is based on achievement and those in whom it is based on a philosophy of life or a social ideology. Also, individuals composing such groups should be distinguished in regard to the varying amounts of status, economic, and ideological security they possess as distinct from psychological security. Finally, groups and individuals should be categorized as to the richness of their satisfaction with life and particularly the vigor and pleasure of their participation in it.

The E, too, must be cast in a different role (see above) and preferably one of nonimportance so as to focus the energies of the group on the problem itself. This might be accomplished, to some degree, if he were to confine his overt dealings with the group to presenting the "problem" of the experiments to them and then withdrawing. Also, the problems put to the group (see above) should be concerned with issues not only within their own interests but with those on which action can be taken, action that vitally commits them to the problem at hand. Further, it may be true that the late adolescent college group (generally the crucible of the contemporary group experiment) is a rather precarious population from which to generalize to human group behavior, especially so in that the anxieties and dependencies that characterize them—at least in the mid 1960's—often render them less capable of implementing the kinds of independent and courageous group behavior that concern us here. For these college groups, then, particular attention should be paid to the reduction of anxiety, removal of authority figures and their manipulative tactics, and the presentation of significant issues within the groups' vital interest and ken. Presentation of theoretical, clever, or irrelevant problems may only aggravate their latent "lonely crowd" mentality by accenting the group's intellectual inferiority, its lack of meaningful purpose, the omnipresent "guinea pig" mentality, and the manipulative designs of the E as well as his omniscience and power which are also attributed to the often intricate, esoteric, and intellectual problems given to the group. In contrast, problems such as those of campus life or evaluation of other group members, in being more meaningful for the group, may elicit courageous, independent, cooperative, and enterprising modes of behavior. Indeed, the optimal "laboratory" conditions for this kind of group study may be the actual living or working environment of the group itself, whether it be the club, dormitory, working place, etc. In such situations, fullness of participation, independence of opinion, and mature responsibility can be purposefully encouraged and become of vital importance to the group. The relevance and significance of the group problem is crucial to the evocation of these qualities as well as to the stimulation of the best group energies. Depending on the values and ideology of the group, examples of problems of this nature would be working for a piece of legislation, a community improvement task, a philanthropy, educational betterment, obtaining some special privilege, diminished constraints on student extracurricular activity, etc. Comparisons of the impact such problems have on the group in contrast with those of a theoretical, irrelevant, trivial, or "conventional experimental" type should be made in respect to vigor of participation, vitality of enterprise, enhancement of cooperation, etc. According to the view advanced here, superiority in such group behaviors should be associated with the former, "meaningful" types of problems.

Another factor in the group value complex of the Greeks that should be studied is the respect for intelligence and ideas. Here emphasis should be placed on evaluating contributions solely on their merit and on disregarding the status, power, attractiveness and other personal attributes of the contributor. Whether this can be best achieved through informal pre-meeting orientation and discussion, through formal instruction and practice, through encouragement of respect for the unique traits of each group member, through role-playing, or through the rewarding experience of practicing this "quality" must yet be determined. Included here would be training sessions in which intellectual honesty is rewarded, deficiencies in participants' ideas are pointed out, and the best contributions are lauded. Elimination of argument for its own sake or for personal reasons should be emphasized. Additional techniques would include training sessions in which intelligent persons discuss serious issues. Only significant ideas would be rewarded during these sessions, and group members observing this might acquire models for their own subsequent interactions. Finally, it is possible that in an atmosphere that fosters ease, flexibility, relaxed confidence, and includes persons who understand one another, these desired results may be attained.

A related rectification of current small-group practice would be to emphasize the importance of facts and "truth" in group discussions. Pre-experimental orientation to the significance of objectivity and the selection of subjects from fields where the pursuit of truth and objective evaluation are paramount (sciences, history, etc.) should be carried out. Using advanced students in these fields and orienting them to the prime necessity of achieving depth and accuracy of discussion in group meetings should also be tried. Hence, by inducing an attitude of serious intellectual involvement (comparable to that of deliberating on a vital problem of life or an important professional or intellectual issue) greater thoughtfulness and accuracy may emerge in group discussion, resulting in more significant resolution of the problems that the group confronts.

Another important feature of Greek group experience was the dynamic and full participation of members in discussion and decision-making. Encouragement of the vigorous participation of each group member in meetings, whether by individual premeeting instructions or by selective encouragement, both before and during meetings, of those particular members whose participation has been low, should also be attempted. Enhancement of the psychological security of specified members also may be valuable whether accomplished through support of their egos or by providing them with some sinecure (financial or emotional) that would assure them of a degree of security irrespective of future events in the group. Something of the same effect can be obtained by selecting for group membership only psychologically secure individuals and those with strong personal or ideological identifications stemming from humanistic interests, from eminent achievements, or from affirmative value commitments. Perhaps, similar strengthening effects on some members can be achieved by the following methods: directing them to act freely and courageously (even though unlikely, it should nevertheless be tried); helping members to deepen social and psychological roots (in preexperimental situations, in their own natural situations, or in other deliberately manipulated natural situations); giving them the sense that no harm will befall them in the group; giving them an activity or role in which they will be successful and so gain confidence and respect; and only selecting those individuals as Ss who play dynamic and salutary roles in the world.

Further necessary changes include elimination of the requirement for group consensus. This condition places an undue premium on conformity,

87

enhances the "lonely crowd" mentality through the denigration of minority opinion and the rejection of individualism, compels premature group agreement before there has been full consideration of all viewpoints (especially facilitated by the brief duration of group sessions), and often makes the "lowest common and most popular denominator" of judgment the most influential. It therefore results in enormous pressure for agreement, in the feeling that deviation is traitorous and wrong, and in a desperation to achieve some result whatever its quality. No wonder that mediocrity is its usual "product" and that leaders consistent with this product emerge or are selected to influence its final result, thus mirroring the group standards. Suspicion or apprehension about the meeting's outcome, if agreement is not reached in the prescribed time, and fear of the reaction of others, if one dares to deviate or protest, combine to produce an intangible "group anxiety or resentment" which, itself anxiety-producing and in conflict with the imperatives for consensual agreement and achievement, is often compensated into "group solidarity" or purpose. This now becomes more important than the value of an individual member's contributions or his well-being, both of which require more time than the group has available to allot to him, and even presuming it did would be disposed to do. Further, the time pressure is more likely than not to be associated with the clever, obvious, and most superficially concrete type of solution. Also, it places a premium on aggressive, assertive verbalizers during the group sessions, on practical and immediate solutions, on debating tricks, and on the most vocal protagonists of resolutions involving facile compromise. The slow, the deeply thoughtful, the hesitant, and the tentatively open-minded have hardly the chance to contribute much because, in part, their very lack of aggressive certainty, of capacity for expedient or superficial compromise, and of aptitude for quick but shallow solutions are far less appreciated under these group conditions than the immediate, practical, strongly pressed, and less probing (and thus less upsetting) positions.

Rectification of these conditions require experiments where consensus is not necessary, i.e., where majority, minority, or individual reports and solutions are encouraged and where the criteria of the group's work are excellence and self-fulfillment. Studies evaluating this proposal may be carried out in which the various conditions for group decision-making would be (1) full consensus; (2) majority, minority, or individual reports; (3) no solution, "decision" or group report required. Studies appraising the effects of using various standards for the acceptability of a group's solutions should particularly include the following ones: (1) only very high levels of solutions and contributions would be accepted, (2) no standard of merit would be required, and (3) expediency would be the sole standard for acceptance.

Additional rectifying methods that should be assessed include compelling the group's patient consideration of each viewpoint that is presented; ensuring that the contribution of each serious minority member be heard out, however much its deviance; enhancing the individuality and confidence of group members before the meeting in order to (1) strengthen their persistence in their unique ideas during the group discussion, (2) entrench and strengthen all "minority view" dissenters against the majority, and (3) teach the more dominant and aggressive faction tolerance of dissident ideas and of "individualistic" members. Another rectifying method would be to help the group understand the seriousness and importance of their activities or discussions (making sure this is the case) and to effectively communicate to them that effort and struggle are necessary if excellent solutions are to be found. The hopeful presumption would be that the more vital and significant the problem the group is engaged in, the greater would be its involvement and concern and, hence, the greater the chances that struggle and effort would be enlisted to bring about excellent work. The use of unlimited time periods for group meetings should also be tried. More thorough and subtle discussions might then occur, dissent would be more likely to emerge, and the shallower and more conventional solutions might be less likely to be adopted. Increased expression of the silent or less vocal would be stimulated, perhaps encouraging, thereby, the group's consideration of the more quiescent and, not impossibly, the more original ideas and individuals. Under such conditions, it is not impossible that the conventional solutions can be replaced by more subtle and penetrating ideas, a type of leadership oriented to greater freedom, diversity, and depth of discussion can take control, and those previously low in the group social structure (dissenters, silent ones, etc.) may be elevated in appreciation and status. It may then be hypothecated that as groups move from one end of a scale designated as "restricted discussion time" to its opposite end, they will correspondingly move from the typical conformist, "lonely crowd" findings of research to freer, richer discussions, more "open" atmosphere, and more penetrating ideas.

Other possibilities of rectification would be the development of group atmospheres where individuality and dissent are the salient goals or groups in which varying forms of anarchy or only the most minimal agreement prevails. Also, the value of an "instructed" stooge endlessly persisting in his views against a majority or an "instructed," incorrigibly "tolerant" person who supports the rights of all minority viewpoints to a fair hearing should be investigated. Many other combinations of variables dealing with various types of dissent and anarchy could be explored with advantage.

Models for such contrastingly oriented studies should be derived from political philosophies, social systems, or theories of communal polity. Hence, a model of authentic democracy for experimental groups would result in quite different group behavior than a model based on pseudo-democratic social systems as appears to be the case in current studies. Despite the fact that all social and group politics are typified by dissent or minority opinion, however variously they cope with it, present group research neither realistically nor vitally deals with such phenomena. Typical dissension is not found because group members are not sufficiently involved in the experimental situation to do more than "act out" assumed roles without genuine concern, frustration, or elation. It is no wonder, then, that authentic dissent or assertiveness does not flourish in such "role-playing" situations. The money they earn as subjects, the fun of playing at the experimental game, the congeniality extended by their fellows for being "part of the group," and the casual interest stirred by the group task are sufficiently gratifying so that *diversion from* authentically applying effort to a given group problem, from disrupting the experimental charade, and from expressing vital concern on any residual meaningful issue is effectively achieved. Good manners win out—the good manners of supine, conforming late adolescents trained to behave like embryonic organization men in return for rewards unbeknown or known, or from *fear* of getting *no* rewards and of *not* being approved. In any case these meetings are part of the same recurrent psychological package: an obligation and routine that is part of the impersonal manipulation and ritualistic testing endemic to current undergraduate experience. In such an atmosphere, to rock the boat is foolhardy, and to pass through such organizational puzzle box situations without being acutely aware of their premises or pointlessness and without challenging their meaning or the "powers" that make their meaning is the sensible thing to do. And it is especially congruent with the characteristics of many of the recent (not most recent, however) college generation on which a great deal of this research has been conducted: a lack of ideals and values, an orientation of opportunism, expediency, and conformity, and a focus on participation largely for status, for "playing the game," and for having a good time.

The group experiment is thus seen, by the usual college subject, as part of the academic organizational ritual—a bureaucratic maze without meaning but one through which he had better pass if he is to avoid "mysterious" difficulties and, with luck, achieve solacing rewards. Hence, the confusion about the meaning and purpose of the ambiguous experimental situation adds to the S's feeling of being lost in its Kafka-like "castle" atmosphere and leads him to uncritically obey the directions of the mysterious E or to find refuge in the anonymity of the group.

A further limitation of current small-group research is its lack of emphasis on the ordinary, natural growth of leadership associated with normal group development. This is owing to the brevity and scarcity of the group meetings so that organic group development—as reflected in the growth of common interests or activities and in the evolving patterns of leadership and social organization—cannot occur. Without such real issues, genuine interpersonal involvements, and authentic group identifications there emerges a pattern of pseudoleadership crystallized in vocal, conventional persons with conformist values who defer to outside authority, i.e., the experimenter. Thereon, static group interactions prevail so that authentic involvements and dynamic change cannot develop. All the more reason for caution in generalizing from such results.

Further, the psychological premises of these experimental situations often have the flavor of the games of children who accept their "pretended" play or "make-believe" situations as real and so respond spontaneously to them. If the subject's orientation, perceptual world, and level of functioning is circumscribed as powerfully and genuinely by the "pretended" situation, social game, and unreal world of the small-group laboratory as is a child's when engaged in play or make-believe, then it is possible that the S's behavior can be viewed analogously as a highly sophisticated and involving role-playing game or make-believe acting, albeit at the adult level. But if, in fact, these group attributes do not so powerfully influence such "child" components of the S's psychological structure, then other hypotheses—such as some of those already noted—may be credited with explaining his behavior.

The independent variables in these proposed studies would be the varied types and kinds of groups previously mentioned; the time allotted for the group session; the types of consensus, if any are required for the resolution of the group task; the "openness," independence, confidence, integrity, courage, and types of security characterizing the group members; the freedom of the group milieu; the tolerance of dissent. A tentative list of dependent variables would include the capacity of the group to take action and to make further task commitments in the course of such action; the persistence of group effort against obstacles and the varieties of courageous and ingenious group action that as a consequence may emerge; the duration and degree of loyalty of the group to the agreements that it has reached; the degree of flexible assignment of roles to all group members; the tolerance of other members' initiatives; the capacity to accept variation and change in the group's procedures, structure, and dynamics. Also included among the dependent variables should be those qualities that were especially distinctive of the Greek group experience: pursuit of truth, respect for intelligence, flexibility of ideas and action, capacity for sacrifice in the pursuit of a high goal, respect for leadership on the basis of its courage and ability, and the openness and vigor of group debate and discussion.

The Ego

To discuss Greek character in the age of Solon is not a happy task. Not only has the enigma it presents been inspected repeatedly, but the discrepancies in the resulting "views" have been so considerable as to discourage new looks for fear of further confounding the already blurred pictures. Nevertheless, inasmuch as the ego is one of the crucial constructs in psychology, it is necessary to enter into this area of uncertain vision and sketch some of the characteristics of the one "possessed" by the Greeks. As a precaution, however, only those features minimally but irrevocably agreed to by all viewers will be included as substantially based on evidence drawn from historical accounts, contemporary description, artistic depictions, etc.

It is not necessary to discuss those Greek qualities that are similar to some that currently prevail in America. Practical intelligence, shrewdness, a kind of plastic adaptability, business acumen and skill, and inventiveness are common features, in some measure, to both cultures. What, however, is not common but was perhaps more representative of the Greek ego was (1) a passionate courage in the convictions that were held by men; (2) a great emphasis on civic responsibility and participation, a love of discussion, and a versatility of aptitude for public affairs and politics; (3) a strong but sensitive appreciation of the arts, including drama and poetry; (4) the capacity for freedom of feeling including that particular lack of repression that revealed itself in spontaneous expression and action and delighted in the uninhibited life of the gods as a coveted precedent for that of their own; (5) a striving for and admiration of excellence in all things as a great source of ego strength but serving, also, to revitalize delight in feeling and the senses which, in turn, stimulated a rejuvenescence of life as a whole; (6) conversely, a sense of the futility of ever being equal in excellence and behavior to the gods—and so god-like—evoked a fatalism as well as constituted, in part, the explanation for the tragedy that was consequent on aspiration to god-like status (a theme particularly prevalent in drama and myth); (7) the sense of wholeness and balance of the ego as a cardinal quality, meaning for the Greeks "nothing in excess," a continuing effort to see things as wholes, as held in delicate balance, and as tempered by reason alloyed with feeling.

Now, by comparison, let us survey the American ego as described in various sociological and psychological studies and as evaluated by a substantial segment of contemporary thought.[9, 10, 11, 12] Insofar as generalizations can be made, its distinctive aspects are:

1. The importance of "adjustment" as a value and as a mental mechanism. To the extent that this factor is of primary significance there will be—granted the current institutions to which "adjustment" must be made—diversion of energies from deep feelings and strong convictions, frustration of a substantial number of inner impulses and inner experiences with a compensatory development of drives directed toward external rewards, and a strong accent on expediency as a modus operandi in life. Other results of this commitment are overemphasis on the external world to the detriment of the inner; an often frantic search for external security; mobilization of vast amounts of ego energy for analysis of external situations, for social or worldly manipulations, and for the machinations of compromise.

2. In tandem with the foregoing is the dependence of the ego on groups, on social approval, or on material success for its strength, particularly as its deep inner claims are neither satisfied nor, frequently, have fully matured. Hence considerable fluctuation in convictions, loyalties, or even values are prevalent. Naturally, the lack of a strong nonmaterialistic cultural tradition together with the snubbing of integrity, inner conviction, and personal dedication as principles of existence make it easier for nonmaterialistic and nonconforming propensities to atrophy in the ego. Also the considerable intrinsic seduction of materialist rewards plus the social or other consequences of rejecting them furthers the diversion of energies into these "societally sanctioned" channels.

3. Characteristic, also, is the downgrading of tendencies concerned with behavior other than that of acquisition, security, conformity, and productivity. Among these are compassion, authentic kindliness, aesthetic and personal sensibility, "spiritual" resources, and similar kinds of "inner" experience. The capacity and talent for love suffers attrition through such a process of subordination and abrasion even though its compensatory and counterfeit expressions may be found institutionalized in organized

charity, "ritualized niceness," etc. Or because its authentic expression is frustrated, love may turn against itself and be transformed into increased acquisitive or security needs, into sundry forms of the pursuit of social approval and love from others, into preoccupation with "bigness" and "expansion," and into increased ruthlessness. Further, the more that such impulses as kindness and love are contained, the greater the resulting resentment, which, not infrequently, is turned back into rejection of the now thwarted impulses, often with compensatory tendentious support of current social values. This resentment, in turn, must be contained for reasons of social expediency. All this results in the arrest or repression of feelings necessary for the tonus and well-being of the ego, which is essential if the latter is to achieve an authentic identity and noncounterfeit convictions. Neither is it uncommon for the ego to be guilt-ridden for "selling out" its own genuine inclinations and, also, in a condition of anxiety for fear of discovery of its authentic values—which would mean candidly confronting its counterfeit tendencies and goals. Its displaced genuine impulses and resentments are now directed toward approval and conformity (with attendant cultivation of traits ensuring their attainment—calculation, shrewdness, cleverness, etc.) thereby trammeling genuine identity and sensibility and leaving a residue of ennui or purposelessness. This general condition, then, reveals itself as a circus of sham instinct expression in which dissembled, fragmented, and bogus impulses shallowly replace the genuine ones. Not infrequently it takes the form of an exhibition of freedom without "real" freedom or a frenzied pursuit of successes and satisfactions without real instinctual gratification. Often the outcome is an ego driven by external influences and the whims of the expedient, compensating through a diversity of frantic but approved activities for having deserted or not found its authentic goals; an ego dissatisfied in its search because it has substituted fraudulent goals for genuine ones, harassed by external social norms and controls so that it cannot express certain of its organic feelings or inclinations, and, in the end, an ego that experiences weakness, purposelessness, and, not uncommonly, some variant of self-hatred. Because it is compelled to expediency as a way of life, it nourishes the development of those capacities that will promote its counterfeit goals in matters of adjustment or materialism: an accountancy intelligence, an interpersonal calculation, a conformist's niceness and respectability.

4. Fear of independence and individuality. The pressures toward conformity and security result in the undermining of personal convictions and principles and serve to orient judgment and action toward that of the collective (group, corporation, public opinion, etc.). Thereby, one is pro-

tected against social, economic, or psychological rejection and censure because of any latently held but potentially bold individualistic expressions or unconventional, original notions incompatible with the collective's norms. The sources of the fears of individualism and independence are many: the large-scale organization of economic and leisure functions into which individuals must fit as cogs and the values of the mass market that must be maintained in the interest of cost efficiency, increasing profits, and expanding industry; reaction to the American nineteenth-century tradition of uninhibited individual enterprise and the havoc it wrought on the underdog; the experience of individual impotence against "bigness" and anonymous, bureaucratic power which, together with the not unconnected sense of vast destruction and violence hovering everywhere, coerces large numbers to believe that only in the collective will survival, approval, and emotional security be assured; the effect of the machine on human individuality with its potential impact of specialization, mechanization, and fragmentation of the human personality.

The preservation of the illusion that independence and individualism are ever present is not only related to the need to retain a continuity with a distinguished tradition of the past which is a powerful source of pride and self-respect, but also serves as an incentive to production because greater work is produced in democratic societies when men are persuaded that they are working freely of their own convictions and for their own purposes. Now having absolved their ideological conscience and fulfilled their "historical" rituals by bowing at the altar of individualism and independence, they are made more manipulable by the pressure of the collective, whether it be exerted via mass media, congenial "togetherness," material reward, or yet other reinforcements and intimidations. The powerful probability that the enormously seductive rewards and pleasures of the technological paradise of present society may be lost if one persists in individualism further enervates the courage to resist the values of the collective. Further, genuine urging of courageous independence incites a fear of greater freedom with its possible attendant threat to the status quo in those who have vested commitments to the present social milieu or its values (e.g., members of the "establishment," supporters or arbiters of the status quo, the complacent, the insecure) and so provokes reactive emphasis by them on security, conformity, respectability, and intimidation. The compulsion and even hunger for being part of the collective increase as authentic violations to basic integrity, individualism, and the "impulse life" grow. Such immersion in collectivity often represents reaction formation to feared individualistic dispositions or counterfeit gratification of personal impulses now displaced to collective rewards and also may be a protective defense against authentic personal identity. Hence, at the core of the unvarnished hatred of individualism is the feeling that it demands more courage, freedom, and genuine "personal identity" than can be easily summoned in the present social condition and, further, that the penalties for its existence are too great.

It should also be said that those who have thrown their lot in with the present social milieu can hardly hope to manage its complexities alone. Alliance with many and large groupings confer a protection, esteem, and power that the "loner," be it a group or an individual, can hardly ever achieve. Such coalitions are entered into with others, in a society of powerful vested interests and contending factions, with the intention of exerting economic or political influence and obtaining material benefits that one could not hope to accomplish alone. Indeed, such self-interest is even more effectively served when several such coalitions, rather than contending against one another with often mutual damaging effects, further ally themselves for the purpose of more expeditiously achieving a common, or failing that, a compromise goal. Such practices support the belief that autonomy and individualism are useless, that the big swallow the small and that more is gained by joining than by fighting them. Herein, then, is one explanation of why commitment and passion become allied with "big groupness" and why autonomy and individualism come to be associated with futility, impracticality, uncooperativeness or, not infrequently, with such appraisals as being "odd" or "difficult."

5. In tandem with the foregoing is the fact that the major commitments and personal identities of the contemporary ego are associated with materialism, social approval, and similar "external" values. Hence, ego convictions often vary with changes in the external world that involve money, possessions, popularity, or group membership. Personal identity becomes synchronous with material wealth, and material wealth with public opinion (because the latter if favorable represents purchasing power in the form of a prospective market for goods and services) and therefore has the potential of conferring or denying material rewards, jobs, or other benefits on those to whom it is disposed. Just as the value of property fluctuates with the market so does the strength of the contemporary ego (or ego identity) fluctuate with its acquisitions of tangible goods and social approvals. Further, since property or material success are, as previously explained, dependent on favorable public opinion in present mass consumption economy (hence the need for "getting along," the need to be popular, and to conform to the group or company), interpersonal procedures and relationships, being instruments oriented to winning such public approval in the social market—and thereon mate-

rialistic rewards—become substantially valued for their effectiveness in achieving these ends and proportionately less for their traditionally humanistic or absolute merit. Thus, such interpersonal relationships, both in process and purpose, not infrequently embody the opportunism and expediency that these "ends" demand. As such, they exhibit an insubstantiality of emotional ties that reflects the erosion of humanistic standards and further reveal that such relationships have often been converted—by virtue of the manipulative "use" of persons in them—into another depersonalized process by the contemporary values of materialism and success. Hence the great importance of public opinion, social approval, and popularity, for to win these, in time, may be the equivalent of obtaining economic rewards. Hence, too, the notion of selling oneself which is, in effect, winning others' favor and so, eventually, their economic favor. It is in this sense that public opinion is the equivalent of property or that one converts oneself into something—an image, a "front," a depersonalized role or function or, in the last analysis, a product or "thing" analogous to the products or things formed by business and industry—that pleases others in exchange for their good opinion and eventually their economic or other favors. Thus, in the last analysis, one may become a salable product or a "thing"—an object of exchange to be wanted and sold and thus needing social approval or demand.

For similar reasons, of which accrual of economic benefits (getting and keeping jobs, making products and sales, winning contracts, etc.) owing to the favorable opinion of others is especially apropos, a great dependence develops on the disposition of these "others" toward the concerned person and, not infrequently, is extended to other attitudes and values of theirs. Hence, to a not unsubstantial degree, certain functions of the ego (e.g., social judgment and belief, certain values and convictions, and some types of executive action) are attuned to and exercised as a reflection and ward of the "others" attitudes, resulting in the shaping of the ego as a malleable and variable faculty. It thus becomes, to some degree, the extension or image of the "other" in that the "other" embodies the capacity for acceptance or approval and, hence, of success and material rewards. Thus it is that the "other"—whether single individuals, a group, popular opinion, corporation, a nation, etc.—becomes the tyrannical arbiter of the ego, often compelling the latter to estimate itself by, and sometimes accept, its attitudes and values. As the "other" changes, so does the ego, and hence it is no surprise that the fluctuation, the dependency, and the uncertainty of the contemporary ego is inherent in the contemporary scene. It follows from all this that the "other" becomes a modern god, symbolizing as well as embodying the capacity to bestow or withdraw love and approval, to dispense reward or punishment (economic or other), and to confer "identity," purpose, and personal worth.

6. Another quality of the American ego that contrasts sharply with that of the Greeks is its capacity to compromise—an art derived from several sources: the necessity for getting along in a pluralistic society with numerous and contending groups who claim equality of merit and legitimacy in respect to beliefs, rights, and, not uncommonly, power; the need to resolve conflicts between such groups so that required production, services, and commerce are sustained or, at least, not disrupted; the attrition of vigorous individualism and strong principle by virtue of the inverse emphasis on expediency, on the primacy of collectives, and on adjustment; the nature and imperatives of coalition politics, as previously discussed; the dissemination of a popular, if inexact, interpretation of democracy which holds that every conviction, opinion, or principle has roughly equal merit or legitimacy in the tribunal of mass judgment so that personal courage in the support of convictions of genuine importance or veracity is undermined by (1) the character of the mass publics that are the judges of them, (2) the fact that, irrespective of merit, competing ideas are accorded equal legitimacy or are supported by equal passion and power, and (3) by the often unjust or dishonest character of the proceedings of the competition itself (between ideas, claims, values, etc.).

Compromise is also demanded in multiple areas of judgment and action: "masculine" boldness vs. "feminine" passivity; work productivity and success vs. work quality and integrity; opportunism and status vs. decency and honesty; niceness vs. aggressiveness and toughness. The fate of such antinomies varies: they may remain in severe conflict (overt or covert) with resulting impoverishment of ego vigor, confidence, and firmness of judgment or decision; one may uneasily predominate to the subordination of the other, resulting in anxiety, in compulsive or defensive exercise of the predominating feature, or in manifold forms of hypocrisy, self-deception, and contrived behavioral façades. If the latter conditions are the "resolutions" of these tensions, then the protracted role-acting (mask) or dissimulation (hypocrisy) needed for their success engenders a vague discontent, a frustration of self-fulfillment, or a lack of *élan* and purpose that, in turn, demands psychological blackmail from the ego in the form of more material and social "success," compulsive "busyness," frenetic socialization or release, and the need for increased personal approval or acceptance from others. To counteract in some degree the counterfeit and self-deluding substitutes for authentic ego expression and integrity, a certain portion of ego energy may attempt to relieve some of the frustration of the psychologically suffocating masks that enshroud the ego: hence do-it-yourself hobbies, canned and discussion-group culture, and emotional self-expression whether through spiritual and religious revivals, amateur painting, theater and poetry, or abandoned indulgence in *la dolce vita*. It would be a mistake, however, not to recognize that in much of this there is the urge to be free of the mechanization, ennui, and suffocation of current ego states and to find a genuine channel and worthy goal for self-expression and fulfillment.

CRITICAL EVALUATION OF CONTEMPORARY STUDIES

These are some of the characteristics of the American ego that contrast with those of the Greeks. Contemporary studies of the ego, unwittingly or not, reflect preoccupation with such features and with the cultural atmosphere in part responsible for them. These studies are often carried out under conditions not dissimilar to those in which the ego is nurtured and functions in present-day life: subtle oppression; engendering of substantial purposeless or meaningless tensions; the stimulation of anxious insecurity but of only minimal independence and courage; the damping of individualism; the disassociation and segmentalization of ego judgment or action through the constriction and mechanization of the experimental and testing situations which, in turn is affected by limiting the range of responses available to the subject and through denuding such responses of authentic *élan*, interest, delight, resentment, and conviction.

These contrived, artificial situations, in which the ego is assessed or experimentally tested, actually sabotage its response potential and, if only for that reason, evoke conditions of existential and self-actualizing anxiety. In addition, the pseudofear, pseudocrises, pseudothreat, and pseudo-punishment, designed to provoke "experimental anxiety" which, in effect, is counterfeit or "unnaturalistic" anxiety—derived, as it is, from the triviality and purposelessness of such experimental situations—further diminish the effectiveness and vigor of the ego and transform it into somewhat of a puppet or shadowy image of itself. Vitality, direction, and executive effectiveness is crippled (in this bogus research charade) by elimination of the ego's authentic understanding, concern, and purpose in the situation that is imposed on it, by the specious problems presented, and by the near impossibility of resolving them with genuine human satisfaction. Thus measures of ego strength in such situations are often meaningless for the authentic understanding of ego functioning. Indeed, the anxiety and constriction manifested in them may only reflect the antipathy and alienation of the S toward being involved in the oppression, mystery, and meaningless problems and resolutions intrinsic to such

99

situations. The upshot is that the crisis of the experimental problem is aggravated, and the ego is torn between the absurdity of the situation, on the one hand, and the pressure to accept it seriously, on the other, with the result that the conflicts, crises, and anxieties that are generated are typical of and as pointless as many other situations in contemporary experience.

It cannot be overemphasized that the ego is sabotaged in effectiveness, in good part, by the frustration of the human need to make the situation it confronts into a relevant, purposeful experience that is meaningfully soluble. Not having discerned these features in it, the ego has no recourse but to submit to the situation (provided it does not reject it outright) with accompanying loss of its capacity for meaningful, human evaluation of the presented problems and for independent decision-making and action. Such loss of some of the constituents of self-identity and capacity for mastery increases the ego's anxiety and, if it is not then fortified by a cynical "don't take it seriously, play it like a game" attitude or by a "hipster" orientation, it becomes more vulnerable or submissive and less energetic or effective.

Further, the constant use of such "meaningless crisis" situations to assess the ego reflects the kind of ego capacities that modern society judges as valuable in coping with the often purposeless, maze-like problems it sets for its members. Nothing in these experimental situations requires the ego to make fundamentally relevant human judgments about the value of the problems it confronts or of its own intrinsic interest in them. Nothing about them gives it license to decide which of its resources should be committed or evokes from it a deep psychic investment. Nothing permits it to reject the whole situation unreservedly, requires a moral decision on its human merits, or engages certain of the ego's "spiritual" energies. Rather, most of these experimental situations call for a sort of quick, supple, athletically inclined ego, suspiciously alert and cat-like, prepared for emergency and fight, equipped to carry on a crafty war of nerves in a world of intrigue, conflict, or office politics, and mobilized for exploiting emotions of the fox and ferret (e.g., cunning, manipulative, controlled), emotions of the "main chance," and those of frenzy, maximum energy, or a cutthroat nature—all of this for issues and problems that, in humanistic perspective, are of a rat maze or petite bourgeoisie character but that present society judges as important.

Such compliance with the values of these experimental situations (as with present society) and corresponding animal-like alertness in them (as in the world of business and power) excites just those threatened, cunning, animal-at-bay responses that a nonevaluating, purposeless, but survival-oriented ego can encompass. Further, these situations, in spirit and substance, reflect a society where rivalry, manipulative advantage, "know-how," and success, whether economically or interpersonally, are in tandem with threat and uncertainty. But also they mirror, paradoxically, conformity to authority (the experimenter) and to collectives (the laboratory, university, or scientific "establishment") as well as the desire to be accepted. Beyond this, the feeling of an anonymous but omniscient control of self and situation additionally oppresses the ego's resources while reflecting the character of mysterious "castle" organizations of society (government, corporation, the psychological laboratory or research group) in manipulating individuals as pawns, sometimes with inscrutable design or, in any case, as part of a larger plan. Because there is especial deference by the S to this inscrutable scientific experiment and to the E's prescriptions and authority as the oracular scientist, further paralysis of the freedom of the ego ensues.

It must be understood that those whose socialization has already brought them in tune with the spirit or values of society as reflected in these experimental situations—the calloused, the petit bourgeois, the anonymous man and conformist, the robot-spirited, the organization man —have no great difficulty in considering such situations as normal challenges nor do they suffer much ideological conflict, alienation, ego constriction, sense of being manipulated, or denial of psychic resources when dealing with them. Because this group has substantial representation among those presently acculturated in contemporary society and available as subjects for psychological research, there may be no great discrepancy between what such ego studies measure and what, superficially at least, the contemporary ego, as represented by such S's, presents for evaluation.

These studies, then, crystallize (1) those "animal" capacities and conforming responses so important to survival in contemporary American society, (2) the automation of judgment and action that emerge when the ego is deprived of the knowledge and free choice essential to meaningful evaluation and wise action and when it functions under conditions of deference, fear, or disguised manipulation, and (3) the disassociation of the relevant, vital, and even emergency problems inherent in the life of the S in the outside world from the lack of authentic relevance and meaning of the problems he is usually confronted with in the experimental situation.

In addition to these deficiencies in the appraisal of ego resources, such situations further limit the ego's potentiality through not challenging its fullest and richest capacities either by presenting a sufficiently significant problem or by arousing it to consciousness of its own predicament, i.e., the authentic (existential) nature of its immediate condition in a specific experimental situation. In these situations, the ego is like a scared robot making its way in the dark or like a calloused, amoral opportunist primarily concerned with survival or success and prepared to do almost anything to achieve it. Actually, some of the anxiety ostensibly evoked by the experimental problem per se is only that displaced from the mystery, oppressiveness, and purposelessness of the situation itself and its attendant repressions plus that displaced from the personal preoccupations of emotionally insecure Ss of college age who are confronted with psychological test problems given and interpreted by seemingly omniscient scientists. In the end, what these scientific ego studies do is to dramatize and distill the role of the ego in present society by fusing a sham Madison Avenue ferris wheel crisis with a manipulated, automatized but striving creature—the marvelous machine-like robot-animal, full of drive and appetite, whose conformity is to accept the rat race and its assumptions without questioning and to strive for esteem and success in its counterfeit environment. By such manipulations, the psychologist unwittingly transmutes his own experience or conception of man in contemporary life into the formulation of theoretical premises and the staging of experimental conditions that can only produce research results out of which can only similarly emerge a dehumanized image of man—an image given further respectability by a corresponding model of scientific theory construction.

The picture of ego functioning, so created, depicts the span of ego resources as diminished, ego probity as penalized, and canny shrewdness as rewarded; it further reveals a premium on conformity, purposelessness, and animal survival while subordinating ethics, independence, and moral courage. Hence it diminishes man's dignity while augmenting his directionlessness and indiscriminate impulse for success. Such then is the picture of the contemporary ego: clever without reflective thought, amoral without purpose, and deferent without candor. But this is far from the total spectrum of ego functions or, indeed, from all its other resources that are manifested in contemporary life or, especially, during various other historical periods. By neglecting or minimizing these different ego components, a distortion of ego structure and dynamics is produced in research and in theory. And by disassociating such unacknowledged ego features from the socially sanctioned and "scientifically identified and assessed" ones, the latter, devoid of the balancing influence and modulating effects of the former, are disproportionately evoked and, hence in present studies, asymmetrical in the weight they have in the ego structure or in the force they exert on its dynamics.

RECTIFICATION

How can such conditions be rectified? What must now be done is to relate the nature of the Greek ego to these research conditions and to draw such lessons from its historical character as will amplify and correct the nature of research on the modern ego. If, in fact, this ego does have the potentiality for those qualities that were regularly found in the Greeks, the germane question is how they can now be evoked for purposes of scientific identification and appraisal.

Among such Greek ego traits are independence, courage, organic integration of impulse and intellect, and participation in experience that was humanistic and expressive of purposive values in life. It is possible that these qualities might emerge under the following conditions.

1. Fully inform the S of the psychological meaning of the experiment and the purport of its detailed procedures.

2. Make clear to him his role in the experiment and the wide range of possible actions that are available in it.

3. Encourage the S—before the experiment—by heightening his confidence, sense of freedom, feeling of "mastery" over events, and by giving him the assurance that whatever he does will not be depreciated.

4. Relate the experiment to a broader context of life and particularly to the S's experience and background.

5. Arm the S with a philosophy or value system (either by selection of certain Ss or by long and subtle orientations of others) that will either give him purposive identity or some fundamental human outlook from which to evaluate and deal with the experimental experience.

6. Experiences of delight and exhilaration should be included in the research situations. They would take the form of healthy, open pleasure stemming from involvement in a stimulating activity or an absorbing task, from a challenge that excites one's best abilities, from an interval of rest, or flowing from some moments of carefree feeling and abandoned gaiety. These forms of happy pleasure are far different from tension reduction or from the dissipation of anxiety, aggression, and frustration which involve quite different psychological premises and processes. However, these latter drive tensions, when present during the experiment, should be given channels for drainage or reduction so that the S's ego—like its Greek counterpart—will not suffer depletion of energy or attrition through countercathexis and frustration, but have the option of fortifying and reviving itself through available release mechanisms. Such tension-

reducing prerogatives are not only consonant with the temper of Greek society but are not dissimilar from large segments of normal experience currently prevalent outside the psychological research environment. Indeed, the failure to provide channels of release for "research-created" tensions or appropriate means for the fulfillment of ego-enhancing, delight-exciting, and comparable enriching experiences make these studies further subject to the previously made criticisms regarding their diminution and distortion of certain potential resources of the ego.

7. The creation of a preexperimental (and experimental) atmosphere where independence, free choice, skepticism, spontaneity, and open-mindedness are encouraged. This may be done by various kinds of orientation and training directed to the acquisition of these qualities.

8. Those Ss should be selected who have the desired Grecian characteristics of ego strength, independence, courage, etc.

9. Induction of moods or experiences in the S that will evoke Grecian-like ego qualities. This might be done in the following ways: by dramatic presentations (plays, motion pictures, or tableaux) in which these qualities are the central themes; by the E and his associates behaving as models of these qualities and manifesting them either in the ordinary course of events or in particularly designed situations where they could be meaningfully and forcefully displayed; by having the S read stories, essays, dramas, poems, and histories that preeminently represent these qualities; by converting the whole experimental situation into a life-like experience in which (1) through the example of others, (2) through pre-experimental orientation or training, and (3) through the atmosphere of the research setting or the power of particularly designed situations (e.g., crises requiring courage, difficulties demanding independence, dangers evoking heroism, or threats arousing purpose and direction) the desired "Grecian" qualities will emerge in the S. Also, in segments of these "experiences" the S should be encouraged to act as a hero or, at least, to imagine he is one and to imagine, further, how these other "Grecian" qualities should be expressed—and then to do so.

10. The S would role-play these qualities in appropriate situations preparatory to an experiment.

11. The S would be oriented to the nature and value of particular traits or actions in various situations, such orientation being based on a Grecian philosophy of life and theory of action.

12. Relaxation, support, and encouragement must be emphasized in the course of these experiments. By permitting various diversions in the research situations (joking, drinking, reading, sociability) and by establishing a mood of relaxation in the preexperimental setting (all laboratory

personnel, for example, should be in an "easy" frame of mind) a certain measure of tranquility might be communicated to the subjects. Periodic and tangible indications of support during the experiment proper (minor rewards, compliments, and verbal encouragement) might augment the S's confidence and courage.

13. Extensive discussions should be held with the S concerning these Grecian-like qualities, the excellence they bestow on character, and their importance for greatness. (Accounts of courage, integrity, excellence, etc., as in the cases of Bruno, Socrates, etc., should be read and discussed with him.) He should also be made to observe when and if personnel of the laboratory in which the research occurs do stand up to authority, make sacrifices of status and rewards rather than forfeit their convictions, and question administrative policy and research premises despite being punished. The S should then be confronted with analogous decision-choice situations during which his courage and independence would be strengthened by the example or support of others and by the gratifying experience of exercising his own integrity. For example, resistance to the effects of electric shock or authoritarian opinion may be augmented by helping the S affirm his right to a reasonable explanation for such treatment as well as by supporting his resolution to sustain his values and independence so that punishment or rejection will not be coercive of his beliefs or personal identity. This, in turn, may make him see the human absurdity of such treatment and so, perhaps, encourage him to effectively protest it.

14. Meaningful problems that are of personal significance to the S or that involve pertinent and vital issues of the community or life in general should be made the substance of ego experiments. In such studies the S would have to confront and probe a challenging problem. In the process of doing so, he would have to face obstacles, reproaches, experience anxiety, decide between easier and less honest or demanding and more honest solutions, and confront various temptations to stray from the path of integrity. Indeed, the whole experimental situation, the laboratory personnel included, might become the setting—both as a social unit and as having meaningful and challenging problems of significance to the S— for the naturalistic or experimental investigation of these Grecian-like ego qualities.

15. In addition, many of the foregoing studies could be carried out in naturalistic situations, such as clubs, conversational exchanges, parties, relationships between friends, or during the ordinary events of a day. Indeed, careful observation in these and other conditions or situations may reveal that there is more courage, integrity, and heroism in the ego

than current psychological theory and research is disposed to recognize. Also, employing experimental challenges and ploys at different points in these situations may evoke the increased appearance of these qualities, e.g., in an amiable controversy, a point raised about the personal courage of one of the participants might provoke its active emergence.

16. Finally, it might be useful to compare the frequency and nature of these ego qualities in the foregoing "enhancing" conditions with their occurrence in other conditions and situations where the problems are neither of vital nor personal significance to the S, where they do not excite a sense of purpose or pleasure in him, and where neither the full facts surrounding them nor a proper perspective on their importance are presented to him.

In pursuing the foregoing proposals, the following may serve as useful, assessment techniques: (1) In discussions or controversies to which he may either be a party or observer (role-playing, dramas, debates, etc.), the amount of sympathy or support the S accords to any protagonist manifesting a Grecian-like quality may be an indication of identification with, though not necessarily possession of, such a quality. Similarly, the bestowing of favors or kindnesses on such protagonists in contrast to opposition or disservice to them may reflect shared sympathy with the protagonist's traits. Ratios and amounts of such "attractions" and "oppositions" in different situations might reveal certain dispositions of the S in regard to these Grecian-like qualities. (2) Measures of the S's persistence must be developed concerning his ability to maintain a position or a line of action despite obstacles, opposition, or temptations from it. The relation between such persistence when maintaining a position in which he deeply believes as compared with one that is expediently maintained only because of group or personal associations, deference to authority, or compulsions of the "experimental milieu," should be determined. (3) The amount of sacrifice the S will incur for some purpose, conviction, or ideal is important to assess. Sacrifice, here, may be voluntary or imposed, deliberate or unwitting. It may take the form of time, work, agony, money, loss of pleasure and success, diminution of status and self-esteem, or increased personal anxiety and conflict. Whether such sacrifice is necessary for the fulfillment of the S's goal, whether he is fully aware of its necessity or superfluity, whether such a sacrifice is accepted calmly or with agony, regret, and bitterness, and finally, whether its incurrence is reasonably and rationally weighed or is increased disproportionately and emotionally for "personal psychological" reasons are altogether pertinent variables for investigation.

Other assessments of these traits would employ indigenous tests in natural and life-like settings. To evaluate courage, for example, small injustices would be contrived: a waitress would ask a diner, not finished eating, to leave because of a line of waiting customers; a policeman would arrogantly chastise a driver without cause; a clerk would unnecessarily delay his service to a customer; a large man would bully a smaller defenseless one; a forlorn stranger would be snubbed at a party; an innocent person, who had been victimized, would be in need of help, perhaps at the cost of time, energy, or even the position of a friend. Observation would be made of the frequency of appearance of courage in the S who would have been a direct witness to such incidents and situations during states of exhilaration, confidence, vigorous independence, etc. as compared with those of complacency, satiety, prudence, or blandness. Distinctions must also be made between types of courage: the kind needed for a military mission, a political cause, for protecting the weak, for ensuring personal dignity or pride, etc., and corresponding experiments and surveys should be developed to assess each such type. Comparable distinctions should be made for other "Grecian-like traits," and similar incidents or situational tests should be devised to evoke, if possible, their appearance in the S.

What is important in all this is that the experiment or study becomes a medium for crystallizing such Grecian ego resources as the S may latently or manifestly possess rather than the agency for mobilization of those qualities that are consonant with the prevailing "image of man" and its progenitor—the status quo. It also may be valuable to survey each S's particular background and activity for just those Grecian qualities that could be made the basis for experiments in which he could significantly participate. These may be found to be latent, concealed, or episodic in the S's life. Indeed, perhaps even the most dehumanized S has some hint of Grecian quality in his character, and formulating a research study to demonstrate its viability would be, if successful, peculiarly ironic. Designing experiments that evince these qualities would, however, demand very high ingenuity from researchers. In this view, the ego experiment is an instrument or locus of values and biases which inevitably evokes resonant behavior-complexes and symmetrical cultural-personal dispositions in the Ss. As such, it reflects the scientific culture and the value biases of its designer—the E—and can evoke only that limited spectrum of behavior implicit in his conception and value system while inhibiting other response-qualities (not implicit in them) from emerging. To the degree that this genre of experiment is rigorous and precise the scientific value bias of the experimenter will more clearly influence the S and so more saliently evoke corresponding behavior while shunting aside different behavioral value tendencies.

Additional methods and considerations that should run through these proposed experiments are: the utilization of the S's personal friends, in both laboratory and natural settings, for support, criticism, and realistic discussion with him when appropriate; the use of all available resources to establish the genuine naturalness of the research situation, e.g., friends, spontaneous conversation, and an E who, in fact, is an authentic and sincere human being. Thus each situation in which the S is engaged must maximally stimulate whatever Greek resources may be present in him. Important too, is the recognition that even in these "natural situations" there are artificial or spurious elements, whether these be a subtly contrived brain washing of the S, an imperceptible, if none the less real, deference of the S to the E—often disguised under the façade of a deceptive independence, and marvelously clever simulations of candid interactions with friends, concern with high values, or commitment to vital goals. Such diagnoses must be made if these Grecian situations do not become a more subtle experimental fraud or charade than those previously castigated, and every effort must be made to ensure the authenticity of the S's participation in these situations. When this genuine engagement is achieved, the required conditions for the study of Greek ego qualities will be present.

To this end, as many reasonable alternatives as possible must be provided in the research situation. An electric shock study, for example, should include behavior options such as refusal to cooperate, ambulation between shocks, drinking of alcoholic beverages, swearing, etc. In other studies, permitted actions would include questioning the value of the research, unburdening oneself to neutral persons who are present, vituperation toward the E, laboratory personnel, or other authorities, engaging in prayer and fantasy, the presence of friends and enemies whom the S may "use" as he wishes, and exhortation of the S to greater courage by persons and groups present during the research. Avenues such as the following should be made available for rebellion or relaxation of the S during the course of the study: rest and play intervals, dancing, listening to music, light reading or story-telling, looking at or sketching pictures, engaging in hobbies, substitute or scapegoat actions, etc.

Other techniques that may be usefully tried in connection with the foregoing include encouragement of the S after he has experienced experimental failure or frustration and affording him numerous opportunities to improve his performance or reactions by specific suggestions made to those ends; appealing to destiny, transcendent belief, myth, legend, and legendary heroes to sustain and inspire him; giving him courage and inspiration through music, chronicles of great deeds or of noble lives, heroic poetry, fables, and examples of the courage of others in analogous situations. Reading and discussion of various Greek philosophers may be found to activate or augment courage, independence, and other Grecian traits in the S during these studies. In addition, activities that helped the Greeks reconstitute ego strength, renew hope, and revive courage would be permitted in these experiments: reading or narrating certain Greek myths or legends, reminiscing about the Greek heroic past, and reliving certain Hellenic religious beliefs or Dionysian rituals.

So far as subject selection is concerned, though some diversity of types should be included for certain crucial comparisons and hypotheses, the larger number of Ss should have some aspects of the Greek image: strong, humanistic values or orientations, vigorous capacity for individualism or dissent, and heroic or courageous personal qualities. As suggested, the problems of these studies must be specifically designed for engaging each S's unique vital interests.

REFERENCES

1. Köhler, Wolfgang. *Gestalt Psychology*. New York: Liveright, 1929.
2. Binet, Alfred, and Simon, T. Several papers, *Année Psychologique*, XI, 1905.
3. Keats, John. "Ode on a Grecian Urn," in *The Poetical Works of John Keats*. London: Oxford University Press, 1961.
4. Riesman, David, et al. *The Lonely Crowd*. New Haven: Yale University Press, 1960.
5. Cartwright, D., and Zander, A., eds. *Group Dynamics*, 2d ed. New York: Harper & Row, 1960.
6. Rosenthal, Robert. *Experimental Effects in Behavioral Research*. New York: Appleton-Century-Crofts, 1966.
7. Coch, L., and French, Jr., J. R. P. "Overcoming Resistance to Change," *Human Relations*, I (1948), pp. 518–532.
8. Lewin, Kurt. "Frontiers in Group Dynamics," *Human Relations*, I (1947), pp. 5–42.
9. Goodman, Paul. *Growing Up Absurd*. New York: Random House, 1960.
10. Josephson, Eric and Mary, eds. *Man Alone: Alienation in Modern Society*. New York: Dell, 1962.
11. Klapp, Orrine. *Collective Search for Identity*. New York: Holt, Rinehart & Winston, 1969.
12. Stein, M. R., Vidich, A. J., and White, D. M., eds. *Identity and Anxiety*. Glencoe, Ill.: Free Press of Glencoe, 1960.

GENERAL REFERENCES

Archimedes. *The Works of Archimedes,* ed. by T. L. Heath. Cambridge: Cambridge University Press, 1897.

Aristotle. *The Basic Works of Aristotle,* ed. by Richard McKeon. New York: Random House, 1941.

Asch, Solomon E. "Effects of Group Pressure Upon the Modification and Distortion of Judgments," in Harold Guetzkow, ed., *Groups, Leadership and Men.* 1951. Reprint. New York: Russell & Russell, 1963.

Barnes, Harry Elmer, with David, Henry. *The History of Western Civilization.* New York: Harcourt, Brace, 1935.

Boring, E. G. *A History of Experimental Psychology,* rev. ed. New York: Appleton-Century, 1950.

Bowra, Sir Cecil Maurice. *The Greek Experience.* London: Weidenfeld & Nicolson, 1957.

Faure, Elie. *History of Art.* New York: Harper, 1921–1930.

Gardner, Helen. *Art Through the Ages.* New York: Harcourt, Brace, 1926.

Goodman, Paul. *Growing Up Absurd.* New York: Random House, 1960.

Hamilton, Edith. *Greek Mythology.* Boston: Little, Brown, 1942.

Hayes, C. J. H. *Political and Cultural History of Europe.* New York: Macmillan, 1932–1936.

Jaeger, Werner Wilhelm. *Paideria: The Ideals of Greek Culture.* New York: Oxford University Press, 1943–1945.

Krutch, Joseph. *Human Nature and the Human Condition.* New York: Random House, 1959.

Lewin, Kurt. *A Dynamic Theory of Personality,* 1st ed. New York: McGraw-Hill, 1935.

Lewin, Kurt. *Studies in Topological and Vector Psychology.* Iowa City: University of Iowa Press, 1940.

Lewin, L., Lippett, R., and White, R. K. "Patterns of Aggressive Behavior in Experimentally Created Social Climates," *Journal of Social Psychology,* X (1939), pp. 271–299.

Marcuse, Herbert. *One Dimensional Man.* Boston: Beacon Press, 1964.

Mumford, Lewis. *The Condition of Man.* New York: Harcourt, Brace, 1944.

Murphy, Gardner. *Historical Introduction to Modern Psychology,* rev. ed. New York: Harcourt, Brace, 1949.

Oates, Whitney Jennings. *The Complete Greek Drama,* ed. by Whitney Oates and Eugene O'Neill, Jr. New York: Random House, 1938.

Plato. *The Works of Plato,* ed. by Irwin Edman. New York: Modern Library, 1928.

Randall, John Herman. *The Making of the Modern Mind.* Boston: Houghton Mifflin, 1940.

Robinson, Cyril Edward. *Hellas.* New York: Pantheon, 1948.

Robinson, James Harvey. *The Mind in the Making.* New York: Harper, c. 1921.

Russell, Bertrand. *A History of Western Philosophy.* New York: Simon & Schuster, 1945.

Smith, Preserved. *A History of Modern Culture.* 1930. Reprint (2 vols). New York: Macmillan Company, Collier Books, 1962.

3
THE MIDDLE AGES

The salient characteristics of the high Middle Ages were:

1. A magnetic orientation to otherworldliness including the notion that earthly life was an unimportant interlude preparatory to the chief residence of men in the afterworld. Hence, resignation and detachment toward the scourges and tribulations of earthly life together with less concern over worldly rewards induced substantial growth of the benign, "accepting," and compassionate sensibilities. There was a vagueness about worldly life: Commonsense actions and down-to-earth behavior were engaged in without the sort of urgent and sharpened sense of reality prevailing in the modern world, and there was the sense that the benevolent acceptance of human error, practical adversity, and worldly events, however painful or unjust these seemed, was nevertheless beatific and blessed. If present life was but a preparation for a future heavenly bliss, then there was little point in Faustian efforts to make earthly life more physically congenial or scientifically lucid, and rather more point in being indifferent to the great efforts necessary to improve man's material lot or to alleviate the severe environmental hardships, social or personal conflicts, and harsh inequities that burdened him. Ensuring this benign acceptance of the status quo was the dogma that the present order was ordained by the Divinity who, in His omniscience and love, could have made things differently, had He deemed it salutary. Further, because the afterlife was to be the chief locus and end of man's existence and earthly life was but a very brief interlude before the blissfully happy eternity of heaven, such a smidgen of time, however frequented by pain and hardship, could be borne with grace and tranquility.

The consequences of this ideology for human behavior were a deficiency of concern for the improvement of earthly conditions; a great optimism about the marvelous promise of the afterlife out of which was generated the famous medieval capacity to benignly bear crushing burdens; a passionate interest in the spiritual, symbolic, and ritualistic aspects of earthly life; a tolerance of enormous amounts of secular human cruelty and, yet, a stimulation and heightening of certain forms of human kindness and personal charity; a lack of adventurousness in intellectual or personal life and a deficiency of effort to transcend the status quo of experience, cognition, and social organization. The upshot, in brief, was a narrow and parochial orientation of mind and feeling.

From this ideological-cultural milieu emerged well-ordered, or even rigid, social relationships and well-defined images of self and others—all conforming to a prescribed formula, and all subject to strict enforcement or consecration by divinely established authority. Each of these human transactions and personal images was considered to be one aspect of the divine plan or an expression of a symbolic meaning or message. This medieval vision conceived a divine world on earth that disregarded material realities and searched for its core of existence in the transcendent "reality" or destiny of love, repentance, charity, divine grace, and heaven. The earthly order—however inscrutable its design—was also an expression of divine purpose and intelligence. So men concentrated, therefore, on the symbolic "meaning" or "significance" of events for the revelation of God's messages and design rather than on common sense and literal ideas. One result was a burgeoning of rich cognitive sensitivity to symbols, ritual, ceremony, omens, portents, parables, and ciphers of experience.

Intelligence was developed along symmetrical lines; symbolic acuity, subtleties of meaning, abstract insight, delicate, evanescent perceptions, the most diaphanous meanings, cognitive intangibles, the spectra of spiritual life, and casuistic disputations. Concern about interpersonal relations, status, earthly ambitions—and other preoccupations of materialistic and secular man—were subordinated and preempted by spiritual and otherworldly sentiments. For every material frustration there was a religious compensation and for every earthly burden a spiritual recompense so that an enormous amount of life was experienced inwardly, spiritually, and symbolically. Through this inner metaphoric richness a dismal earthly life was made bearable and even emotionally and imaginally enriched, not least of all to prepare men for the spiritual drama that demanded much of his waking energies and that also designated him as its protagonist for the trying mission of the earthly interlude before heavenly life. It was easier to benignly anticipate the proposed bliss of the afterlife and to inwardly enjoy the metaphoric and fantasied delights of the present one than to take arms against a sea of troubles and by opposing, end them—if only miraculously so. Such material miracles were not likely to come except by divine intervention and, thus, the wiser part of judgment was to accept, as most men of every age do, without excessive conflict or stress, the world as it was and the current ideology as it existed—thereby making the spiritual best of it.

2. A second salient feature of medieval life was the proportion of grace, redemption, or heavenly bliss in balance with sin and evil. The frustrations of day-to-day life, the cruelties of medieval experience, and the inevitable evils that men universally commit were to be balanced, according to medieval theology, by virtue, piety, absolution, and ultimately grace. Kindness, compassion, and forgiveness became established among the mainstay qualities of men and Church as well as an important source of spiritual (psychological) sustenance in an evil and harsh world. Beneficent acts and orders were much valued (such kindness as flourished during the Middle Ages has been rivaled only during the period of early Christianity) and were paralleled by such actions as the renunciation of material possessions and the materialistic way of life and the commitment to the uncorrupted life of the monastery—where, presumably, temptations to worldly evils were largely removed. With such emphasis on forgiveness and kindness, one visa to salvation was through those benevolent acts that were among the few available palliatives of hardship. If sinfulness and cruelty were inevitable, they could also be pardoned—a benediction that nourished benign sentiment, optimism, expectation of heavenly bliss, and forbearance. In effect, this issued, in tolerance of the feudal system, the nurturing of scholarship, and the development of numerous other aspects of medieval life. Such benign feelings also converted rebellion to resignation and rancor to pious felicity and so mitigated any residual impulse to change earthly life. The upshot was a predominant emphasis on the afterlife or on its representations and surrogates on earth, e.g., fantasies, omens, churchly rituals, miracles, spiritual dramas, "mysterious" signs and symbols—all calculated to sustain belief in the medieval spiritual drama and its epilogue while minimizing the distressing immediacy and realities of earthly experience. Indeed, it was in this drama, with its symbolic representations of life and hope and in its theological expressions of wish, fear, and anxiety, that the vital essence of medieval life and experience was carried out and from which was derived whatever sense, richness, and fulfillment might be extracted from life.

3. Such an ideology produced a psychological view in which the immaterial, the symbolic, and the spiritual preoccupied cognition and emotion, leaving the medieval mind largely oriented to metaphoric or intellec-

tual perception and judgment while depreciating their empirical and materialistic counterparts. This, too, accounted for the downgrading of brute fact and immediate sense perception (though not their theological interpretations) and for the extravagant concern with heavenly bliss rather than with the urgencies of biological, sensory, or material needs and other "base motives." Existence had one paramount purpose: preparation for the otherworldly paradise whose attainment would be eased by the cultivation of spiritual or benign sentiments and the subordination of material passions. Cognition was thereon oriented to the spiritual meaning and order of divinely inspired physical, biological, social, and psychological events on earth, to the evaluation of these events—in terms of moral and spiritual ideal values—as being consonant with or refractory to divine ideology (thus compelling cognitive evaluations of these phenomena in black vs. white and good vs. bad categories), to the search for a physical, biological, and socio-psychological hierarchy that would ascend to ultimate divinity (as in *Summa Theologica*), and to the subordination of empirical experience and thought to the a priori imperatives of this theological-psychological image. Hence, God's order on earth was manifested in the most trivial physical, biological, or socio-psychological events and, in addition, illustrated the divine principle that all things or phenomena moved from a "lower" to a "higher" order whose culminating state was divinity. This divine principle applied both to the hierarchy of inferior to superior processes within single organisms and to the graduated stages of ascent between different species or classes of organisms, objects, and phenomena to the highest culmination or most perfect realization of each. Examples of the former include higher and lower "states" or "levels" of man's condition, moods, behavior, morality, or intellect as well as stages of "becoming" in the development, evolution, or improvement of a given species or organism. Examples of the latter include different classes of organisms, events, and objects which embody superior or more enhancing amounts of the quality in question, e.g., man is a "higher" organism than an ape, a table is a "higher" object than raw lumber, etc. The formalization of this divine principle was given expression in various intellectual, "scientific," and moral theories or concepts: the Ptolemaic theory, the "entelechy" concept, and the idea that "higher" organisms and spiritual emotions have more divinity or "perfection" than "lower" organisms and animal passions.

The highest ascent of spirit was reached, of course, in God, who was perfect spirit. Correspondingly, spiritual feelings, benign sentiments, mystic or ethereal perceptions, and immaterial orientations were "higher" experiences—closer to God, paradise, or to the "upward" striving of St.

Thomas's universe—than were the "lower" qualities of earthly sentiment, concrete or materialistic perception, and base, sense-oriented (hence animal-like) empirical data and experience. Parenthetically, it was precisely the acknowledgment of such sense-oriented empirical data—which would have compelled urgent awareness of the hardships of the social and material "reality" in medieval life—that was spurned, perhaps, just because of the hopelessness of remedying this "reality," were it to be acknowledged. Under such circumstances, a predominant spiritual perception and cognition were the better part of expedient human wisdom. Confirming such wariness was the fact that the feudal order and the system of feudal statuses were seen as a secular expression of the divine scheme of the ascending hierarchy into paradise—this time in man's social organization—and to disturb this would be to mar the divine plan. Since, to enter into heavenly bliss, the capacity to form such perceptions was necessary, it is not surprising that the belittling of material conditions and baser urges was sanctioned; attention to these could only impair the practice of spiritual perception which was an essential preparation for heavenly bliss.

4. Another feature of the medieval system was the economic, religious, and psychological stability and security it provided through love, obligation, control of function and status, and reciprocal respect for social or work roles. This stability was enhanced by divine investment, religious ceremony, symbolism and ritual, the experience of being an organic part of a cosmic and sacred design, and by the feeling of the divinely conferred special value of each man (his soul). This latter sentiment augmented, in part, his self-respect and self-identity by the conviction that the role he played in the divine social order was intrinsic to its structure and function so that any person, if excluded, would be grievously missed, however high or low in the secular hierarchy he might be. It was this impression of divine order and influence everywhere, the sense of the unique worth of each person, the presence in them of that reflection of divinity that was their soul, a full and symbiotic identity with the greatness of the cosmic scheme and the God it revealed, and the indispensable part each one had in this scheme—all of which conferred on medieval man a psychic fulfillment and spiritual promise that produced the marvelous psychological security marking the religious and social life of the Middle Ages. The control of psychological support and catharsis through confession and absolution, the emphasis on grace and piety, and the restraint of greed, avarice, and ambition through the regulation of economic activities, such as profit or usury, and through the management of the hierarchy of status roles together contributed to the experience of

security and self and social identity. Further augmenting such ego and status identities was the feudal system of reciprocal rights and obligations with its attendant experiences of support and protection which also were sanctified by the Church. Guilds, too, were regulated by the Church, and their income distribution and operations were often controlled for fairness and justice in accord with ecclesiastical doctrine—as were many other orders and groupings. To this mixture of religion and justice was added a goodly portion of love, so that from this medieval recipe issued the charitable treatment of the poor, the mitigation of sundry cruelties (when recognized), and the soothing of certain psychic agonies. These palliatives, in turn, made men more amenable to religious influence, more content, complacent, and emotionally tidy—if stuffy—stripped them of some powerful resentments, and by abetting their tolerance of life's hardships—even doctrinally countenancing its minimal delights—it increased their commitment to the world as it was.

5. A further aspect of medieval life was the search for meaning and importance in all phenomena and experience. Whether it was the struggle of good and evil, the protean symbolisms of love and redemption, the superiority of spirituality over sensuality, or the path to the afterlife, such themes as these were given ceremonial expression in the Church and were perceived in every event of nature: in the movements of trees or clouds, in the enigma of individual acts, in the comings and goings of children, in the ravings of madmen, in the nonconformity of individualists, in the ceremonials of secular or clerical courts, and in every other conceivable natural or social phenomenon. Medieval men saw all such events as symbols or ciphers representing revelation, the victory of good over evil, the devil and his works, or God's presence and power (as in instances of recovery from disease, in visionary and ecstatic experiences, or in the behavior of heavenly bodies). Witches, saints, or signs of divinity and deviltry were estimated as not exceptional earthly events and were sought as indicators of the ubiquitous spiritual drama. It was this illusory, symbolic, chimerical world that was the important one and the one, indeed, in which all the great struggles of the spirit against materiality could be dramatically, if symbolically, witnessed, whereas the ordinary events and empirical experiences of the day could, by comparison, be relatively ignored. Into such a mythology, based on belief in the spirit of heaven and the terror of hell, everyday mundane events were translated or symbolized, making even the most pedestrian occurrences full of meaning, expectant with portents, and connoting the intensity of faith and the struggle for the soul.

116

6. A sixth feature of medieval mentality was its distinctive emphasis on benevolence and kindness. Manifestations of these sentiments appeared with uniform consistency in the texture of expected day-to-day conduct that included protection of the weak, control of exploitation, a system of mutual rights and obligations, a benign feeling of goodness and compassion, and a love that filled the everyday experience of men and illumined the spirit of the times—and so was diametrically different from the temper of those societies that are dedicated to secular achievements. This general "spiritual" orientation, this salutary feeling and happy expectation of the victory of the forces of good, this sense of contributing to and being a part of a divine order of salvation in which each moment was a sustaining example of God's presence, this deemphasis on material matters and the corporeal parts of man, this insistent and ubiquitous presence of Christian love with its espousal of abstinence, kindliness, gentleness, and forgiveness, and this sanguine expectation of the marvels and goodness of the afterlife all gave rise to a spirit of contentment, gentleness, and not insubstantial felicity—a spirit that was both qualification for admission to the heavenly paradise and a preparatory training in the qualities that would fully flourish there.

Together these influences produced a sangfroid, a well-being, and an optimism that could not but be refracted in goodness of heart and generosity. Heightening and pervading these sensibilities was the mollifying, serene, tender mood of Christian love from which also emanated an extraordinary calmness and lightness of feeling and a beatific outlook onto the world. Such love also augmented the sense of fullness and warmth, of self-extension and inner exhilaration, of closeness to the world and to God, of nurturing growth and succoring debility—all which, again, further deepened and discharged the emotional well-springs of faith, hope, altruism, tenderness, and a sort of sweet exhilaration in the protean forms of life as well as in their growth and renewal. Part of this attitude, too, was a blissful marvel at the existence of living things as well as at the salutary and cosmic order they revealed. Thus, in the last analysis, love meant acceptance of the universe, of things as they were, and of the intellectual and social status quo. For all this was divinity.

Issuing from this love, too, were the great waves of generosity and the burgeoning numbers of men who gave up their material possessions to better live the spiritual life. St. Francis and the multitudes he inspired were the most shining examples of this selfless altruistic idealism among hosts of other benevolent and spiritually dedicated men. The frenzy of giving as well as the ecstasy of indulging in spiritual adventure and goodness in participation with Christ was an exhilarating undertaking that replaced the dull, banal, purposeless ennui of the discarded, sensate world.

This goodness, affirmation, and altruism was practiced with gusto and purpose not only so that medieval men could become part of the exciting self-fulfilling and purposeful world of the spirit but also to make more remote from them the world of frustration, despair, and emptiness.

Nothing in all that has been said to this point should be taken to mean that medieval life was not replete with brutality, hardship, cruelty, and callousness. Baronial struggles, ingenious tortures, vast and degrading poverty, oppressiveness of the worst sort, vicious attacks on enemies, incorrigible bigotry and parochialism, and victimization of the innocent were, more or less, features of medieval experience. Life was indeed harsh and brutal, and a goodly part of the modalities of medieval mentality was assigned to dealing with it. Indeed, a certain sector of this mentality acknowledged such adversity, though as an inevitable corollary of the nature of man, as an irremediable fact of existence, or an egregious expansion of the devil's works. Rarely, indeed, were those conditions greeted with that amalgam of humanistic secular indignation or mundane appraisal that several hundred years of scientific and humanitarian orientation were eventually to evolve. Indeed, so committed was medieval judgment to the notion that endemic brutality and callousness were the devil's work, or the natural corollaries of the sinfulness of man's nature, that hardly any attention was paid to their materialistic, cognitive, or secular causes. The insensitivity of men to adversity as well as, attendantly, their peculiar medieval species of callousness to one another was exceptional. Insensibility to death from disease, to war, to torture, to back-breaking labor, and to oppression was, without doubt, a part of the medieval nature of things. But this obtuseness was not considered to be such by the medieval mind but rather a necessary acceptance of the ineluctable character of life and the devil's wickedness and thereon quite impossible to be eliminated or abated. Indeed, benign acceptance of such brute reality was a sign of spiritual strength and so enlarged the blindspots of indifference to suffering and cruelty.

Further, much of cruelty and callousness had to do with the established and eternal structure of the universe and of the secular order as God had made it; the feudal system, feudal conflict, the endowment of the vested structure and ideology of the Church with authority and omniscience; etc. Ideas, values, or institutions that were alien to such a system were thought to be evil and devil-inspired, thus justifiably requiring the most virtuous—and heartless—intolerance and suppression. Cruelty and despotism toward such dissenting conceptions were simply thought to be vigorous opposition to evil, to wickedness, and to anti-God attitudes. Hence, their practice constituted, in this view, the protection and nurturing of the true, the virtuous, and the realm and spirit of God. In such a view, the ability to accept these adverse conditions was a measure and test of man's forbearance, endurance, and virtue, as well as a stimulant to the burgeoning of these qualities. Also mitigating against sharp awareness of these cruel realities was the deeply experienced conviction that they consumed but a brief interval—and a necessary one to purify and strengthen men's spiritual character and nonmaterialistic orientation— before the advent of the really paramount end of the entire human (and cosmic) drama—the eternal paradise of afterlife. For these reasons, then, hardship and brutality were not seen as such, minimized when seen, and morally or humanly defined quite differently from their contemporary definition. It was such imperatives that turned men away from realization of the seamy side of medieval life and made them deny the awfulness of what they saw or accept it with benign resignation. Whatever the root causes may have been, the fact remains that in literature, art, ideology, and large domains of common perceptual experience, emphasis was laid on the sanguine and salutary aspects of these adversities.

These ravages did not much intrude into the medieval world of tacit resignation, beatitude, and sanguine feeling. Indeed, the former may have compensatorily provoked, in some measure, the great development of the latter. Also, much psychic effort was expended to mitigate awareness of these ravages through such mechanisms as projection, displacement, and symbolization as well as by support of benign spirituality and love. By so doing, the medieval mind shifted or diverted its awareness of "reality" to other dimensions of human or social perception and appraisal.

What effects, then, did the ravages of the medieval "real" world have? Among others, they brutalized men to insensitivity, to depreciation of earthly life, to opaque callousness toward disease, and to complacency toward baronial cruelties and secular indignities. But because, as previously suggested, these were preempted by the scope and intensity of spiritual experience or masked and attenuated by a rich variety of psychic and social mechanisms, the phenomenal and psychological experience of these adversities were blunted and transformed. It is largely for these reasons that their social or psychic impact and significance cannot be fully measured or judged by our contemporary modes of perception or by our "reality" standards for the causation of behavior.

119

Medieval Intelligence

What then were the main features of medieval intelligence as revealed in the literature, symbolism, science, common experiences or discourse, and general cognition and culture of the time. It must be remembered that these were modal themes of intelligence and that much variation, even as occurs in our day, was present. We will be concerned, then, with the accepted and typical kind of thinking of the period, the kind that would characterize a majority of individuals in their usual reflective thought and in their ideational processes. And it would include the kind that the modern psychologist estimates as relating to adjustment, in this case medieval adjustment. Put in another way, it would be the kind that a hypothetical medieval psychologist would incorporate in his counterpart of the modern intelligence test. Excluded, then, would be modes of thought that were not predominant or eminently characteristic of medieval intellection, e.g., empirical, scientific, and practical modalities.

The general characteristics of medieval thinking were:

1. A conspicuously less practical texture than that of contemporary thought. Considerations of practical utility, of manipulative mechanics, and of proof as it is presently understood—demonstrable, empirical, positivistic—were secondary. The question of economic gain, productivity, tangible results, or some consequent novel outgrowth and sequel was similarly subordinate. Serious concern with external data, including the sensory, and with naturalistic or material evidence was also not typical. Hence, external and independent consideration or confirmation of alternative hypotheses and data was not an important matter. What was important was that certain conceptions of life, nature, and method were accepted a priori or implicitly, and "reasoned manifestations" or "deductions" were subsequently derived from them. The relation of sensory data and other evidence to these "manifestations" was one of example and illustration or, if not feasible, of reinterpretation of the data or "evidence" to fit the predetermined conceptions. Such an approach made empirical criteria of proof irrelevant.

Both the "demonstrable" proofs of scientific method and the materialism of capitalistic enterprise were ignored or devalued in medieval thinking. The inner, impractical, spiritual values and ideas became the vortices of cognitive preoccupation. Hence, those elements of intelligence in accord with these values and ideals were emphasized.

2 and 3. Other qualities of medieval intelligence were the Aristotelian concern with logical demonstration and the imitation of the Grecian example of subtlety and cleverness in disputation. However, all such formal components of intelligence were subservient to the priorities of certain values and spiritual ideas. Intricate and casuistic proofs, with little or inadequate empirical basis were made of preconceived conceptions which themselves often oriented scholarship and science as in the case of Galen's medicine, Aristotle's physics, or Ptolemy's astronomy. Indeed, Aristotelian logic,[1] with its closed-system structure and rigid deductions from presumably eternal (and so God-given) assumptions, was the intellectual cognate and handmaiden of the spiritual premises and absolute values of the medieval system. The primary propositions of such systems, from which everything was to be deduced, were derived from their contemporary culture—in this case the values of medieval society and the medieval ecclesiastical system. The testing of such propositions, too, was circumscribed by the derived modes of thought or procedure and other value orientations of the system. Conflicting facts or alternative propositions were disregarded or suitably transformed, thus limiting diversity of ideas and evidence to not unharmonious variations of the original propositions and their alleged proofs. Questioning such propositions meant questioning the values of the society or, at minimum, the prospect of accepting demonstrable empirical facts as more important than a priori assumptions or ideas. Because these assumptions were right (God-given), they determined everything, and anything contradictory, or even discordant, was wrong, devilish, or evil, including empirical proof and objectivity.

Hence, pragmatic and scientific intelligence, in the sense of empirical proof, experimentation, and practical manipulation, was wrong because the truth had already been revealed, and its detractor's scientific methods were, in fact, nothing less than devil's work calculated to undermine the "axioms" of God's universe. Thus empiricism was deadly: It diverted from proper purposes; it restored interest in the external world and in experiential evidence (materialism, primary sense data, experimental and worldly manipulations); and it tampered with the purity of the inner spirit, which was the source of spiritual intuition, a buttress against disenchantment with feudal society, and from which emanated faith in the hereafter.

The upshot of all this was as follows: the turning away from experimental manipulations and pragmatic methods or proofs as we know them today; the ignoring of quantitative or external evidence as the test of ideas; an intense preoccupation with the sensitive refinement of propositions, their logical proofs, and their most subtle and rigorous derivations; the belief that logic was a sufficient method for the demonstration of truth and had a closer connection with godliness than did base empirical data. Intelligence consisted of understanding these ideas and their refinements, in grasping the methods of their derivation as well as of their supporting logical arguments, and in rejecting competing ideas or other methods of reaching truth. Instrumentally, it involved the most subtle reasoning from these ideas and the ingenuity with which they were shown to have application to the universe as well as hair-splitting deductions, grammarian subtleties, or what has come to be known as Jesuitical argument—all to support and amplify these propositions in refined degree.

4. Intelligence was also demonstrated by creating or interpreting fantasies, miracles, omens, auguries, revelations, strange gestures or acts, and radical modifications of perception. This meant that intelligence became, also, a symbol-creating and interpreting capacity consonant with the notion that if the empirical was spurned, the imaginative and symbolic must become predominant ways of arriving at "truthful" ideas. Thus subtlety of analysis and dissection of words, symbols, disguised actions, and language became the appropriate methods of deriving such ideas as, at that historical period and by their very nature, could not be empirically discovered.

5. Directly associated with these distinctive features of medieval intelligence was the extensive use of the symbolic, theoretical, and spiritual capacities. Symbolic insight was especially important, because it deciphered the drama of God and the devil as it was represented in inscrutable forms or expressions. Because almost everything physical or eventful symbolized something of pertinence in the spiritual realm, the challenge was to uncover the spiritual meaning concealed in the material world. Here is where intelligence came in: to see the divine in a star, the devil in fire, the saints in a maiden, and the Ascension in the way a tree waved in the wind. Subtle intuition was a fundament of medieval intelligence, and its adroitness in seeing secret significances in the "real" world synchronized nicely with the prevailing ideology that the essential nature of the universe was spiritual. As such, this "symbolic capacity" governed a realm of richness in fantasy, imagination, and association that practical intelligence could only limit and constrict just as the former would limit and constrict practical intelligence. Further, medieval intelligence was preoccupied with the theoretical, i.e., the theological meaning of each event or thing and its place in a cosmos divinely conceived and ordered. The need to make this cosmology into a framework in which every act and thing could be theologically placed and interpreted was of enormous

importance. Hence these same acts and things were minimized as far as their mundane, realistic properties were concerned. The most intelligent persons were those who saw the meaning of each act or thing in terms of its place in such a "theologically inspired" cosmos.

In regard to spiritual intelligence, all experience was fitted into categories of good and bad, devil and God, sin and redemption, or similar dichotomies. In these categories, things and events were not treated sui generis but as a cog in a conceptual (theological) system. They were not seen as they phenomenally or concretely existed but, theoretically, as representing abstract concepts (*Summa Theologica*)[2] and, spiritually, as embracing matters of psychic relevance: absolution, redemption, penance, etc. But spiritual had another meaning here, too. It referred particularly to certain dimensions of immediate feeling, e.g., inspiration, solace, guilt, terror, to which these theoretical-spiritual theme categories embodied or corresponded. Such emotions or spiritual themes warmed or repelled, sanctified or desecrated, thrilled with mystic identity or terrified with abandonment and despair—and did so by the representation of concrete things and events. Thus, certain signs such as fish or wine had a symbolic-theoretical significance in medieval cosmology and theology, a symbolic-spiritual meaning in the drama of devil and God, and a spiritual-emotive significance (love, renewal) in the realm of personal feeling. In addition, another component of the spiritual-emotive area, somewhat different from the foregoing, was directed not only toward immediate evocation of feeling but toward the experience of mystic unity, of yoga-like serenity, of transcendent felicity, and of an extraordinary self and worldly understanding. This component illuminated one's destiny and life's meaning (as in satori or certain mystic states) and kindled those elements of the emotional life that fired men to find—in the realm of religion, symbolism, or spirituality—an ineffable, noncorporeal felicity and haven, though at the risk of an impenetrable isolation. It was the capacity to grasp the significance of such experience and to live in the "unreal" and spiritual-fantasied world, transposing all material events and objects into it, that defined this type of intelligence. Another of its properties was the capacity to translate the felt experiential response to these symbolic objects and events into rational intellectual counterparts.

These forms of medieval intelligence do radical injustice to the sense of reality as we know it today, to empiricism or concrete manipulation of data and objects, to the concept of pragmatic, demonstrable proof and self-evident sensory experience, and to the goals of materialism and practicality. Rather the medieval mind gave scope to those dimensions of intelligence connected with nondemonstrable, intuitive, and subtle processes. Thus medieval intelligence involved the grasp of different levels of experience from those of contemporary intelligence, the perception of hidden theoretical and spiritual meaning in them, and the transmutation of this experience and meaning into still other levels of conception and feeling. To this, medieval intelligence added a unique theoretical orientation which assigned all phenomena, through Aristotelian methods, to a divine design as articulated by theology. Intelligence was revealed, in part, by the capacity to grasp this divine scheme and to understand how each part (doctrines and phenomena) fitted into it. Finally, there was spiritual intelligence, which was the capacity to variously see, in even the barest event or thing, a symbolic, archetypical, or aesthetic significance.

The ability, then, to achieve deeply complex apperceptions based on integration of cognition, feeling, and symbolism defined this kind of intelligence. Nor can its emotional component be charged to symbolic factors alone. It emerged from a special complication of sensibility and cognition that reciprocally enriched and extended the cognitive grasp. Indeed, through the evocation of various of these emotions, symbolic, theoretical, and subtle intelligence was deepened and broadened.

6. A sixth characteristic of medieval intelligence was the preoccupation with hidden meanings and subtleties that parenthetically has been already noted. The subtleties and twisting of words, expressions, ideas, or art forms were all related to the medieval compulsion to find evidence, in all things, of the epic struggle between good and bad, to orient mental energy to religious issues, and to dissuade engrossment with the material world. The constant hidden meanings, the forms imbedded in forms, the implicit meaning of words, the secret functions of acts, and the abracadabra of intricate design all reflected the effort to detect the secret significance of the medieval cosmic scheme. Such an effort evolved because the manifest material world did not reveal this scheme, because the "real" (i.e., the sacred) meaning of life was hidden beneath its phenomenal surface, because the ways of divinity were not readily apparent and had to be dredged out, and finally because such an approach relegated the world and men's minds to imagination, "pure" intellect, and spirit, ignoring their material, empirical, and concrete dimensions. Here intelligence looked for such hidden conceptions, such underlying tenets, and such subtle, nonempirical and "pure" intellectual systems as tied together disparate feelings, subjective impressions, imperfect observations of physical phenomena, intense personal experiences or perceptions, and sundry facts which showed a pattern of order and design (though preconceived) beneath them. It was in illuminating this hidden

order and its spiritual-theological significance that medieval intelligence revealed, in part, its nature.

7. A further characteristic of medieval intelligence was its precise logical reasoning. Though already touched on, it needs more elaboration. In part, the rigor of medieval reasoning was the heritage of Aristotelian logic, from whose claim of irrevocably true premises and within whose systematic, closed approach substantially all "truth" could be deduced. Some assumptions of this logic were that there are certain general truths (presumably discovered by Aristotle or his compatriots, through observations and speculation in the Greek manner), that these truths were fully sufficient axioms for finding still additional "truths," and that the remaining necessity was to show how specific conclusions and applications could be deduced from these general truths. The notion, implicit in this logic, that most basic knowledge was "in" and that, in substantial measure, future work need only rigorously deduce from these basic propositions additional specific instances or qualifying particulars fitted quite nicely with medieval cosmology as it did with the premise that every event or thing had a prescribed place in the divine scheme that could either a priori or deductively be determined. It also was in accord with the medieval assumption that general, cosmic truths were revealed or "given" and that only rigorous reasoning or subtlety of perception were required to make a proper inference from them to a specific case or see their manifestation in a specific event. Thus it was important—especially as universals were involved—to use a method that had a kind of mental and possibly spiritual immateriality or eternality, as in the case of Euclidian geometry, which allegedly was true for all places and times and was not based on any earthly materialistic assumptions but rather on hypothetical eternal axioms. Similarly it was important to use "immaterial," eternal logic—a kind of divine reason—without employing debased mundane premises and evidence, so that the truth-seeking methods and their findings were correspondingly divinely eternal and beyond the corruption of a posteriori, empirical reality. The simplicity and frugality of this logic, and its hierarchic organization—so like the medieval system and, indeed, as purist in its nonmaterial, nonfactual character as the immanent spirituality of the age's religion and theology—was a fundamental part of the medieval experience. The constant exploitation of logical methods in the dissection of statement and proposition was only a ferreting out of the truth already contained in the mind of God which, requiring but purity of logic and perception to dissect it from the distorting material matrix in which it was embedded, would thereon explain, if tautologically, the vast

complexity of the phenomenal world. Empiricism, experimentalism, and manipulation were all earthly devices to further obscure, in materialist modalities or contexts, the axiomatic truths that only "pure" logic and vision could search out. It was for these reasons that this same empiricism that (1) raised doubts about the capacity for omniscience of such "pure" intelligence, (2) rejected revealed axiomatic truth, (3) trafficked in sense experience and sought evidence in the eternal world, and (4) was amenable to modifying man's condition, or if possible, his nature, should have been so vehemently denounced and suppressed. Medieval logical intelligence, in contrast, concerned as it was with the subtle aspects of propositions and how they could be transformed or various permutations of them adduced, was unaffected by the inconsistency, jumble, and occasional chaos of the world and worldly facts. All disorder was obviated by this internalized, marvelously consistent, and exquisitely synchronized system of a priori assumptions and logical deductions. Such a system demanded a remarkable kind of internal mental searching, sometimes tortuous, imaginative within its framework, agile in its capacity for disputation, and frequently impeccable in its elegance. And so, though often empirically invalid, such intellection had the momentous purpose of conferring an ordered mental unity on the medieval world in order (1) to hold it in psychological control, (2) to prevent realistic confrontation with its terrors and severe hardships, and (3) to support tenets that would give meaning and hope to the human life—such as it was—that prevailed in it. Today, such intelligence might be considered as the thinking of a gifted logician, of a remarkably bright paranoid, or the sort of reasoning that bedevils us in formidable argument and that, though knowing it is not true, we feel we must answer.

REEVALUATION OF MODERN INTELLIGENCE TESTS FROM THE MEDIEVAL PERSPECTIVE

It is clear in this view, that medieval intelligence presumes qualities far different from those presently assessed in American intelligence tests. The emphasis on symbolism, preconceived ideas, intricate or casuistic reasoning, and imaginative metaphor gave intelligence a far different character than it now commonly has. Thus, modern intelligence tests given to medieval men would not satisfactorily appraise intelligence as it was ordinarily manifested by them. Conversely, a hypothetical medieval psychologist would find present tests a congeries of alien and irrelevant elements (in respect to his culture's intelligence) which he would claim overemphasized realistic judgment, empirical abilities, factual knowledge, and practical talents. His indictment would further charge too much emphasis on things as things and not enough on what they theoretically or symbolically mean; too much concern with the practical or drive-satisfying nature of things and not enough with their dramatic, immaterial, and emotional significance; too great preoccupation with material reality and how to accommodate to it. Specifically he would condemn the tests for too much concern with numbers, words, and practical knowledge but not enough with symbolic and theoretical meanings or broad abstract ideas. He would complain that shrewdness, getting things done, or the best way to win are excessively emphasized, whereas the *goals* of such action are hardly noted, i.e., whether they are good, bad, exhilarating, tranquilizing, etc. So that while medieval intelligence would relegate the mental processes involved in efficiency, profit, speed, etc. to relative unimportance, it would deem it to be the essence of intelligence to press for the purposes of values that such processes subserve. Hence, the significance of actions in terms of morality, theoretical meaning, and the spiritual condition of men would be what our hypothetical medieval psychologist would consider as the proper arena for the appraisal of intelligence. Other such arenas would be concerned with (1) premises underlying the content of test items and the values implicit in them, (2) the internal logic, theoretical aspects, and symbolic meaning of various phenomena, actions, and things in relation to a more general design or higher purpose, and (3) the delicate, intricate logic and perception required to uncover nuances of meaning in these human and natural events.

This medieval criticism of the excessive "realistic" preoccupations in modern conceptions of intelligence would include their overemphasis on business values, money, speed, efficiency, maximizing gain, competition, shrewdness, and trickery—in short on all the intellectual requirements for middle-class success. Such preoccupation with concrete and external things or with materialistic values, irrespective of their purposes, leads to certain concrete forms of thought, as in the case of operational manipulations, positivist methodology, and accounting or numerical processes. It also leads to emphasizing those mental talents—given the present condition of society—that abet acquisitiveness and materialism. Indeed, the present concern with techniques, instrumentation, social and interpersonal manipulations, procedures for gaining "success"—all disassociated from "ends" and effects—is evidence of the abandonment of the medieval world's cherished criteria for intelligence: inner spiritual values and dematerialized humanistic goals. Such orientations encourage the cultivation of an intelligence chiefly developed along lines of empirical proofs,

"reality" testing, and tangible demonstrations while symbolism speculation and intuition are minimized. Such a perspective, the medieval psychologist would contend, does injury to aspects of thinking that have to
do with mystic insight, inner sensibility, or symbolic conception and
makes of intelligence a specialized narrow and often mechanical process.
Those mental functions, he submits, that derive from sensibility, perceptual vision, and inner or symbolic insight are the most difficult to
demonstrate and measure, not only because of their fragile, elusive, and
unpredictable nature, but also because they are neither well understood
nor searched for by contemporary "realistic" psychologists. Indeed, even
when dim awareness of these potentialities of intelligence is present, the
vested establishment position condemns it with righteous positivistic indignation, coercing these dissenting evaluations of the intellectual process
into relinquishing "their" distinctive orientations and into conforming with
the current authorized, conventionalized, and popular intelligence modes.
By using limited, preformed conceptions of intelligence together with their
corollary testing methods, present tests obscure whole segments of intelligence and force responses into concrete thought patterns while deterring
more sensitive, theoretical, and deeper solutions. For illustration the
medieval psychologist would point to the many items that exclude nonconcrete, tentative solutions, that deter moral probing and other scrutiniz-
ing of the tacit assumptions and resolutions of test problems, or that
prevent the conceptual understanding and solution of these problems from
being cognitively shifted to other levels and orientations than those demanded by the test questions. He would also charge that there are inadequate imaginal, spiritual, or symbolic problems given in current tests
so that the processes of vague intuition, imagination, moral insight, and
subtle meaning are severely subordinated to the pragmatic processes, the
repositories of information, and the empirical manipulations that present
test items demand.

Hence, a series of test questions should be constructed that has nothing
or little to do with concrete processes and that brings the whole distinctive repertoire of medieval intellectual abilities, as set forth above, into
play. Further, such test items should have greater latitude and ambiguity
both in the kind of problems posed and in the responses approved in
concrete, "realistic" types of items. Still other revisions would be: Alternative answers to items would be permitted and/or hints to that effect
would be introduced by the examiner; leeway would be given for multidimensional or abstract responses; questions would be constructed directed to the probing of the function of "spiritual" intelligence and still
others could be introduced which would be oriented to assess symbolic

imagination; other items would be developed to evaluate the capacity for subtleties of logical permutations and sophistic distinctions; and questions requiring the transposition of a specific issue into symbolic terms or into general symbolic-spiritual or symbolic-moral terms then would be utilized.

The medieval psychologist would further protest that very little appears in current tests concerning morality, virtue, ethics, values, or other "ends" of action. Such queries as "Is this good—or bad?" "Does it (e.g., an action or decision) augment spiritual feelings?" "What will be the effect on others or on society if this or some other action is carried out?" hardly, if ever, appear in present-day tests. The unexamined and unquestioned values implicit in present intelligence test items are advantage, profit, or victory. The medieval psychologist would maintain that intelligence could not be properly appraised without questions touching on moral and spiritual themes, i.e., the issues of power vs. piety, instinctual pleasure vs. spiritual felicity, materialism vs. grace, etc. Indeed, so involved was the medieval mind with such problems that even a test item concerned with operational "know-how" or tactical matters would immediately be questioned by a hypothetical medieval testee for its ultimate religious value or human and spiritual goals; further, if such a question were to be presented to and scored for a medieval person by current procedures, he would likely obtain a low grade unless these procedures were to include a much greater allotment of time for him to probe the "value" premises of the question and to formulate his answers from that perspective. He might, indeed, reinterpret the question in symbolic terms or see a twist and enigma— some circuitous path or implied subtlety suggesting the divine drama —or he might even inquire whether abstinence from all such "tactical" or manipulative matters would not be the wisest or most moral course. It is true that particular members of some other "Western" culture might raise comparable issues, but the distinction of those "possessing" medieval intelligence was that they would raise such issues as a preeminent, prior, and constant practice. They would dissect the test item with ruthless logic and cryptic subtlety into its constituent parts and ferret out its moral and spiritual connotations.

For example, to items where computation of the speed in transit from one point to another is important, the medieval intelligence might respond valuatively—"Why travel so fast?"—or symbolically—"This really is a journey from a secular shore to a spiritual haven."—or theologically— "The numbers used in this item refer to days of penance." In any case, the medieval criticism would be that the present narrow utilitarian view of intelligence with its attendant formulation of "tactical," concrete and informational questions does not allow for the expression of spiritual or ethical facets of intelligence, inhibits the emergence of its symbolic or subtle components, arrests the exercise of metaphor or refined logic, and prevents consideration of the test item in a broad cognitive and valuative context.

Lack of appraisal of symbolic insight is one of the severest strictures the medieval psychologist would level against intelligence tests. Failure to assess abilities involving symbolic imagery, metaphor, and transposition of the concrete into the symbolic (or vice versa) is what the medieval indictment would read. These medieval foci, he would maintain, provide the meaning, substance, and very raison d'être for intelligence and cognition. If they are ignored, the residual pragmatic capacities become increasingly constricted or overemphasized and operate strictly within the rigid confines or set assumptions of the present problem, neither questioning these assumptions nor allowing intuitive, spiritual, or symbolic insight to nourish and stimulate them or other basic issues of the test item, as well. Because such types of intelligence are not evoked by the "realistic-concrete"-oriented forms of present test items, development of techniques that ensure their emergence must be brought about.

The medieval psychologist would further criticize present tests for failure to appraise certain aspects of imagination and intellectual fantasy. These would include the capacity for subtle inversion of ideas, phrases, and stories as well as for adumbration of pictures, words, and events. The particular medieval content of such imaginative- and fantasy-intelligence was directed to the drama of good and bad, the divine order, and salvation. Examples of such content included the activities of devils or angels, the prevalence of miracles, and the nature of hell. This dimension of medieval intelligence involved the transformation of action or of chronicles of events into allegories of love, salvation, the soul, and numerous other theological or spiritual themes. Other examples of this style of symbolization include particular numerals, which could either signify arrays of angels or a demoniacal cosmic force, and various species of flowers, which might symbolize paradise, love, or contrition.

An enumeration of such attributed significances and transposed meanings that bears on this component of medieval intelligence includes the following: (1) transformations of mundane and literal verbal statements into moral, theological, or symbolic meanings; (2) certain "religious" significances seen in numbers, graphic forms, symbols, and images; (3) metaphorical or mythical transformations of "real" experience by means of visions, miracles, imagined strange objects, fantasied natural events, or imagined and exceptional human actions; (4) inversions and distortions of any simple object and event including the labyrinthine complexities that can be made of them. Cognitive processes such as these would have been embodied and measured in medieval intelligence tests had there been medieval psychologists with the desire and appropriate skills to do so. Just as American psychologists neither well understand nor measure such aspects of intelligence so the hypothetical medieval psychologist would have been similarly resistant and insensitive had he been compelled to confront the kinds of cleverness, shrewdness, and practicality that are the earmarks of American intelligence testing. Thus, what one loses the other gains; what is scientific or correct in one may be immoral or unscientific in another; and what is authentically human and psychologically sound according to one system of social and scientific norms may be deviant, trivial, and unreasoning in another.

To continue with the strictures of the medieval psychologist, he would further contend that the failure to acknowledge the role of values in intellectual organization is an important deficiency in contemporary tests. At present, expedient and "realistic" purposes or needs are generally considered the modalities in regard to which intelligence should be appraised, and alien modalities, with their attendant intellectual functions, are usually disregarded. Our hypothetical medieval psychologist would question the significance of various items found in current intelligence tests with ideas of the following kind: "Why should a respondent's answer be based on hurrying, profit, or practical results—as the substance of the question indicates? Are not spiritual or benign goals more to the point? And if they are, should not different methods of solution be employed and different solutions be found for this specific problem rather than the standardized and ideologically proper ones that these 'correct' answers seem to require?" Because so many of the problems in IQ tests have to do with already sanctioned, predetermined values together with the shrewd speedy intellectual functions they require for solution, the hypothetical medieval psychologist would have questioned whether these were the most humanistically relevant or significant mental functions to assess and whether their inclusion could have any possible bearing on the betterment of man, his moral or spiritual edification, or his increased charity of feeling.

RECTIFICATION

How should rectification of present intelligence tests proceed in order to satisfy the criticisms of the medieval viewpoint? To this end, the following recommendations are made:

1. Picture story tests with different themes and endings would be used.

131

The stories would have different kinds of symbolic allusions and would vary in narrative structure from strict rigidity to vague amorphousness and include, correspondingly, a range of scenes from clear and simple to indefinite and ambiguous. The directions would initially require the S to tell a story that was predominant in narrative importance only, then to tell one that was replete with some kind of symbolic significance or content, then one predominantly embodying a general theme about man's fate, and finally one largely devoted to a topic of life and death importance. The capacity to tell such stories—instigated by the aforementioned pictures—each with a distinct thematic modality or significance, or to tell one story that simultaneously embodied several such thematic complexes or levels of meaning would reflect one form of medieval intelligence. The ability to make one element or episode of these stories signify, symbolically or otherwise, multiple levels of meaning would fit here also. Conversely, the ability to similarly interpret (at multiple levels) elements, episodes, or a complete work—all of which would be presented to the S in the form of stories, chronicles, or picture sequences—would also be important. In addition, hints may be given the S of the types of possible interpretation that exemplify various components of medieval intelligence and the more "levels" of such interpretation or meaning he actively responds to and develops in depth and richness the more intelligent, in the medieval perspective, he would be. Differences between the S's responses to chronicles, narratives, and picture sequences of a simple, clear kind and those of an ambiguous or intricate nature might serve as another index of the richness and complexity of his intelligence.

To illustrate the above testing proposals in more detail, the following example is offered. A simple theme would be given the S to develop: A boy comes home. (This could be presented as a simple verbal statement, in picture form, or as a series of events, i.e., in chronicle form.) The directions to the S would be as follows (the second direction following on completion of the response to the first, and so on until all directions have been sequentially presented): (1) Tell a story (a narrative) about this. (2) Tell a story about this with symbolic meaning and content. (3) Tell a story about this with general "moral" significance. (4) Tell a story about this that embodies tragedy, fate, or survival. The same procedure would be followed for other simple or complex themes, such as that of a man working on a railroad, the case of those who are morally oppressed, those living isolated lives and yearning for companionship, and other themes taken from such literary works as *King Lear, Madame Bovary,* and *Anna Karenina.* As already mentioned, such themes could also be presented in chronicle or picture form.

2. A series of test items concerned with ethical or moral intelligence should be developed. Suggestions to this end are: (1) A problem allowing for numerous, alternate moral courses of action would be presented to the S, who then would be asked to make a choice and explain his reasons for it as well as for rejection of the other possible alternatives. (2) The S would be presented, through the media of either a narrative, a dramatic sketch, or a general abstract theme, with an ambiguous moral issue permitting wide latitude of moral responses. He would then be asked either to submit his own preferential series of moral choices and the reasons for them or to rank preferentially, in order of their moral, immoral, and neutral quality, together with the presentation of his supporting reasons, a large variety of actions submitted to him in the form of an already prepared list. (3) Similarly, the capacity of the S to see a moral or ethical issue in each human experience should be appraised. Open-ended questions would be employed in examining the S's ability to see explicit or unstated moral issues in the human actions and events that would be described in test items. For example, in a question asking the testee to compute the time of running one distance as compared with another, the S might be asked, if he had not brought the issue up himself: "But why run?" This could be followed by further probing: "What end does this running serve? Is it healthful, morally beneficial, and spiritually helpful? Or, on the contrary, is it anxiety-producing, ultimately purposeless for human benefit or happiness, and often evocative of tense aspiration and frenzied activity?"

Much the same approach would be taken toward test items dealing with winning a competition or a game, with winning or accumulating money, and with the testee's accumulation of information, as in the case of "knowledge" of words, i.e., a vocabulary test. Still other issues that are similarly embodied in test questions and that are accessible to this sort of probing include "saving" time and "speeding up," making a profit, and pressures for achievement or security. A multiple choice method of presenting alternative views of these issues (once they have been made explicit either spontaneously by the S or with the help of gentle prodding by the tester) may also be employed, with the S required to rank these views and to present reasons for those he prefers. The probing of the S's specific preferences by the tester is another possibility. Once the testee has indicated his views with respect to the moral, spiritual, or human issues involved in a test item, the tester would examine him further on these views. Such "probing" would seek to uncover the cognitive structure, richness, insight, and acuity of the S with regard to these aspects of medieval intelligence. Types of probe questions directed to these ends would be tailored to the specific issue embodied in the test item. For example, "Should so much drive and effort be employed for this purpose?" would be a probe question for an item which involved the computation of hours of labor or the amount of activity necessary to do some job. Also, "Instead of maximizing speed, would it not be wiser to decrease it?" and "Why should that be done in the scale of a human balance which includes moral factors, experiences of inner spirituality and tranquility, etc.?" are both probe questions that might be used with an item requiring the calculation of the running speed of a person who must get from one place to another in a specified number of minutes in order to win a prize or defeat a rival. For test items that involve such issues as obtaining a very high-paying job or the rivalry between peers to get a bonus, relevant probe questions would respectively be: "Isn't it more sensible *not* to make so much money?" and "Would it not be more salutary to help others rather than to get more than they have?"

In all this the S would be probed for the deepest possible explanations or insights he can muster. Important, also, is (1) his alertness in recognizing implicit moral issues or dilemmas, even when the slightest intimation of them is made if only by the wording or stressing of the problem, and, (2) his capacity to see in neutral and practical problems the presence of moral or spiritual issues and to spontaneously elaborate on them. The number of spiritual, moral, or ethical issues and themes so recognized in a variety of presented problems would give a valuable view of the S's intellectual processes.

Another dimension to be appraised would be the testee's awareness of the effects of human action on other individuals and on personal relationships. To this end, open-ended questions should be formulated and, in addition, a multiple, preferential rating procedure of the type previously described could be adapted. Probe questions such as: "How will this: (1) running (of a race), (2) calculating (each angle of a business or interpersonal transaction before reaching a decision), or (3) winning (of competition) affect the loser, the winner, neutrals, and society?" would be used for pertinent test items, examples of the possible content of which are given in the parenthetical description adjoining each of the foregoing probe questions. Lists of the alternative potential effects that the implicit or explicit values embedded in an item may have on various kinds of other persons, on groups, and on general society could also be drawn up in multiple choice form and the S's responses evaluated. Spontaneous recognition of values in test items that involve beneficial, deleterious, or neutral effects on others would be given bonus credit once a very general orientation is given to the testee. Similarly, the number of hints or explicit directions necessary before appropriate responses occur to the value issue would be weighed in the scoring.

3. Another aspect of medieval intelligence requiring contemporary recognition and measurement is that capacity metaphorically described in another century: "To see a world in a grain of sand/And a Heaven in a wild flower, Hold infinity in the palm of your hand/And Eternity in an hour." [3] It embraced an ability to see cosmic meaning or diverse human and spiritual significance in each phenomenon, event, story, or picture. To appraise this intellectual talent the following proposals are made: stories would be presented to the S who then would be asked to interpret them from as many possible levels or points of view as he could summon. On completion, hints or suggestions of omitted "levels" and "orientations" could be given him (e.g., moral, spiritual, psychological,) and he then would be invited to extend his interpretations. Essays, natural events, landscapes, pictures, simple objects, and certain animals could be additionally used as "test material" for this purpose. The number and levels of interpretation rendered would be weighed in the scoring as would their quality and depth. Thus, in the case of an object, perceptual, symbolic, and structural interpretations would be apropos; for a landscape or natural event, it might be a symbolic, spiritual or cosmic viewpoint or that of an inner psychological state. Test materials would range from the very simplest to the most complex and ambiguous. They would be presented with and without interpretative hints or suggested levels of meaning.

In addition, the medieval proclivity of seeing harmonic order and a synchronous pattern in things and events should be recognized and assessed in the contemporary intellect. Medieval men saw each occurrence as part of a broader fabric of meaning and every object as integral to a larger role in contrast to the specialized, atomized orientation of present mentality which so often disassociates things and issues (problems) from their integrative, organic context and their full human implications. For example, in test items dealing with issues of speed and time, the S's awareness of how these topics embody or reflect a multitude of more general themes, values, and ideas should be examined as in the following possible test areas; the experience that time and speed involve; the mechanics of the economic process as they affect and are affected by them; normalized or conventionalized interpersonal transactions and relationships as they affect the experience of speed and time and, in turn, are affected by them; the qualities of courtesy and respect for personal feelings as they are affected by the "realities" of speed and time; delicacy and aesthetics of social manners and conversation as reflecting the experience of speed or time, and vice versa. If recognition of issues such as these is not spontaneously expressed in response to test items involving speed and time, probing of the S should be undertaken regrading his awareness of and reflections on them as embodied in the presented items. Innumerable other transactions, incidents, or events in which various themes, values, and ideas can be organically represented or reflected as part of a larger pattern or broader meaning of life and experience can be similarly used for this "testing" purpose. These may be specific items taken from present intelligence tests as in questions involving the acquisition of money, crafty dealing, getting along, etc. or as in the case of specific events and incidents from current newspaper or historical reports and from examples offered by philosophers and moralists. Depth questions with probes can be adapted to each item which would be formulated as to allow the S to expound his reasoning at the highest level of organic connection and patterning he is capable of attaining. Some items may reflect or have only a limited organic connection with one or two themes, values, or ideas; others will have numerous and infinitely broad relations with more general themes and patterns in a variety of mystic, symbolic, aesthetic, concrete, philosophical, and spiritual ways. All this would be weighed in scoring according to each item's intrinsic potential for evoking a particular number and richness of interrelationships with general meanings, themes, and patterns. Once more, the object of these "tests" would be to evaluate the S's capacity to see the scope and multiplicity of the general in the particular.

4. Another facet of medieval intelligence was the capacity to see a moral issue in a complicated web of facts and to envision what the demands of "good" and "right" action would be. Appraisal of this capacity would require test materials involving stories or picture sequences of intricate skeins of deception such as are depicted in the novels of Eric Ambler, Graham Greene, and John Le Carré, or as exemplified in the involved frauds of the television quiz programs, espionage activities of various national states, and the complex politics of universities and governments. The S would be required to see the moral issue in all these occurrences, dissect out the moral "good" from the "bad," weigh the implications of each at a variety of societal and personal levels, and morally resolve the specific presented situation, if possible, by a proposal for concrete action. It is important in all this to appraise the S's capacity to see behind the smooth words, the pleasant smiles, the "civilized" operations, the gracious courtesies, and the reasonable procedures to the basic moral issue itself and to dissect, on the model of Balzac or Camus (if not with their acuity), the hypocritically moral from the actually moral and the counterfeit good cause from the authentic good cause. To this end, tests

should be constructed for judging the depicted individuals and issues in terms of "moral," "immoral," "decent," and similar categories, such judgments being based on pertinent excerpts from novels, plays, newspaper reports, or historical accounts. Case histories and other comparable materials would be selected to assess the S's capacity to detect and discriminate moral from immoral issues in a variety of subterfuges, concealments, or instances of subtle distinction as these apply to persons, social groups, interpersonal relations, execution of actions, political programs, etc. Artifice and sincerity, deception and verity, counterfeit decency and real decency, generous words and mean actions would be judged in this light. Chronicles of political and historical events can provide useful material, replete as they are with espionage, diplomatic intrigue, political compromise, guile, and maneuver. Other themes and issues that could be made into useful test material if communicated by means of a concrete episode, narrative, or pictorial form are the advantages and disadvantages of euthanasia; group democracy and the decay of excellence; the achievement of simplicity of life at the cost of giving up further scientific and industrial advance; whether apartments or houses should be evaluated on their capacity to induce a humane, enriched life or on their number, gloss, and gadgetry; the practice of niceness and politeness as social amenities to conceal and consolidate evil; success, acceptance, or, on occasion, love as ultimately impairing individual integrity, moral probity, or principles; conflicts between the imperatives of law and wise compassion when a serious crime stems from desperate poverty or mental illness. Techniques of assessment would be roughly similar to those previously described for other components of medieval intelligence with the instructions intended to evoke from the S, spontaneously at first, some manifestation of the "moral intelligence" these tests would have been devised to measure. Subsequently, multiple choice and sentence completion methods would be used to elicit additional evidence, as required, of various aspects of this ability, including the capacity to detect counterfeit morality, fraudulent benevolence, sham "nice" people, etc. Additional test materials could take the form of a series of arguments or accounts of events and experiences in which several alternative outcomes would be prepared from which the S could choose only one; all would have as central to their content a "moral" issue or problem that would have to be resolved in one of a number of optional ways. Still other procedures would include giving the S the opportunity to carry forward to its conclusion a story, chronicle, or argument, intentionally left unfinished at a crucial point in the exposition of a basic moral issue; encouraging the S to improvise a narrative, theme, or argument revolving around such a problem; having the S

137

analyze the moral issues or themes of various political tracts. Hence, the capacity to see moral issues in the simplest decisions, to see the implications of an act in its total moral ramifications, and to resolve moral dilemmas would all come within the compass of this "medieval" faculty. Some of the following moral themes and dilemmas may be useful to develop for the assessment of this capacity: the dilemma of using "toughness" in the interest of "kind" or "good" causes in contrast to its employment to advance self-interest in matters of power or status; the use of deceptive language (words) when expedient as compared with its use for "worthy" ends; and, in general, any means-ends dilemmas, especially where means are "immoral" and ends "moral." The materials and the procedures that are necessary for conveying these issues in test form would be comparable to those previously described: stories, episodes, historical incidents, problems, multiple choice questions, and unfinished narratives.

In scoring, a distinction should certainly be made between those Ss whose insight and aptitude for detection is broad, penetrating, and subtle, and those whose is more limited or superficial. The capacity to see the fundamental moral issue irrespective of the complexity or surface deviousness of the presented test material as well as the ability to comprehend even the slightest moral consequence of an action should also be appraised, e.g., the effect of an ever so slight deprecatory comment on a very sensitive child or of a subtle diplomatic maneuver on the aggravation of a petty skirmish.

The preferential ordering, by the S, of his spontaneously given or multiple choice "resolutions" to *all* the foregoing "moral-intellectual" tests would reveal, in part, his cognitive-valuative hierarchy by the way he orients and uses his intelligence in connection with moral or expedient solutions. This would also throw light on the character of his intelligence as having scope, depth, and richness or as being more practical, programmed, and shrewd. Further, all sorts of issues and problems ranging in emphasis from the most moral to the most expedient could be presented and the responses assessed for corresponding or noncorresponding emphasis on the particular moral or expedient focus of the question. It should be remembered, too, that the more searching and reflective the S's "moral response" to the question is, the greater the probability that a longer time will be required to give its expression full justice, whereas the superficially greater cleverness, shrewdness, and practicality of conventional responses probably need relatively shorter times. If only for this reason, no time limit should be set on answers to these "tests."

Medieval Perception

Medieval perception included the following salient features:

1. It was not predominantly "reality bound" or structured in the dimensions of externality, objectivity, concreteness, or manipulation. Perceptions that were clear, tangible, usable, or "real" were not necessarily preeminently acceptable or important. What was salient for medieval perception was symbolism, i.e., a perception's representation or embodiment of some religious or mystical meaning.

2. A second feature of medieval perception was the prevalence of noncognitive, elusive, and subliminal or barely liminal percepts. These often ambiguous percepts ranged from the sensory to the mystic or symbolic. Special subtleties or intimations of meaning as well as plays or variants on the form and import of words, pictures, and material objects were all common to medieval perception. Indeed, it can be said with some assurance that the literal dimensions of an object were hardly ever the exclusive ones by which it was apprehended. Thus, in paintings, there were often hidden figures, symbolic connotations to colors, spiritual or theological meanings assigned to content, and hints of religious values in geometrical or spatial patterns and perspectives. In natural phenomena and social or personal experience things were often perceived at different levels from which they concretely appeared and often as manifestations of divinity, love, redemption, and evil. Indeed, even in a simple sunset the acculturated medieval eye might see a miracle, God or the devil, blood and victory, or the transformation of the world. In the case of language, words were judged as conveying hidden meanings or omens. Even the form of a work might symbolize some significant religious event or revelation. Works of literature, theological texts, etc. were rife with veiled import: "coded" messages, cryptic metaphorical sequences, and ciphers of verbal arrangements, conveyed portents, spiritual ideas, or supernatural themes. The whole text of such a theological or literary work might be a spiritual allegory, an elaborate parable, or a cryptogram of religious allusions. As for numbers, they frequently had supernatural or theological significance: thus "3" might signify a fundamental religious doctrine, e.g., the Trinity, or evoke particular feelings of forbidden, mysterious pleasure; "6" might connote the completion of divine work or symbolize fortitude, proud dignity, and strength.

Goodness, evil, redemption, salvation, and the reality of afterlife—these were the things that medieval men were concerned about; the effort to make mundane perceptual experience fit into such categories was of prominent importance to them. In effectuating this, such processes as symbolism and imagination became more prominent in perception and concrete reality factors less so than is the case with contemporary perceptual experience. Though this medieval perceptual orientation required sacrifices of such concrete dimensions, it brought added imaginal, symbolic, and spiritual perceptual sensitivity to the form and content of objects. The perceptual "real" or concrete were thus attenuated in the effort to perceptually avoid acknowledging the harsh and frustrating world of realistic experience that confronted medieval man. The result, for a substantial sector of medieval perception, was that the imaginal, affective, ideational, and symbolic factors became prominent. Thus many stimulus objects were reinterpreted so as to be perceived in congruence with medieval ideology and values. Color, form, hidden dimensions of content, and words were often imaginatively transformed or perceived as having such ideological and valuative characteristics. Further, the de-emphasis of cognitive concreteness in certain areas of perception together with the involvement of nonmaterialistic factors turned substantial portions of perceptual experience toward the inner world of fantasy, symbolism, and imagination with resultant concern with those ambiguous, less structured, and more elusive external stimuli that are more attuned to inner experience. Such stimuli as nuances of color, indefinite forms, elusive episodes, suggestive movements, and amorphously structured objects became a major object of perceptual interest during the Middle Ages because they were more diversely and imaginatively interpreted than "hard," cognitive, perceptual stimuli. One consequence was the exploration of numerous aspects of spiritual, mystic, imaginal, and symbolic perceptual experiences and the utilization of any stimulus as the starting point for an act of structured perceptual imagination.

3. Another aspect of medieval perception was its spiritualization and symbolization through the plot and meaning of the Christian epic. This was manifested in every way: thus, the color blue might stand for divinity, purity, or birth, and red for fortitude or earthliness. In nature, a common event such as the movement of the leaves might be judged as a heavenly voice affording reassurance of salvation. A red sunset might mean duty, blood, divine destruction, or rebirth, and the movement of a stone could signify redemption or spiritual transfiguration. Animals and their behavior could represent some aspect of the good-evil complex, whereas specific instances of human resignation to cruelty, privation, and

tyranny might signify the sacrifice and martyrdom of Jesus. Even movements of birds or winter winds had some symbolic significance. In this way almost every object and event, at one time or another, could be perceived to represent some theme or experience of the Christian cosmology or drama.

4. Another characteristic of medieval perception was its proclivity to see things or happenings in a moral light. Evaluation of the world as good or evil or in terms of charity or meanness was evidenced in almost every aspect of medieval perception: painting, literature, theology, politics, and in the interpretation of ordinary, everyday experiences, such as the kindness of a smile, an animal's captiousness, a parable, the night overshadowing a fiery sunset, the fall of a stone, or the pyramidal structure of a tree. Even colors, textures, and forms were perceived as symbols of good or bad. Often enough, the sensory, concrete, and empirical factors in perception were subordinated to this moral component.

5. Further, because of Aristotelian influences in medieval experience, perception sometimes had the quality of "becomingness," "emergingness," or a changing process. In this medieval sense, perception was a stone becoming visually harder and larger or "emerging" as a scriptural tablet, and the sunset perceptually "becoming" an interval of blinding, rekindled life or a glorious final consummation. The death of a gentle animal—in this "evolving" view—might be seen as one episode in the unfolding odyssey of the transmigration of souls. Implicit in all this, also, was the teleological orientation of medieval life, which affirmed that all phenomena occur for or evolved toward some divine good.

Seeing things or events as dynamically "emerging" toward some variant of perfectability was a related facet of this perceptual view. Hence squares might be seen with the prospect of attaining "roundness," and evil might have some prospective good: in the red of a sunset there were the indications of its change to blue; there was life in death and death in life. Many phenomena were perceived as becoming "better," "purer," and more perfect or as having this potentiality. Perceptual objects were seen with attention to the dynamic processes of change and development that they underwent as well as the perceptual changes they instigated in the viewer. To see cruelty was to see how it could be transformed; to see good was to see how it could be improved. To see a painting was to see it transformed under scrutiny, was to see its figures, design, and meaning change in quality and emphasis while, simultaneously, this whole perceptual process evoked changing aesthetic experiences. In the same way, a leaf had visually implicit in it the bud of its spring flowering, the delight evoked by its tender fragile greenness, the abstract design of its delicate gossamer network, or the brownness of its death in which, perceptually, there was already a promise of rejuvenescence.

It was this dynamic or "pregnant" power of the perceptual process that could transform the actual perceptual stimulus into something quite different from what it objectively or initially appeared to be—though already implicit or potential in it—that made it so important to the medieval mind.

From the viewpoint of medieval perception, modern perceptual research fails to adequately deal with many perceptual phenomena because of too rigid and concrete formulations and implementations of its studies. Thus, it speeds and pressures the S through the experiment so that too often only quick and superficial responses are elicited in the form of concrete and "realistic" perceptions, which represent, in turn, the dominant values and dimensions of our culture and, hence, those to which contemporary perception is most reflexively attuned. It is such perceptions that are most often rewarded because they are most oriented to the goals of adjustment or the status quo—in short, to present "reality." Moreover, contemporary perceptual tests and experiments to which the S is exposed, being strange and challenging to him, often call forth the predominant culturally sanctioned response-sets of practicality, caution, and conformity which are appropriate and sensible for such unknown situations—especially in the context of the S's understandable feeling that, as a participant in a psychological study or "test," his "normality" is also being appraised.

Further influencing these outcomes is the desire on the part of the S to get the job (i.e., experiment) done as quickly and successfully as possible with a minimum of difficulty or disturbance which, in effect, means conforming to the wishes of the E and to the requirements of the experimental design or, in any case, being wary, if not suppressive, of any free, spontaneous perceptual experience he may have. Moreover, because such designs rather deliberately emphasize and reward practical, conventional perceptual behavior, the S's responses will be in the same vein if he is to get through the "job" satisfactorily. Thus, deviant, vague, mystic, spiritual, and symbolic perceptions are truncated, and the predominant response readiness is that of a conventional reality-oriented, no-nonsense approach quite in keeping with the regimen of mechanistic orientation, good sense, and unambiguity that the laboratory and the instructions of the E induce. The S is, in a fashion, too often made a variant of an efficient, rational, perceptual machine: a machine schooled for concrete, realistic awareness and for conforming materialistic response. Often, the perceptual result is an engineering, manipulative, dehumanized appraisal of the stimulus object, an appraisal that, because of its oversimplified, positivistic, concrete reductionism, its omission of *human* and *symbolic* meanings or values associated with the stimulus, and its exclusion of other latent spiritual, moral, or mystic meanings and affects ultimately makes the perceptual process antihumanistic, business-oriented, and machine-like.

In further appraising current perceptual work our hypothetical medieval psychologist would suggest that it is excessively based on animal and instinctual behavioral processes, preoccupation with which, he would argue, is partially derived from modern jungle-like economic competition and survival-oriented, self-aggrandizing individualism, which, from the perspective of the sociology of knowledge, explains the instinctive, materialistic, concrete orientations of contemporary perception and perceptual research. Also accounting for this preoccupation are the loss of traditionally accepted social values or purposes and the collapse of numerous historical standards for evaluating human worth as well as serious doubt about the desirability and virtue of this traditional "worth" itself. Thus much of perception is instinctually, mechanistically, and economically oriented in a culture that manifests this orientation in its concrete, practical perceptual norms and modes of perceptual experience. In such an environment, nonmaterial and humanistic perceptual values are alien, having no economic, survival-abetting, or animal-instinct satisfying worth and, if viable, might well jeopardize proper adjustment, success, and, not impossibly, existence. Because they are not resonant with or welcome in contemporary behavior or congenial to the theories and descriptions of the perceptual process set forth by contemporary psychologists does not mean that these "immaterial" perceptions are not often present, if latently so, in contemporary men and, indeed, might be observed, if only they were sensitively, imaginatively, and methodically sought.

STUDIES IN MEDIEVAL-LIKE PERCEPTION

Specifically, rectification would take the following forms:

1. Persons of medieval cast of mind, of "mystic," consummately inner-oriented, or exalted sensibility, and of capacity for spiritual, symbolic, or metaphoric perception should be recruited as subjects. These might include certain monks and nuns, those of Zen Buddhist training or of some schools of Hinduistic persuasion, certain Jungian-oriented persons, and others of intangible and delicate sensitivity. In this grouping would be certain kinds of artists and religious persons or those dedicated to inner spiritual sensation and experience.

2. The studies proper, whether they are conducted under experimental

conditions or in specifically designated naturalistic environments should, in the large majority of cases, be preceded by intensive training in medieval sensibility and perception. This might be accomplished either by placing the S for lengthy periods in medieval-like rooms (furnished with medieval decorations and *objets d'art,* inundated with medieval music, and populated with persons selected to convey the medieval presence of spirituality, benevolence, and sensitivity by their conversation, manner, and reactions to stimuli) or by the S's being oriented in medieval lore, history, art, literature, exposed to medieval lectures, and living for a time (in imagination and intellectual experience) in a medieval-like milieu. Medieval paintings, role-playing of medieval-like parts and episodes, participating in medieval-like conversations and interactions, and seeing medieval drama or motion pictures also may help in achieving this perceptual orientation. Natural settings of an eminently medieval character also should be utilized, including those of cathedrals, certain kinds of medieval-like rooms (such as in the New York Cloisters or other art museums), and various kinds of monasteries, castles, or guild halls. These settings, too, might be used as environments where experiments could be carried out and perceptual experiences (either deliberately introduced or occurring spontaneously) could be studied. In addition, there may be certain moments or incidents in the everyday course of life —quiet moments, introspective moments, muted periods of the day such as dusk, unusual interactions and conversations that have an air of delicacy and intangibility, moments in dimly lit rooms or in certain chiaroscuro moods, however induced—where these perceptual experiences may more fully flower. An interval of leisure when sensation gently flows in and is intangibly meditated on, a period of quasimystic experience and thought or of inner sensation and wool-gathering, walks or drives when the protean qualities of sensation and feeling take on an ineffable, fleeting quality, moods of gentle sadness—all these and more may be culled and assayed for medieval-like kinds of perceptual experience that spontaneously occur or, indeed, could be used as contexts in which to introduce designated perceptual stimuli to elicit them. Other preparatory orientations would consist of induction of the S into mystic, near-mystic, and semitrance states through training in Zen Buddhism or Yoga, induction into twilight sleep or near-hypnotic states through music, mystic incantation, muscular relaxation techniques, or verbal suggestion, and induction into various kinds of transcendent or preconscious conditions by going through an intensely personal spiritual or religious experience or by "proper" use of psychedelic drugs.

3. The utilization of as many unstructured stimuli as possible should

be encouraged in perceptual studies. These may be ambiguous figures, amorphous lines, muted drawings, shadings of color, suggestive diagrams (not recognizable as specific "things"), cubist or dadaist designs, expressionist pictures, certain forms of contemporary music, etc. With these stimuli, the S should be asked to take his time before his perceptual report occurs, and if further orientations are needed, he might be asked to try to "see" these stimuli in symbolic, cryptic, mythic, or other non-tangible terms. Failing this, specific hints may be given or, even further, multiple choice questions presented to this end. The hints and multiple choice alternatives should represent different levels of symbolization, spirituality, mysticism, morality, etc.

4. In addition, stimuli with strong mystic or symbolic import may be presented. Among these would be vivid sunsets, intense blue skies, the throbbing sounds of water, the absolute jet blackness of a pool, mysterious shadows, dark opaque caves, intense green foliage, symbols such as the mandala, the wise old man or the earth mother, various religious symbols (from the Zoroastrian, Buddhist, Hindu, and Christian religions), dream symbols, symbols of nuclear crises or of man's life cycle, mysterious figures, unconscious or archetypical images, drawings and carvings from "primitive" tribes, allegories, fables, various portents or omens, and legends or myths with universal meanings. Such stimuli as these, under appropriate medieval-like conditions, might evoke corresponding medieval-like perceptions. Again, the relationships between these responses and the S's value system, the richness of his inner world, the degree of his commitment to the external or the inner world, and his human and spiritual sensitivity or humanistic perspective should be investigated.

5. Concern should be paid to the S's capacity to interpret stimuli in terms of moral significance or of some ethical orientation. Here, a variety of stimuli may be presented varying from those with high moral or ethical content (a parable, a fable, a moral precept) to those comprising the simplest events, acts, or innocuous issues. Thus, pictorial forms varying from those of the simplest object-concreteness to those symbolically or graphically representing such moral themes as compassion, evil, and altruism would be relevant stimuli. On a similar continuum, brief interpersonal conversations and interactions could be presented to the S, who would be asked to respond to them from a moral perspective. Thus a perfunctory nod or greeting, a slight discourtesy, the cruel chastisement of another, a warm salutation, a generous compliment or acknowledgment when not required, and a hard, indifferent, or warm response to the pleading eyes of a beggar or a weak person—these or other "vignettes"

may be depicted in words, pictures, or sound and would be the appropriate stimuli to determine the S's capacity to see some moral and ethical point in issues and events, or on a grander scale, to generalize from them to a broader moral conception. All these episodes may be presented in a pictorial or narrative multiple choice format or may be made to "spontaneously" occur in natural situations in which the S is present. Thus, some event occurring at a moment in which the S is in a room—e.g., the sudden appearance of a religious "sign" or symbol, a rude comment of one person to another, a generous act of assistance to an older person or to someone in distress—may be used to evoke and appraise the S's moral perceptions. The various dimensions of these perceptions (personal, social, community, political, reverence for all life, etc.) and whether they are actuated at the most remote level (by such neutral stimuli as casual remarks, material objects, or physical movements) or at various intermediate points on this moral-amoral continuum should also be determined. In all of this the S's capacity to abandon concrete, tangible, and materialistic perceptions in favor of concern with moral and spiritual ones should be assessed.

To summarize, stimuli on a gradient from the most concrete and tangible to the most moral and ethical would be presented to the S. Those S's with massive disposition toward moral perception may hesitate to abandon such responses even in the presence of the baldest, most amoral concrete stimulus while quite the opposite might hold for Ss with unreconstructed, concrete perceptual orientations. Appraisal of such perceptual sets under varying moods and in different environments for these different kinds of stimuli should be carried out by the previously suggested procedures of spontaneous responses, suggestive hints, and multiple choice methods.

6. Also to be appraised are the evolving "pregnant" dimensions of perception, i.e., the capacity of the S to see changing forms and emergence of new images in a presented stimulus. For color and form stimuli, this would mean the disposition to see nuances of other shades or colors in the presented color stimulus or to perceive emerging "new" or variant forms transform the "look" of a presented form stimulus. It also might mean that there would be a kaleidoscopic succession of responses to a given stimulus. It might mean, too, seeing all sorts of perceptual possibilities in words when they are presented as stimuli including their potentiality as puns, syncratic verbal forms, homologies, and structural or geometric language forms. It might mean the capacity to see a picture, image, or object evolve perceptually into something quite different from what it initially was. Thus a noble lion may become a cruel beast or an

archetype of fierceness; a Titian portrait of a noble man may instigate an intense interpersonal transaction between the spectator and portrait, assimilating deep sectors of the former's personality into the figure of the painting, which may then itself change into a symbol of sublimity holding out the prospect of an exalted experience for the spectator; a leaf may first be seen as a symbol of fragility, then of capacity for growth, and finally of mystery; a small bud is perceived as having the promise of a large tree, then becomes a weak object to be protected, and a moment later is seen as a feminine symbol or as a promise of life. A color—white, for example—may perceptually change its character from purity to dullness, then stimulate a symbiotic absorptive interaction with the spectator and even leave him in a near mystic state.

Studies of related aspects of this perceptual dimension might take the following course: a stimulus object (colors, forms, abstract designs, sounds, or words) would be presented and the S asked to recount the course of his perceptual experience as he continues to attend to it. In suggestive, open, and "emergent" settings (multifaceted rooms, psychedelic lights, moving backgrounds of furniture or scenery, revolving rooms, kaleidoscopic backdrops, evocative and protean atmospheres) the S would be presented with a variety of stimuli ranging from the most concrete and structured to the most misty, ambiguous, mysterious, or suggestive and be required to report the course of changes in his perceptual reactions. At one end of the stimulus continuum would be exact, clear colors or concrete objects with definite lines while at the other end would be muted colors, intricately suggestive designs, vague forms with fuzzy contours suggestive of figures from Zen Buddhist art and lore, religious symbols, Jungian archetypes, figures from the paintings of Bosch, and mythical figures. The same would be done for words, phrases, or sentences which could vary from the most tangible and specific to the most suggestive, ambiguous, and cryptic (metaphoric words or phrases, picture designs in words, poetic symbols and images). The S would be asked to freely pursue his perceptions of these stimuli and report them. Thus he could make "plays" on the stimulus words, respond with various meanings and levels of affect to them, perceive different structural designs in their arrangement, see contradictions between their conscious evocations and their unconscious affects, and react to the kinesthetic feel of words as well as to their auditory and visual imagery and denotation.

Perception of sounds may similarly be studied. These may be specific denotative sounds (a call, a whistle, etc.), pure tones, truncated sounds, the most complex cacophony, sounds suggestive of various feelings (fear, agony, ecstasy, spiritual experience, tenderness, eruptions of the uncon-

147

scious and mystic states), animal sounds, and sounds connoting or symbolizing events and ceremonies (birth, death, marriage, victory, tragedy, etc.).

7. Becoming deeply absorbed in a stimulus object so that one feels an experiential fusion or symbiotic identity with it is another dimension of the medieval perceptual orientation. One feels in oneself the color of the wood, the texture of the cloth, the hardness of the table—and may experience these sensations kinesthetically, viscerally, and tactually. Such intense "inner" experiencing of an object may be cultivated through deep concentration, absorption in a particular aspect of the stimulus (color, brightness, texture, volume, etc.) and through deep, inner absorption in which the S internalizes or becomes one with the stimulus, while minimizing or eliminating the objective and realistic perception of it as an object or thing. Immensely helpful to these efforts would be sensory, muscular, and perceptual experiences taken from Zen, Yoga, Esalen-type, Hindu, or other mystically oriented teachings. In addition, perceptual practice in the activation and refinement of kinesthetic, tactual, visual, and visceral responses to a variety of stimuli should be pursued. For example, a given stimulus—a fabric—would be presented and the S would sense and experience it in other sensory modalities besides the visual. He would kinesthetically feel its weight and texture, thermally respond to its warm or cold colors, tactually experience its patterns of roughness or smoothness, etc. till the stimulus would have evoked all the sensory and perceptual modalities that were within the S's response potential and he, himself, would have become perceptually identified with or merged into it. A wide range of stimuli possessing varying degrees of potential for evoking such manifold perceptual responses can be presented to the S with a variety of orientations and backgrounds. The influence of medieval-like perceptual orientations and environments, particularly preexperimental mystical orientations, on the S's perceptual responses to these varying stimulus modalities can then be compared with the effects of other environments and preexperimental orientations on them.

8. The behavior of the E in these perceptual studies, as in all the foregoing proposed medieval-type experiments, should be a blend of spirituality, benevolence, tentativeness, and sensitivity that embodies the dimensions of medieval mentality previously identified. He should be benign and permissive in his attitude, and his treatment of the S should reflect kindness, grace, immateriality, and a concern with the inner life and spirit that would put into subservience any orientations of concreteness, preeminent rationalism, or striving for achievement. In conversation,

in the directions he gives, and by the kind of inner spirit he diffuses, he should extend the impression to the S that success and materiality do not matter and that the important matters are the inner life and its experiences, symbolic or metaphoric meanings, and spiritual and benign feelings.

For each of the previously described aspects of medieval perception, rather specific orientations and settings should be developed to evoke optimal perceptual responses. Thus, for cryptic or symbolic perception, settings and communications that emphasize intricate designs, involuted word patterns, arabic motifs and mosaics, veiled many-faceted conversations, and interpersonal moods of subtle complexity would be desirable. For mystic perception, the background might consist of religious decorations, figures, furniture and designs, archetypical and symbolic materials, kaleidescopic presentations of dream-like images passing quickly before the S, presentations of religious expressionist films and images, and an atmosphere that would be muted and mysterious. To facilitate mystic perception, the E should be serene, somewhat enigmatic and inner-oriented in manner and from him should emanate a spiritual, benign but somewhat detached or "immaterial" air, as if he were both concerned and not concerned with reality and could, were he so disposed, be fully involved with it, particularly so when it related to human beings.

Medieval Group Psychology

The characteristics of medieval group psychology were:

1. A transcendent and idealized concern with the group. In the medieval group, the attitude toward feudal obligation and mutuality, sanctified by the Church, was so strong that it was thought to be divinely ordained—as in the case of the reciprocal allegiances and duties of serf to lord and lord to king, including their respective social and economic units. Feudal interstatus obligations were the secular counterparts of duties owed God. Indeed, the hierarchical feudal organization in which each had a distinct place was analogous to the clerical hierarchy of the Church and to its complex system of interconnected, ascending acts and rituals necessary for attaining salvation and eternal life. And to the degree each fulfilled his status role without rebellion or complaint—to the extent, for example, that the noble discharged his responsibilities to the serf and vice versa—God's will was fulfilled and the harmonious hierarchy

149

of His social structure was sustained. Thus society was integrated, in part, on the basis of an upward spiritually striving process in which each had and felt a sacred role and duty. There was no disgrace felt in the lowly position of serf. It was accepted without envy or further aspiration; it was good to occupy a status to which the Church and the nobles had as many obligations as one had to them—and if God placed one in that position it was for a divine and marvelous purpose that, in fact, contributed to the earthly harmony of Christian life and thereon to the preparation for the afterlife. Thus, even "low" status privileged one to play an integral role in this divine earthly scheme just as nobility and royalty did, if at somewhat different levels of influence. Further, those of "low" estate were endowed with the special virtues of poverty and, presumably, therefore with the immateriality, lack of corporeal temptation, and greater spirituality that conferred assurance of possessing true Christian virtue while undergoing preparation, through the practice of these traits, for its full exercise in paradise.

Thus this system functioned and was sanctified as a preparation for salvation. From such influences emerged a group milieu in which conflict, envy, resentment, social aspiration, etc. were substantially deemphasized.

2. Because leaders occupied sanctified statuses in this divinely ordained system, they were given the deference that accorded with the Thomist conception that increasingly "higher" secular roles should correspond to spiritually "higher" positions. Such deference did not, however, appreciably incite envy, resentment, feelings of exploitation (and consequently rebellion), fears based on hostility to authority, or the type of servile self-abasement that emanates from oppression. As explained, this was because societal status was consecrated, aspiration to rise was unsanctioned, the main purpose of earthly life was not the acquisition of power, wealth, or rank but preparation for the heavenly kingdom, and the secular life had to be endured as a condition of salvation. A fundamental test of this endurance was the capacity to ignore social ambition or material desire and to tranquilly accept one's assigned secular status as a sanctified part of the social order, to change even one component of which would be near sacrilegious.

3. Attendant on this was the subordination of the individual to the dominance of the mystique of the group and its interconnected system of mutual role relationships and obligations—both of which made him a cog in an intricate mechanism designed to fulfill God's conception. Though the individual was, in a sense, an "end" or purpose of this mechanism, he was also, at the same time, a means for its tangible realization.

150

Thus, in this system of highly organized obligations, values, and purposes, there was no questioning of assumptions or probing of goals pertaining to individual and group relationships. Indeed, there was no individualism or personal fulfillment as the Greeks or cultivated Europeans since the Renaissance knew them because the system of medieval group values and purposes fully absorbed the individual, satisfying the most urgent of his personal needs, quieting his doubts, and sustaining his faith and endurance. Individual needs for self-expression or fulfillment of capacities were channeled into religious rituals, group activities, artistic projects (both collective or individual, as in the construction and adornment of cathedrals), etc., all of which were richly satisfying experiences and made men feel that they were participants in and contributing to a sacred and shared enterprise. Thus hardships, privation, and discontent were alleviated by religious observances, by a divinely ordained social order, by the tranquility bestowed through grace, by hope for an afterlife, and by communally shared enterprises in which each felt he played a vital and organic part in making an essential contribution to the welfare or spiritual well-being of the group.

By such methods, the feudal Christian social system totally absorbed the individual within its framework, making him coextensive with the group. Further, by threatening any authentic individualist quest with ostracism or, at the very least, with the obloquy of sin, anyone courageous enough to adventure in heterodox paths not only courted heresy but forfeited the fundamental group memberships of medieval society as well as the prospect of salvation, and so instigated, by such independence, the gravest personal anxieties, doubts, and loneliness—exactly those feelings the medieval system was so exquisitely designed to excite and then appease.

These factors, collectively made for a group cohesion, an identification with group purpose, a sense of holy or transcendent mission, a feeling of personal belongingness and worth, and a fund of personal and group security which may be historically unparalleled in the West. Allied effects of this individual-group solidarity were the strength to bear difficulties and privations, especially material ones; the tendency to reject unlike sentiments or ideologies and to ostracize or suppress nonconformists and skeptics; a disposition toward rationalizing away or "magically" denying "realistic" and concrete adversity, ideological conflict, and tangible obstacles; the proscription of any critical appraisal of the values and ideological premises of the medieval system including the suppression of dissimilar modes of thought; substantial consistency and predictability of group behavior as well as great courage and righteousness of conviction underlying it.

RECTIFICATION AND PROPOSED STUDIES

On the basis of this summary, how can we broaden our conceptions of contemporary group behavior and integrate them, when suitable, with some of these medieval dimensions? It is clear that religious idealism, the individual's absorption in a transcendent group mission and the equating or, indeed, subordination of his psychological needs and interpersonal transactions to it, the emphasis on nonmaterial values, the abatement of envy, resentment, and status ambitions, the diminished concern with individualism or with the achievement of a "personal identity," and certain other group qualities are not sufficiently acknowledged or studied by contemporary psychology. Whether this is owing, at the present time, to the deterioration of a vitally significant, absorbing, and richly fulfilling group life, to an exaggerated but often counterfeit emphasis on individualist fulfillment and ideology, to the decline of heroic and exalted collective purpose or of noble and selfless mission, to the erosion of satisfaction of individual, collective, and spiritual needs, or to the fragmentation and mechanization of the contemporary person and his disparate, affiliate groups is not unambiguously clear. Whatever the eventual explanation, however, medieval group experience, to the extent that it deepens and illuminates understanding of the modern process and condition, must be reinvestigated and its findings applied to present research. The following proposals are to this end.

1. Attempts must be made to study groups deeply committed to an idealistic or elevated purpose or mission. This, in contrast, to the current practice of selecting ad hoc, contrived, and transient aggregates to experimentally confirm a hypothesis which so often is quite alien to the actual reasons for which such collections of persons participate in the experiment. Such reasons, often enough, are to please the experimenter, to acquire money, fun, or "interesting experiences," and to satisfy still other *individual* needs. Such aggregates are thus "counterfeit groups" engaging in a charade of activity which, in effect, is a tortuous accommodation between the pressures of the experiment and its arbitrary manipulations, on the one hand, and the aggregate's own conflicting interpersonal and individual needs, on the other. What too often results from these studies is a complicated mélange of pretense, self-deception, acquisitiveness, conformity, and curiosity-seeking but hardly the functioning of an integrated and purposeful body with a clear, if not, high mission.

To rectify these conditions the following proposals should be carried through: present and past groups with high purposes should be restudied, e.g., reform or revolutionary groups at their idealistic and elevated beginnings, some peace groups, utopian groups, the "new" communes, certain religious groups with exalted programs, or, indeed, any group that has had an edifying or benign mission before the time it becomes excessively formalized or loses its unadulterated "elevating" passion. More can be learned about group mission, resistance to internal decay and external adversity, and capacity for sacrifice and sustained optimism or morale by studying the beginnings of collectives like the kibbutz, certain nineteenth-century European socialist groups, or the early stages of populism, chartism, and the American antinuclear testing movement than all the group laboratory studies in which the goals, values, and interpersonal prescriptions do not draw on the vital concerns, purposes, and organic experience of the group members involved. What happens to such "idealistic" groups as they achieve success and respectability, when the purity and intensity of their benign mission is dimmed, when complacency, organizationalism, soundness, and appropriateness supersede enthusiasm, openness to new experiences, and inventiveness and when personal ambitions, status preoccupations, or interpersonal complexities become more important than uninhibited freedom of communication and unselfish dedicated zeal? All these should be studied not only in the histories of great religions and revolutionary movements but in the small reform or other beneficent groups of the past and present. Contemporary groups of this type should not only be naturalistically studied by interview methods, participant observation, documentary records, etc. but, if possible, should also be studied in the laboratory on a number of group issues: cohesion, cooperation, perseverance, personal sacrifice for the group's purpose, benign personal feelings, etc. Studies of the same research issues can also be made on these groups in their natural settings and the results compared. Groups ranging from most to least in degree of dedication, benevolence, and elevation of purpose can be compared with the aggregates ordinarily used in laboratory studies, and groups in various developmental stages from their first idealistic missions to their later prudent transformations should be similarly investigated. As a result of such studies—in natural settings and the laboratory, in the past and in the present, and at different stages of group development—a more authentic and broader conception of the phenomena of dedication, purpose, sacrifice, solidarity, etc. will be obtained than is presently emerging from group studies.

2. Because one of the conspicuous features of medieval society was the

individual's complete identity with or submersion in the group, the question arises whether this particular quality is, in general, associated with other attributes of these groups: cohesion, capacity to endure, hope, harmony, high morale, spirituality, benevolence, inflexibility of procedure, imperviousness to new ideas, etc. There is a large fund of material on all varieties of groups (both historic and contemporary) that could be analyzed for correlations between individual-collective identity (or coalescence) and the foregoing group behavior variables. Among examples of groups that might be studied along these lines are the Communist party prior to and after the Russian Revolution, the Jacobins of the French Revolution, Jesuitical orders at certain historical times, the early Christian groups, and certain monastic orders. Toward the opposite end of this individual-collective identity continuum, i.e., the "decoalescent" end, associations of anarchists, artists, or writers and certain scientific and university groups could be similarly studied. Whether groupings in this sector incline more toward interpersonal conflict, benevolence, hope, inflexibility of procedure, factionalism, individual anxiety, etc. than those at the opposite end, or vice versa, would be useful to determine.

Similarly, studies should be carried out on comparable contemporary groups in both natural and experimental settings as well as on analogous types of "experimentally composed groups." In these present-day groups, further questions about the identity or separateness of the individual from the group can be explored. Such issues as (1) the degree and scope of the coalescence of the individual with the group (absolute, substantial, minimal), (2) the areas of coalescence (humanitarian, religious, social), (3) the quality of coalescence (intellectual, emotional), and (4) the extent and quality of separateness of the individual from the group can all be intensively studied with groups varying in position on the coalescence continuum.

3. Another characteristic of the medieval group was that it served as the media within which the exercise and fulfillment of almost all individual abilities and needs were achieved. This group involvement brought much personal happiness though often it was mediated through collective fantasies, rituals, and projections.

Generally, there are very few existing groups that afford the intensity of individual-group involvement along with happiness and hope that medieval groups and communities provided. Those groups that presently achieve a comparable condition of involvement do not, however, provide sufficient reassurance for their members and lack the halcyon contentment and blissful expectancy that medieval groups afforded.

Historical studies may be particularly useful here: different kinds of collectivized, absorptive, and intensely involving groups (political, religious, or scientific) can be compared with pluralistic, loosely knit, richly variable groups (artists, anarchists, literary persons, etc.) in respect to the completeness of the identity of members with the group, the fulfillment of individual needs and potentialities, and the degree of hope, serenity, joy, and supportiveness that the group enjoyed. The intensely absorptive groups in these studies can vary as to singleness or multiplicity of purpose, capacity for satisfying many or few of the member's needs and abilities, and the degree of salutary, benevolent, transcendent, or dedicated feelings the group sustained. Studies such as these should also be made on comparable contemporary groups as well as on appropriate experimental and laboratory aggregates.

4. Love must be studied as a salient factor in group purpose and process because, if only as evidenced in the medieval experience, it contributed substantially to the group's capacity for satisfaction, happiness, hope, tranquility, and the ability to make worldly or corporeal renunciations. Investigations should be directed to a whole series of historical and contemporary groups: monastic orders such as the Franciscans, very early Christian groups; certain Zen groups; various utopian communities in their beginning stages; the "new" communes; certain hippie groups; the Fellowship of Reconciliation of the American Friends Service Committee; certain altruistic women's groups; certain "benevolent" and early social work groups. These groups—in which love is a compelling factor—can be compared on a number of variables to others having emotionally different but equally strong purposes; scientific or professional groups, trade associations, radical groups, political associations, athletic groups, various business groups, etc. Comparisons should also be made with groups that have a minimum of love or, in fact, whose dynamics are copiously influenced by hate: certain military groups, Nazi groups, other extremist groups of the right or left, and ultranationalist or xenophobic groups. Qualities on which such groups ought to be compared are disturbance or turbulence of group atmosphere, amount of personal self-realization or fulfillment of members, charity and acceptance of members for one another, degree of constructive activity and productivity, amount of vigor and enterprise, and amount of serenity and happiness that the group enjoys. Originality of achievement and vigorous affirmation of purpose should also be evaluated because some contend that these group qualities are substantially reduced by large supplies of love and especially so in benevolent groups. Studies should be carried out in both natural and laboratory situations and also include experimental groups.

Experimental ingenuity will be needed to create experimental groups that are generous, benign, or tolerant and those that are spiteful, angry, and hateful as well as some intermediate types. Through the proper use of leaders, through an appropriate selection of group members, through the fulfillment of various of their needs, and through indoctrination of hope, benevolence, serenity, and other "medieval" values, it may be possible to establish groups that are benign, happy, and altruistic. Such conditions may also be achieved with groups formed to engage in "do-good" or self-help projects or in the case of groups placed in permissive, benign atmospheres marked by benevolent cooperation and contentment. Contrasting "hate" groups might similarly be composed through pertinent methods of leadership, selection of appropriate subjects, encouragement of hostility, scapegoating, or internal resentment, depreciation of benevolence and gentleness, esteem for dominance or callousness, and by judicious selection of an effective "hate" cause, target, or environment whether it be a political institution or group, a specific rival or opponent, an underdog or dissenter, or an environment of turbulence and conflict. Through the use of measures previously described, comparisons would be made between experimental and natural groups that occupy various points on the group love-hate continuum.

5. Another issue that medieval group experience crystallizes for contemporary research is the type of emotional constellations that are involved in absorptive, collectivized groups as compared with those at the more autonomous, loosely knit end of the coalescence scale. In the former case, as with medieval groups, there may be greater collective emotionality and responsiveness to images, emotional themes, slogans, superstitions, fantasies, etc. In general, these absorptive, transcendent groups have greater enthusiastic confidence in their beliefs or "fantasies" than do their opposites, and they evidence, as well, more emotional fluctuation response when their "illusions" and ideologies are fundamentally challenged. Comparisons between the two types of groups ought to be made in respect to fantasy appeals, power and frequency of superstitions, extent of emotional manipulation of reality, the use of symbols and rituals to satisfy varying needs for emotional support or security, and differing psychological manipulations used to maintain group morale and discipline.

So far as leadership is concerned, it may be speculated that absorptive groups (other than scientific or similarly objectively oriented and disinterested ones) have a more charismatic, emotional leadership, which is characterized by high responsiveness to collective psychological symbols and moods as well as by a greater capacity and disposition for using rituals, myths, or fantasies to manipulate groups. Leadership of the less "absorptive" groups probably involves less exploitation of emotional themes and complexes, is less concerned with unvarnished love, hate, superstition, and myth except during times of crisis, is more preoccupied with reality and objective experience, and is more interested in what is practical, tangible, and prudent than what may have the appearance of illusion, remote fancy, and hope. Studies of the differences between these opposite types of leaders should be made on corresponding historical and contemporary groups. In the case of experimentally composed groups (if these can be constituted), each of the postulated opposite-type leaders should be matched with each type of group (e.g., absorptiveless and absorptive) for purposes of comparison and control. Various ploys, frustrations, threats, loves, hates, hopes, kindnesses, cruelties, crises, and panic-provoking stimuli as well as slogans, myths, superstitions, emotional issues, inspirational incitements, etc. should be introduced into both types of group-leader combinations at varying stages of the group process. In addition, prudent courses of action, factual briefings, "reality" orientations, and practical suggestions should be introduced as possible options for each type of group to consider and adopt. All such "interventions" must be most subtly, diplomatically, and realistically accommodated to the spirit, milieu, and nature of the dynamics, structure, and proceedings of the group if they are to be at all meaningful and "realistic." Other assessment methods would include asking these "opposite-type" groups to interpret or resolve various situations embodying themes of a collective (subordination of individualism to the group mystique) or autonomous nature, as previously described. These would be presented to the antithetical-type groups in the form of role-playing, drama, or motion pictures and could be either in a completed or incomplete format. The responses of these groups to such portrayals would be continuously appraised throughout the presentations or the groups would be requested, afterwards, to resolve the dramatically presented problem, complete the incompleted plot, or analyze the issues of the role-playing sequence and, in all cases, make interpretations of the presented themes and propose solutions of the problems they involve.

The Medieval Ego

The main characteristics of the medieval ego were:

1. Extraordinary superstition and susceptibility to certain external signs and representations. This meant, among other things, intense responsive-

ness to objects, events, and symbols of any kind that could convey good or bad spiritual meanings such as were involved in redemption, damnation, sin, grace, and the unceasing struggle between God and the devil. A very large number of events or things were also interpreted as boding either good or bad fortune for the person concerned or for others. This was because so much of life was lived in hope, wish, and fantasy, the content of which was imbued with the morality and imaginary prospect of good or evil, that a great deal of ritual, imagery, and dramatic occurrences was required to sustain and give meaning to these aspirations and dreams. Hence the emphasis on symbolism, superstition, miracles, omens, portents, and irrational experience. These "symbolic" events or things were interpreted as signifying God's will, as reaffirming the existence of paradise, as warning of perdition, and as conveying some illuminating bit of knowledge about the cosmic scheme or the universal conflict between God and the devil. Accordingly, the ego's responses to these "signs" would variably be anxiety, panic, hope, encouragement, elation, and reassurance together with the employment of those remedies and mitigants that medieval society provided for disturbed feelings and convictions: holy rituals, sacraments, and priestly solace. Inevitably, when these were not effective, terror, rage, or exaggerated anxiety resulted.

2. The medieval ego was collectively infused and group directed. It was scantily concerned with individualistic sentiments or rational critical viewpoints except those stipulated as legitimate by the prevailing monolithic ideology or the pertinent medieval group. Most of its dispositions or interests were given expression in the forms of religious or group fantasies and defenses that were either unconsciously projected into collectively certified demons, horrors, and paragons or intropunitively channeled into radical asceticism, guilt, masochism, etc. The ego's capacity for rational doubt or dissent was suppressed, punished, or weakened by the inculcation of sin and ensuing guilt or by the required penance and subsequent renunciation of the sinful dissent. Though free intellectual activity and personal self-expression were permitted in certain areas, complicated rules and prescriptions were developed to channel them into preformulated theological categories. Indeed, there were the greatest limitations placed on uninhibited individualism, on the expression of impulses and sentiments unless they had predictable reference to collective values, on the freedom to question whatever and whenever one was inclined to, and on the liberty to take a different position from that legitimized by the absolutist ideology of the medieval "establishment."

3. The medieval ego was sustained to a very considerable extent by wish fulfillment, fantasy, nebulous hopes, and the ideology and emotional

support of the Church. Consequently, its character was basically optimistic, felicitous, and capable of tolerating an enormous amount of material frustration. Material and practical objects or considerations did not preeminently matter to it in view of the numerous spiritual, religious, and altruistic compensations that the medieval world offered. It was, in large degree, by means of the vast, intricate, and richly textured system of medieval symbolism, ritual, and imagery that these ego convictions, values, and identities were sustained. Additional support was rendered by the feeling that earthly life and experience were also touched by a scintilla of divine grace and that even within its compass, participation in the sublime was possible. These sentiments together with the firm expectation that perfect bliss irrevocably awaited one on entry into heaven evoked a rarified, inner spiritual exaltation in men that made them bear a harsh and difficult mundane life more easily.

4. Inherent in the medieval ego were also the "spontaneous" qualities of charity and goodness, as well as the capacity to sublimate envy, anxiety, greed, and bitterness into altruism or benevolence. These characteristics were spectacularly seen in the acts of saints and other holy men or less dramatically in the everyday practice and praise of altruism and goodness. Often as a result of the practice of these qualities came feelings of happiness and virtue together with a sense of holiness, sanctity, and sharing in a divine eminence. All this, in turn, made the practitioner of altruism and compassion feel that he was far above the trivial, petty, and demeaning emotions that were the mark of a baser species of men: those who had not been touched by divine goodness and grace. Such an orientation enormously enhanced medieval man's ego strength, his identity as a benevolent and spiritually elevated human being, and his feeling of being unscathed by human or material hardship because he had experienced this divine contact.

5. Abetting the equanimity and sense of well-being that characterized the medieval ego was the stabilizing character of medieval society. The permanent social and economic positioning of individuals was internalized in the ego as a rigid psychic stability and security and as an absence of ambition for personal status and material acquisitions. As a consequence, there was also a muting of related anxieties, frustrations, and invidious comparisons. Duplicated in the ego, also, and in harmony with the image of the social environment were attitudes of positive self-regard, diminished feelings of competitiveness, absence of overweening pride, and low concern with acquisitiveness or worldly ambitions. The ego's commitments, reflecting medieval aspirations, were to spiritual values, good deeds, and benign sympathy. By virtue of these internalizations, the

medieval ego was infiltrated with a holy sense of security and a gentle self-complacency—stimulated, too, by the omniscient theology of the Church and the certainty of ultimate grace and salvation. All these influences further cultivated in the ego the qualities of felicitous resignation, self-worth, optimism, selfless task commitment, and unequivocal dedication to the prevailing social system and the life it nurtured.

6. The ego's fund of emotional and cognitive security, hope, tranquility, fortitude, and buoyancy was additionally augmented by the symbols and images of Christiandom, by myth, superstition, and religious ritual, by the prospect of the afterlife, by the ever-present redemptive and beatifying example of sainthood and martyrdom, and by the dramatic "occurrence" of miracles. These environmental models, through internalization, imitation, and other forms of social learning, became powerful influences on the ego if not constituent parts of it.

7. In return for abandonment of freedom of thought and expression, the collective image of society and religion came to claim those functions of the ego that, since the Renaissance, have been the domain of individuality and self-fulfillment. In compensation for this truncated individuality, there was substituted a rich and complex tapestry of collective ritual, myth, archetypes, images, and rules. At the cost of abandoning personal choice and fulfillment, a collective social code of previously determined norms and prescriptions infused the ego and had enormous stabilizing, fulfilling, and beneficent effects on it. In part, this was because, when it internalized ego structures and practices, this code satisfied many individualistic needs and impulses. Thus religious ritual or ceremonial and religious art and architecture satisfied certain aesthetic and emotional needs; Christian theology indulged needs for hope, order, and psychological security both in the present and afterlife; Thomist logic and science fulfilled ego needs for rational understanding and control as well as for intellectual curiosity. The collective mental ideology and standards that supplanted the would-be individualistic ego's independent, rational, and empirical processes and curiosities was a remarkably interdigitated system that provided enormous psychological and intellectual security, a comprehensive world picture, and a monolithic perspective in which men could completely lose themselves. Such an ideology supplied the fortitude and understanding to enable men to cope with the mysteries and dangers of life and offered an ideal world of spiritual justice, altruistic love, and hope to which men could benignly and happily commit themselves while submerging in it their own frustrated rational and individualistic desires.

8. Participation in a society partially oriented to spiritual goodness,

love, and identification with a powerful governing Church and its theological models of altruism and spirituality gave the ego a sense of deep involvement in an exalted and supremely important enterprise. It experienced a sense of full participation in medieval life and a harmonious integration with it through performance of good deeds, engagement in ecclesiastical rituals, harboring of spiritual feelings and benign sentiments, full conviction in the teachings of the Church, and even in mere "followership" of medieval behavioral norms. Through such an experience of involvement and social identity, the ego achieved a harmony of elevated purpose and exhilarated commitment with the Christian world. This bestowed on it, in turn, additional resources of fortitude and strength, gave it serenity and dignity in vital spiritual areas of life, and infused it with self-feelings of love and respect.

RECTIFICATION

It is clear that one of the important rectifying requirements for contemporary work on the ego should be the assessment and, if necessary, introduction of medieval ego qualities in experimental and naturalistic research designs. Studies should be made of individuals in different situations who are immersed in the kindness and loving sympathy of others. In experimental studies the S should emanate decency and altruism. The conventional and "scientifically" honored procedure of utilizing an impersonal, cold "laboratory" to present stimuli or "tests" to the S in the course of existentially meaningless or noncomprehended experimental situations should be changed to a more sympathetic and altruistic orientation. There should be a major development of studies in which the investigated issues are decent respect, fairness, intelligent sympathy, altruism, and warmth. Indeed, if the E were only to show consideration for the S's welfare and if he were but to incite kind and benign feelings in him, it is not impossible that different results would come out of "ego research" than are presently being found. The mere fact that the E has a warm smile or that he neither acts coldly nor mysteriously to the S may very well produce different findings from an experiment that was identical in all respects but for these factors. Further, if the experimental room were decorated and furnished in the spirit and motif of the medieval period and if every step of the experiment, from the initial invitation of the S to participate to the completion of the research "directions" given to him, were conducted in a spirit and atmosphere of brotherhood, gentleness, and consideration, it is entirely probable that surprising experimental results would ensue.

The substantive content of the "ego experiment" itself should also be radically reevaluated. Such variables as appreciation, benign satisfaction, spiritual delight or fulfillment, love, warm acceptance, and inner felicity should be introduced into contemporary research studies. By contrast, such variables as aspiration, envy, ambition, and competition should be proportionately diminished.

Such conditions are not easy to implement in present-day experiments and the following proposals are made with recognition of the numerous obstacles and traps to be avoided before optimal effects can be achieved.

1. The S may be made to feel benign, hopeful, kindly, or "spiritual" in a series of social and personal medieval-like orientations, interactions, contacts, influences, and environments before the actual experiment begins. These would include religious inspiration whether evoked by sermons, readings, discussions, or mystic experiences; participation in an elevating altruistic project; experiencing a deeply moving idealistic vision or hope. Such preexperimental orientation may also include appropriate role-playing of medieval traits and the use of proper medieval-like models (those who embody a deep spiritual, mystic, or benevolent image and experience of life, be they living persons, historical figures, or characters from literature) to incite the S to the activation and practice of any medieval-like qualities he may latently possess or to influence him to acquire such qualities through the emulation of these model figures. To the same end would be employed dramatic productions, medieval readings, mood inductions appropriate to the medieval temper or spirit, participation in medieval-like scenes or tableaux, and an array of other procedures, psychodramas, and actions in the exercise of medieval-like mentality and qualities. In some contemporary natural situations it might be possible to find conditions approaching goodness, gentleness, altruism, compassion, and other aspects of the medieval milieu. Such situations should be systematically investigated for their possibilities in influencing certain prospective Ss toward various dimensions of a medieval-like orientation. Among them would be the environment of certain orders of priests and nuns, the formerly benign Haight-Ashbury situations, the few utopian communities remaining in this country, certain of the "new" communes, and other altruistic, warm, or compassionate religious and benevolent situations or environments.

2. Various social situations and interactions can be created in which there are disappointments and difficult choices to be made, where harassment or depreciation is manifest, where the S must subordinate himself and his views to others, or where he gets little or no reward for vigorous effort, commitment, and productivity. Such "conditions" would

be presented naturalistically or experimentally after the S had been exposed to the previously discussed medieval-like orientation. Results would then be compared with matched conditions without such orientation. Among the behavioral reactions to be appraised would be envy, anger, hope, tranquility, altruism, capacity to sustain effort and work, detachment, scapegoating, self-depreciation, benign feelings, etc. Further, these same frustrating "test" conditions should be studied in milieux that abound in benign feelings, sympathy, and gentleness, i.e., in environments that convey a medieval-like atmosphere, in comparison with the "hard," cold, research environments typically used.

What types of subjects should be studied in the experimental situations to be created? They would be selected from among gentle, altruistic, mystic, compassionate, and spiritual persons including dedicated humanitarians, mendicant religionists, Zen Buddhists, those imbued with spiritual or transcendent bliss, deeply serene individuals, and otherwise spiritually exalted ones. For purposes of comparison, another group of Ss would be chosen from the opposite end of this spectrum including the toughest, shrewdest, and most materialistic, practical, manipulative persons. Overall, the Ss for both groups would be selected from among those in the following fields: nonviolent civil rights workers, social reformers, ministers, humanitarians, monks, "flower people," philosophers, pacifists, businessmen, policemen, newspapermen, military men, engineers, politicians, accountants, lawyers, and bankers.

3. Studies should be made of actual historical and contemporary persons whose character, ideology, conduct, or values variously fall into the medieval-like pattern. Saints, monks, benevolent persons, benign philanthropists, certain reformers, some social workers, some nonviolent members of the peace and integration movements, certain dedicated physicians and nurses, some of the "flower people" and former hippies of Haight-Ashbury or similar districts, and some of the Fellowship of Reconciliation membership should be studied in respect to spiritual courage, fortitude, equanimity under stress, hope, capacity for love, inner happiness, warmth of personality, spirituality, altruism, compassion, serenity, lack of envy, greed, or personal ambition, and maintenance of values despite privations and obstacles.

The personal genesis of these behaviors as well as the personality structures from which they emanate should be investigated. What is the cost in time, material possessions, and personal interests for these behaviors to be sustained? How much authentic love lies behind each of them? Subtle distinctions between the numerous types of altruism, love, goodness, warmth, sympathy, compassion, etc. must be explored. Altruism, for example, might be mainly determined by the need to sustain a self-image of kindness, be nurtured by a narcissistic satisfaction in being good, be derived from guilt and reaction formation, be motivated by the need to get gratitude, esteem, and status recognition from others, stem from the desire to influence, oppress, or demean others, spring from a genuine desire to unselfishly enhance the condition of the other without psychological or material benefit for oneself, emanate from a deep, warm flow of love toward the world, spring from a desire to see all living things grow and blossom as well as being rejuvenated oneself by such an experience, stem from the deepest of compassions embracing a vast sensitivity to suffering and oppression in others with the ensuing need to ameliorate their condition, originate from a reverence for life as expressed in the fostering of health and happiness of others or, finally, emanate from a desire for wholeness and balance of people in general as well as of life itself. Scheler [4] has made a comparable analysis of sympathy and Bernard Rosenthal [5] has done the same for compassion.

All these and other medieval-like characteristics should be studied in a multitude of behavioral areas: relations between friends, strangers, groups, and in the effects of remote or impinging institutions on individuals; in the realm of money matters and during various intervals of the day, week, season, or year; in such areas as work and leisure and in enterprises or projects of various kinds.

Issues requiring further exploration are whether the performance of or predisposition toward these altruistic or other medieval-like acts causes their executor to feel more expansive, strong, happy, elevated, warm, tranquil, loving, resistant to frustration, spiritual, generous or hopeful as well as instigates in him a reduction of pettiness, rancor, concern with materialistic and concrete matters, pessimism, envy, and greed.

To be investigated, too, is whether these benign qualities have a reciprocal effect on those to whom they are addressed: Does it make them more generous, tranquil, content, hopeful, friendly, encouraged, energetic, self-loving, and self-respecting? Has it no effect at all or, perhaps, some contrary and debilitating impact? Here, historical, sociological field studies, and psychological case studies would be valuable. The types and degrees of such benign acts should be examined in respect to (1) the effects they have on recipients in various historical periods, social classes, and religious groups, (2) the value system, personality structure, and state of personal needs of the benefactee, and (3) the specific sociopsychological circumstances and situations in which these acts are carried out. Certainly the effect of a beneficent act on its recipient (and its instigator) would be different in an age of kindliness or sympathy than in an age of materialism and individualistic ambition. And, similarly, its effects would vary with different social classes, ethnic groups, economic organizations, social milieux, sociopsychological interactions, social norms, etc. All this should be studied in careful and diverse ways: opinion polls, meticulous social observations, historical records and writings, newspaper reports, biographies, clinical case studies, travelers' chronicles, novelists' or essayists' accounts, intensive interviewing, and experimental approaches and manipulations in both laboratory and natural situations.

Experimental interventions in naturalistic situations would include the following: Beneficent projects could be set up in schools, lodges, communities, industries, etc.; altruistic persons would be introduced into sundry groups or communities to inculcate and act as models for benign behaviors; subgroup microcosms of altruism might be interjected into certain groups by means of indoctrinating a few persons, through some sponsored humanitarian program, through general social pressure, or through bonus-premium or prestige-gain plans that encourage benign actions. Medieval-like oriented consultants on altruism and love could also be introduced into various situations.

In the case of laboratory situations, special kindness and benevolence should be demonstrated by the experimenter, his agents, or the S's friends and acquaintances when he is participating in an "ego" experiment. A benign climate and spirit should permeate the experimental environment: Apparatus should be removed or concealed, questionnaires should be administered with consideration, and personal concern should be expressed in response to the S's apprehensions and interests. The E's agents and, if possible, the subject's friends, whether in or out of the laboratory situation, should express encouragement and optimism, radiate calm, and supply understanding and hope to the S.

The relation between the E's attitudes and the S's feelings during and after the experiment proper must be assessed. Does the E's benevolence and that of the experimental atmosphere make the S feel kinder, more serene, and happier? Does it enhance his self-esteem, optimism, and warmth or, to the contrary, does it make him feel tense, uncomfortable, hypocritical, or even angry? How do its effects compare with those of the conventional treatment he usually is given? Some of this assessment could be done by interviews, by observations in and after the experiment, and by clinical introspections. The Ss' responses should be weighed in terms of their senses of identity and reciprocation of feelings with the E as well as in terms of the similarities of their ego structures and sentiments.

165

Carefully appraised should be the effects on the S of differences, however subtle, in the behavior or role of the E during the experiment: * varieties of kindness the latter displays, objective or sympathetic interest he exhibits, relaxed or casual attitudes he reveals, etc. Also, groups of friends, peers, colleagues, and other types of aggregates might be transferred to the laboratory for participation in "ego" experiments and for the study of processes similar to the above. Analogous studies can be carried out in the context of a class project, a club meeting, an athletic group contest, or other relevant and personally significant enterprise.

Differential effects of short-time, superficial, or episodic benevolent feelings, atmospheres, and actions should be evaluated. In the case of actions and sentiments, for example, a brief smile, a friendly word or gesture, a timely entrance into a warm room, a cordial joke, the brief sight of a mother alleviating a child's pain or a stranger spontaneously helping a destitute person should be assessed to determine their effects on the S.

To determine the effects on the S's of all the foregoing medieval-like influences or interventions (both short- and long-term) in naturalistic situations, methods of assessment will be needed beyond those already specified for formal experimental studies. These would include records of the S's behavior in a reasonable time period before and after the study. The behavioral report would include number of kindnesses, harshnesses, rudenesses, upsets, periods of calmness or ease, and the duration of feelings of love, happiness, and optimism. Standardized personality inventories or behavior checklists, various picture and projection tests, and detailed reports of the S's behavior as observed by friends, family members, and associates would also be utilized.

4. Another crucial neglected area of study is the role that values (transcendent, religious, spiritual, and moral), idealism, and exalted hope play in the dynamics of the individual ego. During the medieval period, it was identity with a world Church, a sense of divinity, the experience of spiritual felicity, belief in the afterlife, and the immersion of the self in a benign, beatific value system that induced sanguine and salutary feelings and gave the ego strength, resilence, optimism, benevolent expansiveness, and serenity.

Historically, the effects of all varieties of such transcendent, "do-good," spiritual, or idealistic value systems and ideologies on the individual ego ought to be assessed. Have they made the ego stronger, more expansive, warmer, kinder, more hopeful, tranquil, or humble? In these and other respects, how do they compare with the influences that materialistic,

* Robert Rosenthal [6] has already carried out in certain areas many of the studies proposed here.

secular-oriented, self-interested, and acquisitive values have had on the ego? Further, are altruistic persons (saints, "do-gooders," spiritual people, humanitarians, everyday benevolent individuals) or even nonmaterialist, nonpower-oriented persons superior in these respects to those who have opposite values? Historical records, chronicles, biographies, novels, case studies, contemporary accounts, and other pertinent documentation would be useful in answering these questions.

It is imperative to distinguish the varieties of transcendence, idealism, and "do-gooding" in their effects on the ego. Clearly those kinds that are inspired by the Enlightenment are different from those of religious, spiritual, or mystic nature; those idealisms that authentically express some variety of interpersonal or universal benevolence should be distinguished from those that largely have a tangible societal purpose; and, as previously specified, there are a number of different psychologically motivated kinds of altruism with, doubtless, corresponding different effects on the egos harboring them.

Further, the personal motivations and specific roles that participants have in altruistic movements are vital in determining the particular influence that benevolent sentiments and ideologies have on the ego. Administrators in such movements are affected differently from activists in the field and followers differently from initiators; founders are differently influenced than their successors and those who become involved largely for reasons of personal power, status, or achievement are differently affected than those to whom participation signifies a deeply felt conviction and concern. Further, those who use such altruistic movements or value systems to resolve personal problems, assuage guilts, etc. are influenced quite differently from those to whom such enterprises represent a vital center of their personal identity.

5. Another important issue is to determine the historical, social, and psychological conditions under which medieval-like experiences occur as well as the conditions under which they have persistent effects on the "experiencer." Do such experiences occur more frequently in youth, middle age, or later life, during personal experiences of elation, depression, serenity, or grief, at times of affluence, poverty, or adversity, and during historical periods of wealth, stability, exuberance, discontent, poverty, turmoil, or decline? Under which specific sociopsychological conditions do these experiences have persistent effects on the "experiencer" and under which do they not: during personal crisis, in periods of spirituality and idealism, at times of loneliness and alienation, during periods of prosperity or adversity, etc.?

6. To "experimentally" evoke various medieval-like ego states in the

167

S in order to evaluate their psychological, aesthetic, and spiritual properties as they actually emerge, the following experiences may be useful: exposure to art of a spiritual, altruistic, or mystic nature; listening to exalted and religious music; reading novels with medieval themes and spirit; walking in a forest while in sympathetic resonance with nature or empathically responding to the serene beauty of a starry night; exposure to suffering, injustice, or hardship and to what should be done to redress such injury and anguish; attending a particularly moving religious ceremony (or sermon) or "going through" a deeply personal religious experience, both of which may evoke certain aspects of the basic humility, compassion, and quiet love of medieval-like ego states; intimate exposure to the lives, feelings, and thoughts of great saints, mystics, and humanitarians, including St. Francis, Ghandi, a particularly dedicated, altruistic physician, and other extraordinary kind and gentle persons whose beliefs and lives are chronicles of benevolence, compassion, and love; viewing a drama that inspires its audience to hope, spirituality, or compassion; reading certain poems by Blake or essays by Tolstoy; watching a movie about the work of Schweitzer, Helen Hull, or the Abbé Pire; hearing a lecture by Martin Luther King, Jr. Provided such procedures encourage or activate some aspects of latent medieval-like ego states, if only for a day, a few hours, or even a few minutes, they will have furnished a chance for appraisal of some of their dimensions.

Perhaps in more persons than is presently known, there is a sympathetic response to such stimuli, or, at least, a passive appreciation of them. Even if such "sympathetic understandings" occur only in fantasy or other marginal and latent realms of the psyche, it is not impossible that they may be empathically evoked at certain times in response to altruistic heroes, noble humanitarians, selfless religionists, underdogs and the maltreated, benign or magnanimous actions, grave injustices, and spiritual or mystic atmospheres. These latent sympathic responses will manifest themselves in a myriad of manifest, subtle, and obscure ways which it will be the task of research to uncover.

In the laboratory, how can the nature of these medieval-like ego states be investigated? First, by making the studies as meaningful, purposive, authentic, and naturalistic as possible. This means introducing projects and behavior processes as integral phases of the laboratory environment, e.g., "do-good" and "reform" activities; spiritual meditation and mystic insight; establishment of warm relationships between subjects and between subjects and the experimenter. In these kinds of laboratory contexts and as part of various research designs, the S would be infused with a sincere concern for the cultivation of medieval-like values, for an inner meaning or spiritual identity in his personal life, or for a vital altruistic morality and activity. Some of this might be accomplished by making the laboratory a setting to rediscover the latent "medieval" facets of the ego through reflection, reading, artistic experience, discussion, mystic experience, and certain kinds of group immersion.

In such laboratory studies of the latent "medieval-like" ego, the distinctive features of the atmosphere must be serenity, felicity, hope, warm altruism, and spiritual sensibility. The E's attitude should project a sense of high and dedicated purpose, a tranquil optimism of how "things work out for the best," an intuitive grasp of the elevated, happy aspects of experience, an inner warmth, and a benign altruism as regards people and experience. This can be facilitated by individuals in the laboratory being engaged in medieval-like pursuits and behaviors. Humility, serenity, and courage should be in abundant evidence and kindness and encouragement manifestly apparent through the course of the experimental sessions. It is important that at least some of the "introduced" stress and adversity that the S may have to undergo in these research situations should be part of a compassionate, spiritually elevating, or humanitarian project or activity that approximates the spirit and the psychological significance of medieval-like functioning. Also, it might be useful to compare studies of frustration and adversity in such medieval-oriented activities with studies of these same variables in the context of the activities employed in contemporary ego research.

7. In various of the medieval-like ego types, there will likely be important weaknesses that, however, are different from those characteristic of nonmedieval egos. It may be that the most religious or spiritually oriented egos cannot so easily solve concrete, practical problems or so expeditiously deal with "realistic" issues as the most pronounced nonmedieval egos can. To such egos, these "practical" problems—primarily involving status, survival, power, or materialistic concerns and often requiring the subordination of fairness, decency, or morality for their solution—are cognitively alien, irrelevant, or meaningless. Nevertheless, in order to implement medieval-like altruistic and "spiritual" programs or to achieve idealistic goals it may be necessary to be toughly oriented to external facts and social reality, to occasionally downgrade people and morality, or to hurt those one cares about. To assess these issues, naturalistic and historical studies should be made of events in which hard, unkind, practical actions had to be taken in order to achieve idealistic goals but where morality, sympathy, and decency exerted an opposing influence. For example, certain reform, humanitarian, and spiritual movements have not been "realistic" enough about power, vanity, greed, fear,

or hostility and have consequently failed; certain altruistic persons have been indiscriminately tolerant or generous and, thereon, have not taken effective, "ungenerous" action when required for the attainment of their altruistic goal or have not maintained sufficient control over a situation to achieve their benign ends. Such altruistic types have often been too optimistic and trustful of virtue and decency in others and insufficiently aware of malevolent and other "negative" qualities in men. Often, too, benign men have underestimated the agonies of and resistances to beneficial personal and social change or the harsh action required to transform old institutions, social patterns, scientific orientations, or personal responses to more salutary ones. Historically, numerous religious and utopian cults have foundered on these illusions, miscalculations, and human foibles. Illustrative of this dilemma are the cases of certain noble, untainted scientists, social idealists, and poets who have lacked the toughness and practical sense to implement their high purpose. Studies of the lives of such persons with respect to the problems of executing hard, cunning actions (means) to achieve altruistic or other idealistic ends should be undertaken.

But the converse issues are equally important. When do reformers dedicated to freer, more equitable, and more altruistic societies give into venal and power inclinations or pressures, divert or dilute their ideals, and become preoccupied with establishing their own tight, disciplined networks? When do scientists begin to zealously bias their perspectives and select their experiments to support or augment their vested concepts or special scientific commitments irrespective of opposing evidence or more comprehensive alternatives? How frequently do earnest idealists with the grandest moral passion (pacifists, religionists, and humanitarians) employ dishonesty, cruelty, distortion, and comparable means to gain their ends? And how often do ostensibly gentle and decent persons, whether through lack of knowledge, courage, awareness, empathy, and vital concern or, alternatively, out of expediency, vanity, latent power needs, conformity, or some other personal and selfish pressure become cruel and callous or fail to redeem their often repeated moral and altruistic pledges?

Naturalistic studies should assess these issues, particularly in dedicated and idealistic persons who confront alien values or brute pressures and in exactly those situations where ideals demand one position and practicality demands another. An example of such dilemmas are those humanitarian movements or altruistic enterprises that are bold and imaginative but not ruthless enough to remove negative diehards, strong enough to resolve factionalism, or cunning enough to build, by venal, organizational, or other expedient means, strong and continuing support for their own salutary, benevolent policies.

In this perspective, certain studies can be suggested: A debate on the general issue of morality and expediency can be staged for the S, or specific moral dilemmas can be presented to him in the form of biographies, movies, or historical incidents. The S would be assessed for his understanding of, his identification with, and his resolution of such a general or specific moral issue or some particular facet of it. For example, should one, to preserve the principle of "openness" in a group, accept everybody into it, thereby incurring the risk that some of those admitted might threaten the existence of the "open" spirit itself. Another issue would be that of the scientist or scholar who must choose between carrying on research with high integrity and purpose or, by trimming, conventionalizing, or otherwise making it "acceptable" would complete it quickly, thereby securing recognition and, perhaps, a research contract. Such moral dilemmas can be presented in the form of actual historical episodes, stories, essays, dramatic sketches, role-playing, debates, and case studies (hypothetical or real) of various persons or groups. Methods for assessing the S's identifications and preferences for a given moral or expedient position under these conditions have been previously discussed. Such preferences and identifications may also be studied by placing the S in natural situations involving these dilemmas—or observing him in situations where they spontaneously occur—so that he must make a decision, take some action, and subsequently explain the reasons for doing so.

In the laboratory the following proposals could be carried out: various real social challenges and tasks that require the utmost integrity of conviction and unequivocal altruistic commitment would be presented to the S who would have to choose from a range of solutions or actions varying from the most honest, selfless, altruistic, and noble to those marked by self-serving, compromising, or expedient motives and behavior. For another study, a project would be undertaken by the S in which he would be given the choice of (1) doing it in a short time by either adopting an idea that was second rate or by otherwise adulterating the project's conception and plan for execution or (2) of taking the more honest and superior approach which, however, was more uncertain as to the time required for completion, would present greater obstacles to overcome, would entail a goodly risk of failure, and, if successful, would win little, if any, more reward or appreciation than if the easier option had been followed. Such studies may be carried out with benign, altruistic, and selflessly dedicated persons as compared with those not having such qualities or having quite opposite ones.

171

REFERENCES

1. Aristotle. *The Basic Works of Aristotle,* ed. by Richard McKeon. New York: Random House, 1941.
2. Aquinas, Thomas. *Summa Theologica.* Chicago: Encyclopedia Britannica, 1955.
3. Blake, William. "Auguries of Innocence" in *The Portable Blake.* New York: The Viking Press, 1946.
4. Scheler, Max. *Wesen und Formen der Sympathie.* Bonn: Cohen, 1923.
5. Rosenthal, Bernard G. "The Psychology of Compassion," *The Human Context,* forthcoming.
6. Rosenthal, Robert. *Experimental Effects in Behavioral Research.* New York: Appleton-Century-Crofts, 1966.

GENERAL REFERENCES

Aquinas, Thomas. *Summa Theologica.* Chicago: Encyclopedia Britannica, 1955.

Augustinus, Aurelius, St. *The Confessions of St. Augustine,* and Kempis, Thomas A., *The Imitation of Christ.* New York: Collier, 1909.

Barker, E. "Unity in the Middle Ages," in Francis Sydney Marvin, ed., *Unity of Western Civilization.* New York: Milford, 1915.

Barnes, Harry Elmer, with David, Henry. *The History of Western Civilization.* New York: Harcourt, Brace, 1935.

Boring, E. G. *A History of Experimental Psychology,* rev. ed. New York: Appleton-Century, 1950.

Clarke, Maude V. *The Medieval City State.* New York: Barnes & Noble, 1926.

Faure, Elie. *History of Art.* New York: Harper, 1921–1930.

"Feudalism," "Land Tenure," and "Manorial System" in Edwin R. A. Seligman, ed., *Encyclopedia of the Social Sciences.* New York: Macmillan, 1930–1935.

Freiss, Horace Leland, and Schneider, Herbert Wallace. *Religion in Various Cultures.* New York: Johnson Reprint, 1965.

Gardner, Helen. *Art Through the Ages.* New York: Harcourt, Brace, 1926.

Gwatken, H. M., ed. *The Cambridge Medieval History.* New York: Macmillan, 1911–1936.

Hayes, C. J. H. *Political and Cultural History of Europe.* New York: Macmillan, 1932–1936.

Heaton, Herbert. *Economic History of Europe.* New York: Harper, 1936.

Herr, Friedrich. *The Medieval World.* Cleveland: World, 1962.

Marcuse, Herbert. *One Dimensional Man.* Boston: Beacon Press, 1964.

Montalembert, Charles F. R. *Monks of the West from St. Benedict to St. Bernard.* London: Blackwood, 1861–1869.

Mumford, Lewis. *The Condition of Man.* New York: Harcourt, Brace, 1944.

Murphy, Gardner. *Historical Introduction to Modern Psychology,* rev. ed. New York: Harcourt, Brace, 1949.

Pirenne, Henri. *Economic and Social History of Medieval Europe.* London: Kegen Paul, Trench, Truber, 1936.

Randall, John Herman. *The Making of the Modern Mind.* Boston: Houghton Mifflin, 1940.

Robinson, James Harvey. *The Mind in the Making*. New York: Harper, c. 1921.

Russell, Bertrand. *A History of Western Philosophy*. New York: Simon & Schuster, 1945.

Smith, Preserved. *A History of Modern Culture*. 1930. Reprint (2 vols). New York: Macmillan Company, Collier Books, 1962.

4
THE RENAISSANCE
❧

1. The Renaissance distilled for modern man a sense of passionate humanity, worldly enjoyment, and fully spectrumed fulfillment of individual impulse and potentiality. From it emerged in rich diversity the theme of multifaceted individuality as a fundamental goal of life and the unique organization and maximization of each person's talents, tastes, sensibilities, and appetites to that end. From it, also, in goodly measure came the powerful emphasis on empirical thought and action that so conspicuously marks the image of contemporary man.

By virtue of the fact that individuality was one cornerstone of Renaissance mentality, a basis was predicated for self-determination, self-knowledge, and self-realization. Democracy as a political and social process also flowed from such individuality in that it is only when men freely search out and express their interests that its functions can be optimally pursued. Much of this general orientation was attributable to an intense revival of humanism though the Renaissance accentuated those components that involved instinctual fulfillment, enjoyment of life, sensory gratification, delight in the efflorescence of the mind and feelings, and the indulgence of the sensual, artistic, and exploratory predilections of men.

The Renaissance image, then, was comprised in large measure of individual enjoyment and enrichment and the broadest diversity of human experience, sensibility, thought, and enterprise. From this generating vortex came the Renaissance qualities of enrichment and delight in sensual, artistic, literary, and conversational activities, desire for wealth and material possessions, subordination of an ascetic or altruistic morality to instinctual liberation, ingenious and subtle interpersonal manipulations interwoven with callousness and ruthlessness, and decorative splendor in dress, furniture, and physical accommodations. Attendant on these qualities came the appreciation of men who had the capacity to enrich visual, auditory, and other sensory or perceptual experiences: artists, craftsmen, musicians, writers, etc.

Though the Renaissance view of man differed from that of the Greeks in certain fundamental respects, it nevertheless affirmed some of man's most basic humanistic urges: in the arts, in originating and adventurous energy, in personal happiness, in the most far-flung exercise and refined development of the mind and senses, in a greatly increased consciousness of all life experience, feeling, and sensation, and in an enriched alertness to the full promise and exercise of being human itself. It is indeed ironic that the heritage of this image of man that has been passed down to present-day psychology has been in the form of a narrow concern with need reduction, instinctual gratification, reward of a largely external and materialist kind, and the influence of social approval.

If there is an ultimate essential theme of the Renaissance conception of man it is uninhibited individualism: the right of the person to be a law unto himself, particularly in artistic and aesthetic expressions, though it also applied to certain areas of science, politics, and morality. This doctrine, to some extent, also influenced modern psychology's views on the nature of individual needs and motives and on the unique constellation of abilities, predilections, and complexes that characterizes each person. At the time of the Renaissance, in contrast with the present period, this doctrine meant that the self-fulfillment of the individual was a chief goal of life which, in large measure, would be reached through a broad range of pleasure and expressiveness, of openness and adventurousness of mind and feeling, and by the exercise or indulgence of all one's sensory, perceptual, and mental functions.

In contrast, the doctrine of contemporary psychological individualism is substantially based on the notion of a well-functioning machine, marvelously synchronized with other machines, the individuality of each being adjusted to fit with or enhance the others. To this end, each machine's individuality must be adequately analyzed and plumbed, whereupon its "needs" or conditions for optimal functioning can then be fulfilled. However, satisfaction of the conditions leading to optimal functioning of the larger organizational whole (i.e., society or some other pertinent social unit) must take precedence over the individual needs and will determine their type and breadth of fulfillment as well as what particular individual needs will be required for such "optimal" organizational functioning.

In this view, individual needs are satisfied to "fit" the person into a social system as an efficient cog, to evoke his interest and satisfaction in doing a job, to aid him in conforming to the demands and stresses of

175

society or an organization, to reward this compliant adjustment with approbation and self-esteem, and, not infrequently, to identify this entire process as happiness. Parenthetically it should be noted that this contemporary psychological process of exciting the spirit, if but the counterfeit spirit, of individualism and not fulfilling it cultivates the soil of much conflict between individualistic aspiration and social conformity, elicits and then frustrates expressive and self-fulfilling urges, and induces unrealistic aspirations and confusion as to what constitutes authentic personal fulfillment and expression and what does not.

During the Renaissance men were inundated with symphonies of pleasure from sensations of sight, sound, touch, taste, and the carnal. Every experience was desirable, and each sensual or sensory whim was indulged with abandon. Renaissance art with its richness, delicacy, and exquisite manipulation of aesthetic and visual possibilities was itself a reflection of this passion for taste, feeling, exploration, artistic sensibility, and lust. In the large sense, any intense feeling, enthusiasm, or delight— were it curiosity, artistic activity, sexuality, or music—embodied or symbolized the Renaissance idea of high passion. By passion, too, was meant any overwhelming sensibility or feeling inherent in any aesthetic, affective, or intellectual activity. This could include conversation, thinking, scientific curiosity, interest in nature, and unfettered naturalness—all in their vast breadth and variety. Ideas, too, had their own passion, germination, gestation, and flowering, and thus it was during this period that all sorts of scientific, poetic, naturalistic, and artistic conceptions were played with or delighted in, not only as a reaction to the rigid control and over-discipline of the medieval intellectual temper, but as a rediscovery of the pleasure that came from uninhibited exercise of the mental functions and from being spontaneously human and natural. There was delight in the infinite explorations that could be made with the senses and other observational faculties, and pleasure that came with the discovery and understanding of the ways of nature and of natural man. Here the delights of curiosity came not so much from relentlessly putting the impersonal question of "why" to all phenomena nor from an Enlightenment-like passion for rational and systematic formulation, but more from the wonder and awe at nature itself and from an uninhibited fascination in the exercise and implementation of the intellect, of adventure, and of discovery. The pedantic need of the Church doctors to give rigid, systematic answers and to codify with hair-splitting arguments an a priori cosmology was not preeminent. Rather what marked the Renaissance spirit was a way of looking freshly or newly at things—and the headiness of that view was enormous. New questions could be posed based on phenomena observed with a refreshed and accessible eye, and without any inculcated blind spots obstructing naturalistic or scientific vision; the eye and ear were free to see whatever and however they could and the mind to wonder and to be curious at almost whatever or wherever it chose. Just as everything was grist for the mill of art, history, poetry, or pleasure, so almost anything could now be questioned, studied, or looked into to whet or satisfy one's curiosity. In this way natural phenomena and empirical realities became the meat and marrow of the new experience, the new science, the new outlook on life, and the basis for a resurgence of the vital experiencing and exploration of the human, animal, and physical world.

What cannot be emphasized too much is that all such scholarly and scientific explorations and studies were undertaken with ardor and enthusiasm: Scholarship was wonder and discovery; the "why" of such work was not to answer a moral or theological question nor primarily to illumine a preordained celestial plan. Rather it was the "why" of unfettered curiosity and delighted naturalistic wonder, of bold and uninhibited authentic observations without metaphysical interventions.

2. Consistent with this perspective was the dethroning of medieval morality with its inhibitions, collectivist priorities, fatalism, and highly developed sense of Christian goodness and decency. The indulgence of passion, adventure, and immediate experience represented the discarding of prohibitions on innumerable impulses and mental functions and also indicated, to a substantial degree, the deterioration of such moral obligations as fair treatment, compassion, and personal respect. Safeguards against the exploitations or the excess profits of certain institutions and economic practices were also withdrawn: for example guilds lost their protective economic control over labor and other "production" prerogatives, and usury was formally sanctioned. As a result of these and other developments, exploitation of the weak and impoverished vastly increased. Compassion became a foolish or vacuous vanity, and kindness, consideration, and altruistic love were put down as weaknesses of character, i.e., either as impractical acts or as perverse self-abnegations which could be used against their practitioners and thus mark them as targets for exploitation or domination. Further, the very great commitment of energy and time to indulgence of passion, adventure, and empiricism was such that little concern remained for moral conscience, consideration and compassion for others, humane collective values, or Christian love. Weakness, humility, adversity, poverty, and wretchedness were condemned—not only because deprivation and mortification were now considered to be "bad" or foolish —but also because compassion for the sufferings and weaknesses of others was no longer tolerable at a time of self-indulgence and self-assertiveness.

Appreciation or approval of altruism and humility could raise disturbing questions about the value of assertiveness, license, and personal ambition, could also arouse reservations to the view that self-indulgence and self-aggrandizement were desirable ways of life, and finally might disturbingly challenge the "new" view that anyone suffering hardship or privation could properly be charged with lack of talent, energy, strength, or other qualities necessary for prospering in the Renaissance milieu. Indeed, such questions were implicitly too threatening for they went ultimately to the question of power, to the problem of selfish indulgence for the few at the expense of the many and, in terms of moral criteria, seriously broached the issue of whether the edifice of privilege and the elite class should not be dethroned for the more equitable benefit of all.

For contemporary behavior, the offspring of this ethos has been a rampant economic individualism, a strong desire for appetitive and materialistic gratification, a dethroning of collective morality and the commitment to it for the sake of individual advantage, a spur to ego aggrandizement by means of fame, fortune, or singular achievement, and finally, a sanction for the individual to be as rugged or tough with others as possible, neither granting nor expecting compassion. Also deriving from this tradition was the conviction that self-enhancement by means of personal gain and advancement justified corruption, subterfuge, and exploitation of others. All such iniquitous practices had to be executed with great finesse to give the impression of propriety or even morality. Here was one of the great arts of the Renaissance: that while the moral conventions were seemingly complied with, the spirit of morality was lacerated and violations of decency and justice unceasingly abounded.

Independence, cunning, self-reliance, and toughness were part of this heritage. Reflecting this outlook is the fact that in contemporary psychological studies very little help is given to the S while his independence, resourcefulness, aggressiveness, and craftiness are constantly being challenged. And though there are rules of the game and rituals of social or economic transactions, the trick is to circumvent them without conspicuously violating them. What is relevant is that one gets what one wants by operating cleverly and deceptively, without evident transgression, rather than by the exercise of morality and decency. This lack of concern for scruple or for other's just rights and socioeconomic equities is partly based on the premise that each will be playing the ruthless, self-aggrandizing game which was a heritage of the Renaissance. "Getting away with it" is evidenced in contemporary business practices and, indeed, is covertly solicited in many psychological experiments and tests by placing premiums on ingenuity, cleverness, or cunning. Similarly, ethical considerations of what is right, of how an activity or solution may affect other persons, or whether a problem-solving orientation and goal is exclusively concerned with self-interest are hardly ever determining influences in contemporary psychological studies or tests. How to get it done, how to win, or how to solve it quickly are the issues. Any expedient or "reality" manipulation that will work, including cleverness, ingenuity, or shrewdness shading to artifice, become the condoned operations, derived in spirit from the Renaissance, subtly invoked in experimental situations, assessments, questionnaires, or in the covert procedures and manipulations of many studies—an unstated theme of which is the often complex and shrouded struggle between the S and society (the latter symbolized, in part, by the E and the manipulating scientific and bureaucratic establishment of which he is a part) as to who will prevail. The ingredients of this struggle are the mystery and tension of the experiment and the various pressures on the S; the conditions are that he must win something and that somebody may be putting something over on him in a somewhat "stacked" chess game while he, reciprocally, must outwit them. All this he must take in stride while proving his mettle and solving the tricky Renaissance-type psychological mystery puzzle. For it is true that the trickery and subterfuges of the modern psychological experiment, in some measure, are owing to the Renaissance's pleasure in and absorption with intrigue, deception, and success as well as to its preoccupation with making the mind as agile a mechanism as possible for the contrivance of intricate and veiled problems or the unraveling of them. Thus, the mystery of the experiment to the S is that of confronting a puzzle or of being involved both as a pawn and a player in a complex gambit—and thereon being manipulated, or alternatively manipulating, as adroitly as possible. Indeed, the Renaissance man—and his manipulating counterpart, the contemporary psychologist—used (or uses) the prevailing ethical values, emotional symbols, or potent slogans to fool others (including the S), to enlist their support when necessary, or to confound them into thinking that he (including the E) is honest, decent, has integrity, or is genuinely concerned with the honorable discharge of a stated or implicit commitment, moral and other. This contemporary manipulation or "confidence" game may be more complicated than the one of the Renaissance because one must presently carry on its transactions according to the fiction of "civilized" competition which embraces—much more than in the Renaissance—a complex and subtle code of counterfeit friendliness, amenities, and respect. The consequence is an inordinate manipulative and cynical use of morality and the embroidery of self-aggrandizing acts by counterfeit altruism, pious myths, and humane humbug. If one hopes to advance,

179

one must submit to the rules of this racketeering charade while, simultaneously, declining to authentically respect or morally credit them. If one is not constantly master of such intrigue and, at the same time, supremely aware that it is a "ritualized game," one falls into the limbo of internalizing these norms with cynicism, disgust, or apprehension which, in turn, often results either in a further depreciation of moral rules, in augmented, if concealed, self-disgust, or in anxiety about the operations of the "game," i.e., an exaggerated fear of losing it or a harboring of guilt for having internalized its rules. Consistent with this spirit is the covert and heavy "atmosphere" of many psychological studies, replete with gambits and deceptions, oppressive with anxiety, laden with values that are honored in speech and breached in devious action, fraught with subtle intimidations masquerading under "scientific instructions," and infused with urgency for success whether by means of subterfuge, desperation, Machiavellianism, animal shrewdness, or other survival mechanisms—all of these being disguised by superficial or counterfeit cooperation, cordiality, respect, and even independence.

Further, in experimental studies, by focusing on mental and biological urgencies, on stress, or on what essentially are "animal-like" hardships and frustrations, there is elicited a survival-oriented attitude state—quite in the tradition of those aspects of the Renaissance temper that embraced success-striving, fighting for survival, cunning alertness, and vigorous practical energy. The modern tradition of fighting to win by whatever tactics or faculties can be summoned is the heritage, in part, of this Renaissance complex and is embodied in many of the implicit proceedings of the contemporary psychological experiment, especially of the stress variety.

3. One of the distinctive characteristics of the Renaissance was the rediscovery of unfettered intelligence, of "openness" to experience, and of the powers of observation. This reawakening comprised, also, the reclamation of natural reason, curiosity, and empirical appraisal. In part, this represented the rediscovery of some aspects of Greek science and in part the revival of Greek humanism, i.e., a fascination with ancient Greek and Latin texts and their modes of observation and orientation to physical or human problems—without the burdens of scholasticism or morality. The Greek experience and mode of thought was immensely attractive to the Renaissance and its response was resonant and enthusiastic. The open examination of man's life and destiny and the naturalistic scrutiny of his character and capabilities were all revolutionary views for men accustomed to medieval ideologies. The rediscovery of ancient learning was the rediscovery of man, and for this reason Greek and Latin texts were avidly

devoured, particularly those concerned with humanity and letters. New experiments were carried out and natural phenomena were freshly observed and checked with classical authorities. Science as an empirical, naturalistic study was reborn. Mathematics was revitalized as an essential ingredient of the new science, and, without the restrictions of scholastic dogma, it could more easily formulate an exact system of relationships for whatever natural order was discoverable in the universe. Thus a great impetus for empirical study of this presumed order was provided together with the faith that further formulae and, indeed, a complete mathematical design systematizing it would eventually be uncovered. Via such orderly exploration, the ultimate secrets of the universe would be yielded up to the rational unfettered mind and thereby give it the power to understand nature as a predictable and controllable process.

The spirit of the Renaissance was permeated with the feeling that men could do almost everything, that the laws of the universe were within his grasp, and that by his discovery of them he could confirm that he was the master and center of all things. Such views confirmed men in an enormous self-conceit and in the irrevocable authority of their intellective powers, which, in turn, gave them an enormous sense of emancipation and exhilaration. Such exhilarated power and egotism inundated man's views of the universe and made of it an hospitable and indulgent place whose manipulation and exploitation for his benefit had been made possible by the "new" scientific and empirical orientation. With the acceptance of this direct sensory and perceptual experience and the intellectual freedom that the "new" orientation involved came a sense of intense reality or empiricism which, in time, came to supplant the previous a priori symbolic organization of perception and experience. A leaf was examined for what it was: in terms of physical and operational dimensions. It was not experienced as some "higher expression" of God's will, thereby confirming an antecedently revealed truth. Experiments and natural observations were now engaged in with insatiable curiosity and drive. There was the enormous zest of overthrowing anachronistic shibboleths, the relish of exploration, and the bona fide confirmation that things were as man found them—not inscrutable nor capriciously manipulated by an unidentifiable force more powerful and omniscient than himself. There was, as well, man's imperative obligation through work, resolution, ingenuity, imagination, and other human capacities to search out the universe's secrets. In substance, all of this emphasized what he could do by himself, by his own natural abilities, or, in short, by his nature as man. It placed a premium on observation, intelligence, logic, realistic orientation, resolution, and objective, pragmatic demonstration and proof.

If nature was susceptible to empirical investigation, so was man himself. He, too, was a natural phenomenon, subject to natural and physical forces as were other natural events and as much an appropriate object of scientific method and formulation as the other phenomena he studied. Thus man rediscovered himself as a natural object, one susceptible to observation and analysis by eye, ear, logic, intelligence, and imagination. He was not inscrutable or touched with divinity but rather deserving of the very highest intelligent curiosity and investigative insight.

Derivatives of the Renaissance scientific perspective retained in contemporary life include the faith in investigative research and mathematics, skepticism of dogma, and the conviction that man can know and, in time, control almost everything.

One aspect of contemporary psychology that reflects this tradition is the omnipotent expectation of fully understanding men by experimental research, testing, and statistical appraisal, and thus, ultimately, of being able to control him. It is true, however, that contemporary exaggeration and, indeed, distortion of these scientific ideas of the Renaissance can be substantially attributed to the era after the Industrial Revolution. Such a "scientism"—as it eventually evolved—which ultimately came to treat men as impersonal processes or objects, had its seed in the notion that all human phenomena could be as objectively and positivistically understood as any physical or nonhuman natural phenomena. Though the Renaissance treated this viewpoint with open-minded and often humanistic interest, the industrial age was to transform it into the tenet that man was, in fact, a "thing" or mechanical process and was therefore to be conceived of as a depersonalized physical or economic datum which was to be impersonally analyzed and manipulated for pragmatic or material purposes. And the master instrument of this intellectual enterprise, i.e., scientific method, was cumulatively transformed into an ice-cold, rational, investigative mechanism: ultimately without sentiment, ethic, or value and rather like a dissecting omniscient force—indeed the nineteenth- and twentieth-century equivalent of God. Such an orientation neglected to grasp that this hypertrophied investigative method might also be an agent of a parochial and mythical faith. This state of affairs has been particularly reflected in psychology's emphatic biases toward certain methods and phenomena of study and aversion towards others. To an indeterminate degree, this instrument became another way of organizing or, perhaps, of influencing human behavior—and man's understanding of it—and of permitting a value bias, concealed superficially by a rational and operational "scientism," to impose a specious type of mechanistic order and rationale on explanations of human experience.

The classic model of this value orientation—the experiment—is where the puzzle of man is dissected, simplified, and made to conform to orderly, determined behavioral rules and principles implemented under a priori frozen conditions. Thus the S is placed in those types of impersonal circumstances that permit derivation of ordered and simplified regularities of behavior though these may not be authentic expressions of the nature of human experience. One of the offshoots of this is the proliferation of interminably trivial and sterile researches contrived to achieve the highest "scientific purity" and "mythical" behavioral—and often only mechanical—order, however irrelevant, artificial, or specious these may be. Also flowing from these conditions is the treatment of the S as an impersonal object, mechanizing and restricting his potentiality of response into limited categories for more effective conformance with often preconceived behavioral symmetries. Some of this explains the rigid and orderly treatment of the S and the pressures for mathematical (mechanical) order in the design and execution of the studies themselves. A good deal derives, however, from the scientific models of Newtonian physics and from the mechanical image of man of the Industrial Revolution, both of which immensely influenced conceptualization and methodology of contemporary psychological science. Further, the restriction and simplification of the S's responses reflect the values of a bureaucratically and machine-oriented industrial society in which the goals of efficient mass production require strict control of response and conformance of behavior to an organizational system which, in effect, is the status quo. Thus the experiment—as a microcosm of the prevailing social and behavioral values of society—instigates a test of and, at the same time, fosters the S's tendency for "establishment-sanctioned," efficient, or "mathematically symmetrical" responses.

4. If some portmanteau term could be applied to the Renaissance, "humanism" or "humanness" would most aptly apply. The reawakening from the deadening of the Middle Ages was a reaffirmation that was carried on with gusto and without inhibition. All of it was a vast delight —these rediscoveries of men and the zest associated with them, and because their limits were not known, every possible sensation, experience, and feeling was an exciting prospect. This then was a search—without divine rationalization or religious sanctity—for a secular and animal awareness, for a consciousness of the vast range of sensations and talents that medieval theology had suppressed, for an empirical rationale of meaning, action, and purpose, and for a human significance and destiny that could not be reached with theological doctrine.

In sum, all this meant that man had become the center of things, that there could be rational answers to his problems, and that a uniquely human salvation could be achieved in his destiny through his own human capacity and energy. It was this humanism that would supply the basis for refining the faculties of the mind and personality to abet free inquiry, create beauty, indulge desires for adventure and enjoyment, and revitalize the idea that man could integrate his animal, intellectual, aesthetic and social dimensions into a rich and significant life. But, at the same time, by positioning man as the center of the universe and making his knowledge, vision, and power the keystone of his destiny, it gave him an egotistic and arrogant responsibility and laid down to him the vast challenge of finding "experimental" answers to the pressing problems of his life and the world, and of cultivating and employing all his capacities to that end. Thus it exposed him to a compelling search for a pragmatic or empirical security as well as for a cultural or intellectual domicile that, at times, left him in despair or confusion and, in part, accounted for the array of scientific researches, ideologies, urgent personal ambitions, social movements, materialistic preoccupations, and intellectual expressions that were efforts to fill the void consequent on emancipation from the medieval world view. Thus technical and scientific knowledge came to substitute for spiritual security, liberated indulgence in animal and sensory pleasures for the hope of eternal life and virtue, and materialistic striving or personal self-aggrandizement for a moral and cosmic perspective.

5. What passed down, in part, from the general Renaissance tradition when, in time, its values emphasized business more than art, manipulation over originality, acquisitiveness rather than enjoyment, and caution over self-expression was a premium on shrewdness, intrigue, and cleverness as traits desirable for the purpose of maneuvering and exploiting others. There can be no doubt that this was a vast narrowing of the rampant individualism of the high Renaissance with its broad emphasis on the rich personal fulfillment of talent, artistry, intelligence, and adventurousness. In this historical transformation, the qualities of intrigue, canniness and exploitation of others became, during later periods, one of the most prominent heritages of Renaissance individualistic values, while the vital spirit of self-actualization, self-expression, and artistry diminished in preeminence.

In contemporary psychology, intrigue and artifice are employed in the manipulation of the S and in the dissimulation that often characterizes the experimental situation. This takes the form of not presenting the whole truth to him, of employing specious incentives and false pretenses to motivate him and of ever so subtly, and with the veneer and justification of scientific research, brainwashing him by the tactics of oblique and direct coercion.[1] It means presenting problems to him by specious methods (group dynamics studies in which stooges and spies play the role of normal group members, unbeknownst to the S, or the administration of bogus intelligence tests to put the S off so that the E may study another process) so as to obtain something of profit for the entrepreneur-scientist: a significant result, a scientific paper, or another grant. In effect, this means that the S may be exploited, influenced, molded, oppressed, aggravated, or threatened for the advantageous purposes of the E.

One of the useful issues that had been increasingly clarified in recent research is whether this system of dissimulation, manipulation, and trickery is already known to the S and thereon evokes reciprocal defensive reactions which are as equally deceptive and manipulative as the E's contrivance of the experimental proceedings.[2] Further, there may be some validity in the contention that the E manipulates the S to fulfill the unverbalized role of the omniscient scientist or the powerful employee-administrator, the S being paid (in money, attention or some other reward) to produce responses and to come up with desirable or, at least, appropriate results. Thus the experimental process and its results may emerge, to some degree, as a corollary of an employer-employee or manipulator-manipulated relationship.

In contemporary psychological studies, the freedom of the S, though ostensibly permitted in certain kinds of open-ended interviewing and in certain latitudes permitted in a few experiments, more often than not does not occur. In these latter studies, the S is presumably made to feel respected, is treated quite well, and is often encouraged to be spontaneous and self-determining. In fact, however, he is often circumscribed by impediments, hidden punishments, and unspecified rewards. Moreover, the effect of such situations on the S is often conflicting and confusing. In part he is somewhat disposed to convince himself that he is really free and capable of actualizing his personal identity in the study, but he also knows that this is only within circumscribed limits and that a game of intrigue, manipulation, and invisible chess is going on that he must play. He must define freedom within those limits that the E overtly or implicitly sets so that he can decide whether to act defensively, obstinately, subordinately, or assertively. The struggle to retain his identity, to gain advantage, and to advance his interest through the processes of intrigue, submission, or deception is thus carried on in this microcosm of the larger world: the psychological experiment. The formidable fact is that certain Ss—in respect to personality, ideology, and values—are better attuned to this specific situational challenge than others. Thus

185

those who are generally sincere and deferent but indifferent to middle-class values of success or achievement may comply with the E's requirements, not caring enough about their participation in the study to exercise their courage and initiative in so trivial or limited a situation. Authentically individualistic self-actualizing Ss may openly rebel in these situations while others might see them as full of a potentiality which, however, is undermined by their oppressive conditions. The shrewd, devious, manipulative S, in contrast, may be the most effective person in this type of situation. These are, of course, the most heuristic typologies, but the salient point is that the results of research studies may reflect more the value system of the specific S and his attitudes toward the E and the experimental situation than any designated hypothesis that is ostensibly being tested in the study. Thus, if certain Ss behave differently from others this may simply represent a greater correspondence of values or sentiments between the spirit of the experimental situation, the E, and the S in these cases.

Conditions for Assessment of Renaissance Mentality

To implement an appraisal of Renaissance mentality in contemporary research, it is necessary to construct environments, atmospheres, and social interactions conducive to its emergence and functioning. To do this, physical environments that simulate those of the Renaissance should be developed. These would include rooms and anterooms that would be replete with Renaissance decorations, furniture, and richly sensual and elaborately constructed *objets d'art*. Renaissance music would be played and reproductions of some characteristic Renaissance paintings and statuary would be discriminatingly placed in these areas. The S would be allowed to spend considerable time in such rooms—even days or weeks—before the actual research would begin. He would be allowed to handle Renaissance books, read Renaissance literature, poetry, chronicles of Renaissance personages: Cellini, Leonardo, the Medicis, and the Sforzas. Specific vignettes and incidents of Renaissance life would be narrated to him, and much effort would be exerted to expose him to what Renaissance behavior was like: particular habits of life, moment-to-moment activities, the routine of the day, specific modes of thought, and characteristic experiences of Renaissance artists, noblemen, and ordinary citizens. Films of Renaissance life would be shown, stories of Boccaccio read, and Renaissance plays enacted. Such an orientation would not be an academic course in the Renaissance but an attempt to acclimatize the S to a Renaissance-like milieu. This, too, could be experimentally varied, e.g., with some Ss the orientation time might be quite limited (an hour or two), with others it might be weeks, with some the reading would be eliminated, with others, emphasized, etc.

The behavior of the E and others taking part in the orientation procedure would be free, uninhibited, joyful, adventurous, and sensual. Part of their orientation effort would be to replicate the bright, abandoned interaction, the lusty talk, the freedom of expression, the intricacies of personal manipulation, and the deviousness of the schemes and enterprises that characterized the Renaissance spirit. This spirit would also be evidenced in private conversation and negotiations with the S, in group meetings, in the racy, robust atmosphere of intimate social occasions, in a project or plan of action of a deliberatively composed Renaissance-like group into which the S would be initiated, in games of artifice, and in simulated situations designed for the acting out of Renaissance-like themes or for the execution of some of its characteristic stratagems. As a result of these foregoing activities, the S would hopefully be affected to the extent that he would evidence genuine exhilaration, joy, spontaneity, adventurousness, and willingness to partake of the numerous delights that would be made available in these situations. In all this, the E would be the very model of Renaissance man while fostering identical qualities in the S.

Renaissance Intelligence

Let us now briefly reconstruct what the Renaissance view of intelligence would have been had a hypothetical psychologist of that time been inclined to construct intelligence tests. Its main features were:

1. Intrigue, artifice, and social craft as evidenced in politics and interpersonal relations of all kinds. This involved the manipulation of social situations as well as the astute selection of strategies for long- or short-run goals. Included were the ethical snares and deceptions that might be employed to attain one's ends as well as the deceptive use of moral and ethical reasons to subserve reprehensible purposes. Ingenuity would de-

termine the type and timing of such specious rationalizations to give the deceptive appearance that the actions they justified were the same as morally affirmative ones just as it would determine the attribution of immoral purposes, unethical or illegitimate procedures, etc., to the actions and motives of the adversary. The sagacity to choose an effective strategic act, however nefarious it would be, to turn it into moral capital for oneself and thereby to increase strategic advantage is included in this cognitive component. Cunning in imputing immorality to one's rivals who, in fact, might have been quite decent was especially pertinent. Further, the capacity to perceive these artifices and dissimulations was a salient dimension of this intelligence component as was the ability to dress up the most ruthless and immoral acts with plausible-sounding, worthy reasons. These manipulations occurred as well in conversational gambits, in emotional or intellectual exploitation of others, in the arts of persuasion, and in gaining power over a group. They included the proper witticism, excuse, deception, maneuver, guilt-inducing phrase and clever ploy to achieve one's ends, whatever they might be.

2. Another characteristic of Renaissance intelligence was the relatively free and unprejudiced use of the mind. Reacting violently against a tradition of dogma and fiat from which they were descended, the men of the Renaissance conceived that the function of intelligence was to record and directly interpret experience as it was given via the senses, and to ensure that all empirical relationships in such experience or the causal connections logically derived from it would have a significant influence on consciousness and thought. The consequences of this "change" in outlook included a searching examination of all experience and a scrutiny of the assumptions of the various traditional and contemporary methods for its monitoring and conceptualization. This accentuated orientation of candor and "reality" toward experience, this reliance on careful observation and on logical analysis of the relationships between events, particularly as expressed in mathematics, made for a skepticism of any moral or cosmological preconceptions unless their tested meaning could be unequivocably demonstrated. In time, this would come to mean that all social conventions or values could be held suspect unless their "meaning" or effects could be empirically shown to be useful or desirable; the same would also hold for methods or theories of science, techniques or modes of thinking, and numerous other areas of behavior and endeavor. Eventually there was to be no unimpeachable convention, canon of thought, or procedure except the one that worked, and each such prospect for this requirement had to be examined without preconception and by those criteria that empirical thought and procedure would esti-

mate as useful and efficient. Whatever yielded knowledge, success, or was effective ought to be employed and thereby was judged to be right, valuable, and worthy of acclaim.

Vastly important to such an approach was empirical and mathematical logic as applied to experimentation or to other cause-effect and correlational relationships. However radical or startling a conclusion might emerge in science or commerce, it was the logical evaluation of empirical evidence that justified its novel or unorthodox formulation. In contrast to medieval reasoning, this "new" empirical and liberated logic, based on experience and in concert with the innumerable possibilities generated by a now liberated imagination would, in time, have an unlimited range of empirical sequences and correlations available for analysis. It would thereon develop the most unconventional schemes, ingenious researches, and bold contrivances while no longer being inhibited by predetermined values or criteria of what was proper and improper.

A fundamental component of this cognitive orientation was its tendency to validate imaginative conceptions of all kinds. Empirical proof, practical implementation, and other pragmatic, experimental, or observational tests were to become essential aspects of the structure of Renaissance mentality.

3. Another feature of Renaissance intelligence was its concern with artistic cleverness, ingenuity, and other varieties of artistic play. Ingenuity and innovation in making up stories or games, subtlety and innuendo in written language and conversation, and legerdemain and nuance in painting, architecture, and design were part of this cognitive component. It also involved the capacity to compose different artistic or technical forms and designs, to intuitively understand certain varieties of aesthetic complexity, and to grasp the affective or thematic aspects of styles of architecture, designs of gardens, furnishings of rooms, etc. Included here would be the ability to tell what was wrong with a given pattern or style as well as the capacity to correct it, or to make a design according to various specified criteria of richness of patterning and "good taste."

Indeed, the exercise of "good taste," itself, was one of the more important, easily available ways in which Renaissance men could exhibit their intellectual capacity. It had numerous forms of expression including richly variegated conversation, general aesthetic sensitivity, adept manipulation of relations with others, discrimination in the decoration of rooms, houses, and places of work, artistry in culinary preparations and dining arrangements, and sensitive balancing of recreational and work activities.

4. Another important component of Renaissance intelligence was man-

ifested in debate and disputation. Facility in meeting intellectual difficulties and objections of all kinds, agility in detecting the weak points in an opponent's position, and effectiveness in making one's arguments with lucidity and artfulness were facets of this Renaissance cognitive capacity.

5. An important dimension of Renaissance intelligence was the capacity to optimize happiness, delight, and self-fulfillment. It involved insight into what would be most pleasurable for oneself and consciousness of the many ways and potentials one might have for finding happiness and self-actualization. Awareness of the sensations and experiences that could give one delight as well as the nature of one's personal hierarchy of "maximum" and "minimum" pleasures or self-fulfillments were salient aspects of the Renaissance view of intelligence. Associated with this cognitive component was the capacity to avoid self-defeating experiences and oppressive situations. In part this also involved discernment of what would be defeating or demeaning for oneself in a wide variety of situations, activities, and interpersonal relations and the astuteness to think of ways of avoiding such ill effects. Also, this cognitive capacity would include the foresight to envisage the consequences of one's own actions in respect to bringing defeat, unhappiness, or other difficulties on oneself.

6. Another salient aspect of Renaissance intelligence was its organic and spontaneous character. This component embraced the functions of open-minded questioning or wonder, the grasping of raw empirical fact or sensory data, and the apprehension of whatever relationships and correlations might be inherent in them. The capacity for unimpeded exploration of empirical problems, direct experience, and primary data were significant facets of this cognitive component.

CRITICISM AND RECTIFICATION OF CURRENT
INTELLIGENCE TESTS

From this perspective on intelligence how would our hypothetical Renaissance psychologist evaluate contemporary American concepts of intelligence and intelligence tests? He would contend, no doubt, that these tests are too intellectual in a narrow sense and too dependent on conventional knowledge and thought patterns. He would submit that present tests are neither sufficiently flexible nor bold and do not appraise cognitive functions outside the established value systems and cognitive premises of contemporary "sensible" behavior. He would doubtless assert that American tests are more the expression of an accounting, security-oriented value system in which (1) cautious and respectable modes of mental process are prominent, (2) acquisition of materialistic or intellectual products (vocabulary, information, etc.) is a prominent cognitive guideline, and (3) conduct of the most prudent kind is a salient standard of "intelligent" behavior. In this perspective, these tests are not a measure of the adventurousness, the risk-taking capacity, the boldness, the inventiveness, or the zealous experimentation of the Renaissance mind. There is nothing in them that assesses intellectual tilting at or intellectual excitement about the world. Nor is there any determination of the alert curiosity and ingenuity that could be evoked to deal with authentic "new" problems as they are found in the contemporary world. Rather, too many contemporary psychological views of intelligence conspire to conventionalize it, to be repressive of its potentials for curiosity, innovation, boldness, or uninhibited ingenuity, and to liquidate any penchant it may have for questioning the cognitive processes associated with the status quo. To the Renaissance psychologist, then, authentic intelligence, as he conceived of it, is not understood or gauged in contemporary psychology. By contrast, the organic, uninhibited, or unorthodox expressions of intelligence of the Renaissance mind would be considered alien, on the American psychological scene, to positivistic conceptualization and appraisal and, indeed, would often be penalized by the scoring standards of contemporary tests.

The Renaissance psychologist's view of intelligence also consisted of understanding the role that the cognitive processes could play in humanistically illuminating any given issue as well as in their potential for facilitating pleasure, delight, richer personal experience, heightened awareness, and liberated and acute curiosity. Not to have such an orientation, the Renaissance interpretation would hold, may result in the view of intelligence as an accumulation of information and cognitive technique for their own sakes and in an emphasis on technical proficiency and practical skill as ends in themselves. Such a technical, almost exclusively practical view of intelligence entails the narrow application of cognitive resources to a given problem without reference to such goals as the facilitation of pleasurable or salutary human conditions and experiences and the promotion of heightened awareness or sensibility— consideration of which the Renaissance would have deemed essential for the proper understanding of intellectual functioning.

Another Renaissance criticism of present-day tests would be their lack of concern with those intellectual components embodied in all manner of aesthetic and artistic functioning. Such intellectual components are included in sensitivity to art, architecture, all varieties of design or decoration, and aesthetic responses to nature (landscapes, mountains, seascapes, etc.). Such functions the Renaissance psychologist would contend, involve cognitive components, such as imagination, analytic ability, and intuitive understanding, which have been historically associated with intelligence. If arithmetic computation, knowledge of words, and general information are presently assessed in intelligence tests, it is hard to see, he would submit, why the cognitive capacities embodied in aesthetic and artistic functions should not also be measured in them. In his view, sensitive judgment about design, grasping the compositional structure of a painting or poem, insight into architectural balance or contrast, and similar cognitive, imaginative, and intuitive capacities have as much legitimate claim to be included in these tests as those factors currently assessed.

One must never forget that every age, indeed every culture, has its unique *au courant* view of intelligence. But a technical, materialistic, practical culture—such as ours—excludes from its cognitive focus and legitimized modes of intellection the many-faceted aesthetic-cognitive sensibility that was valued by the Renaissance culture and that marked the Renaissance mind. By affirming that these functions do not have a place in the basic cognitive processes and relegating them to the somewhat scientifically dubious categories of the aesthetic or valuative, the scientific status quo in the field of intelligence measurement is stoutly maintained together with its foundations in the practical, bourgeois view of cognitive functioning. Further, by assigning these factors a relatively unimportant or irrelevant role in relation to intelligence rather than the significant one that intelligence tests should assess, this approach reduces the substantial contributions these functions can make to a richly proportioned and broad theory of intelligence and intelligence measurement.

In the Renaissance view, these presumed defects of current tests may be rectified, in part, by the following proposals which are arranged under each component of Renaissance intelligence that has been previously discussed:

1. Intrigue, artifice, and social craft. (1) The S would be questioned about his understanding of particular verbal deceits, metaphors, or ploys in poetry and prose such as occur, for example, in the works of Shakespeare, Marvel, Donne, and Lovelace. Specific passages would be presented and the S asked to explain them. (2) Picture puzzles requiring detection of secret passages or of hidden objects and figures and involving clever gimmicks (such as are used in treasure hunts) could be used to appraise this Renaissance-like mode of cleverness. Puzzles or games in which the S must find and interpret salient "clues," "keys," and other devices to reach the solution would also be used for this assessment. (3) Mystery "problems" of the classic English variety would be presented and the S required to solve them. (4) Test problems involving the

detection of ingenious lies in a variety of given situations would be presented, e.g., cover stories, political or personal deceptions, hypocritical amenities or courtesies, conspiracies, phony excuses, and other varieties of guile and artifice. The S would be required to detect all such dissimulations and subterfuge. (5) Incompleted stories of maneuvering and intrigue would be narrated in which the S would be required to take the part of one of the story's main characters. He would then be asked to concoct ways to deceive, mislead, or disorient his fictional enemy or rival (in the story situation) to gain a specified goal. His hypothetical enemy, in turn, would be "prepared" with a graded series of stratagems and ploys (constituting countermoves to the S's tactics) to which, in turn, the S would be requested to react. The hypothetical enemy's moves would be flexibly contrived in response to the S's strategy and would be directed by the E. Situations would range from those permitting the widest to only the most limited options for response deceptiveness on the part of the S and would encompass a broad variety of themes and subjects. (6) Problems involving ethical snares and deceptions that could be employed to gain strategic goals would be presented to the S. These might include the deceptive use of moral and ethical reasons to subserve reprehensible ends. For example, a problem about achieving a specific goal might be presented to the S. He would then be allowed one of a series of alternative actions, some being conventional or moral and others not, but in the case of the latter requiring the development of a new morality or standard of conduct to justify them. Though the "conventional" choice would only rarely facilitate attainment of the goal, the "nonmoral" choice would almost always do so. After the S had made his choice of one of the alternative presented actions, he would be required to compose a reasonable, "morally" acceptable justification for it. His skill in artfully and ingeniously contriving convincing "moral" reasons for often amoral, immoral, or ruthless acts would be among the criteria of scoring. This technique could be also applied to test items involving conversational gambits, the guile involved in certain love relationships, devices used to downgrade or support another person, etc. The justification that the S made for his choices and, in some cases, for his own proposed actions would be assessed in terms of originality, expeditiousness, and flexibility of adjustment to different conditions.

2. The Renaissance capacities for cognitive novelty or unconventionality and for validating imaginative concepts and ideas of all kinds would be appraised by the following approaches. In all test questions involving these components, the most radical ways of evaluating a given problem or the most imaginative ideas for demonstrating a specific proposition or

for verifying a given concept would be demanded of the S. Also, he would be required to apply some form of radical logic to a presented complex phenomenon which would be derived from the inherent nature of the phenomenon in question. By encouraging the S to choose or originate unconventional methods or modes of thought to solve such "problems" and to implement all the novel and experimental conceptions he could in connection with them, some evaluation of this component of Renaissance intelligence may be made. Conventional solutions to problems or conventional procedures for reaching such solutions would be presented along with unorthodox procedures and solutions. The S's selection of the procedure and solution for each given problem as well as his reasons for selecting them would be determined. A general objective or problem would be vaguely outlined to permit the S to respond with whatever methods he could summon to achieve success in it. For example, he might be asked to engage in a witty or ingenious conversation, to win the affections or respect of a woman or man with whom he is acquainted, to devise a conversational or other social gambit to persuade someone to do something, to contrive ways of making money under various conditions, or to find novel ways to advocate one's self-interest with different kinds of persons. In respect to the cognitive capacity to validate imaginative conceptions and ideas, examples of problems that might be put to the S are: how to concretely implement a specific artistic idea that is described to him; how to demonstrate the tenability of an original concept or theory; how to practically implement a social innovation or a technical invention, each of which is described to him. In these and other conceptions and theories that are put before the S, his methods for verifying or demonstrating them may be logical, traditionally empirical, boldly adventurous, or innovatively intuitive and may involve documented perceptions of situations, bold conceptions in the gathering of empirical data, the design of innovative experiments, subtle sequential reasoning based on personal experience but eventually leading to some sort of external validation, and the demonstration of sensitive insights and ideas about the external world through the media of words, painting, music, bodily motions, or any other cognitive and expressive channel he can effectively use.

3. The cognitive components of artistic cleverness, ingenuity, and good taste might be partially evaluated by the following methods. (1) Stories would be presented to the S who would be asked to modify them, shift different sections around, or to compose them anew on the basis of the most oblique hints from the E. The S might be asked to insert tricky parts or to introduce complications and embellishments. (2) The wit of

the S would be elicited and appraised including the subtlety of his puns, the nuances of his concealed references, and his remote allusions or verbal deceits. (3) The S would be encouraged to generate improvisations of different Rube Goldberg type designs. (4) Outlines of various kinds of pictures would be presented and the S asked to specify in detail how they should be filled out and delineated. (5) General ways of depicting a particular object would be suggested and the S would then portray, either graphically or verbally, his detailed conception and representation of it, for example, a general suggestion would be made to represent a tree as a bountiful and ornamented growth, as a figure encompassing various hidden objects, or as a grotesque form of growth and the S would then proceed to verbally or pictorially depict these in detail. (6) The S would be asked to represent, verbally or graphically, such "fantastic ideas" as walls that are not walls but screens, or "torrents of milk and champagne." (7) The S would be asked to invent pranks and practical jokes as well as to contrive various "fun" games. (8) Questions such as how to climb across water or jump into the sky would also be put to the S. (9) Innovations in social manners and in varieties of dress for different occasions would be asked for. (10) An effort would be made to engage S in absurd, "wild," or fantastic conversations which would reveal his capacity for imaginative, ingenious, and coherent flights of discussion and would require him, as well, to imagine how he would act in fantastic social roles or in outlandish situations.

4. The Renaissance cognitive capacity for debate and disputation would be evaluated in the following ways. (1) During the course of a discussion, an instructed adversary poses arguments against an idea that the S has advanced and the latter is required to counter them. His effectiveness in doing so with artfulness and ingenuity would be one measure of this intellectual component. (2) The S is presented with arguments against a previously stated position of his; he is given time to study these, and in a subsequent discussion with his opponent is permitted to rebut these objections. In such discussions, a series of graded oppositions to his position would be raised covering logical, factual, or ad hominum points and involving subtle disruption of his thought processes and ideas or embracing any other opposition, attack, diversion, or feint that could contest the S's advocacy of his position. An analogous format could also be adapted for written argument. (3) The S would be asked, using many of the foregoing procedures, to defend a position he either likes or dislikes, a position that is intrinsically strong or weak, a position on which little material or data is available, a position that is either inherently rigorous or amorphous, or a position on which he is

either well versed or quite ignorant. His ability to do this with artfulness and power, irrespective of his original orientation to and knowledge of the position in question, would be evaluated. Appraisals would also be made of the S's ability to build, sometimes only from a single error of his opponent, a cogent and victorious structure of argument as well as of his capacity to surmount diversions, dissimulation, and abuse and turn them to his own advantage.

5. The following proposals are directed to the appraisal of the Renaissance component of intelligence that was concerned with the capacity to optimize happiness, delight, and self-fulfillment. (1) An intensive interview would be utilized to determine the amount of pleasure that the S obtains from a wide variety of stimuli as well as how aware he is of his own potentialities for experiencing these pleasures. In addition, a detailed record of the S's pleasurable behavior would be obtained by observing him in a wide variety of situations or by securing information about this behavior from those who know him well. The findings from such a record would then be compared with those of the clinical interview. An assessment could also be made of the S's capacity to discern under which conditions or moods various stimuli would have the most pleasurable effect on him. This could be derived both from the clinical interview or from a questionnaire designed to survey such behavior. The relation between these self-evaluations and the S's actual behavior would then be compared as it bears on his capacity to be aware of his own personal hierarchy of pleasure and self-actualization. For example, he might be correctly aware that when bored, music, but not conversation will give him pleasure but also that after hard work a quiet conversation will be of more delight than having an alcoholic drink. (2) Associated with this intelligence component is the capacity to avoid self-defeating experiences and oppressive situations. The disposition to avoid negating experiences might be gauged by presenting various situations to the S—either verbally, pictorially, or through dramatization—and requiring him to make choices of alternative courses of action that are made available to him. Self-defeating and self-enhancing options would be specifically introduced in both manifest and disguised forms. The issues in these situations would be the choice of friends, salutary and damaging interpersonal relations, scheduling of time, selection of recreations, the balance between career and personal life, love relations, and a host of other activities. Open-ended procedures could be used to assess the responses to these situations which would be described in detail. (3) Also, intensive clinical interviewing could be used to determine the extent and nature of the actual situations in which the S is

involved in such self-defeating orientations as well as his specific awareness of these tendencies. (4) Authentic and role-playing situations in which the S would be assessed for this cognitive component should also be employed. In such cases, he would be directly placed in various natural situations in which it would be possible to make self-defeating or self-helpful responses or in different role-playing situations in which the same options would be present. (5) Movie and dramatic presentations as well as fictional accounts of various situations could also be used. These would be presented so as to either allow the S to complete an incompleted dramatic plot or narrative dealing with the theme of self-defeat or to directly identify with characters who are or are not oriented to self-defeating cognitions and judgments. (6) The various forms of cognitive self-defeat that are presented in these assessment situations and in the foregoing written tests would be veiled in a series of disguises that would range from the most transparent to the most impenetrable. Also, the various alternatives to self-defeating cognitive orientations would range from those that are barely affirmative and successful to those that are eminently positive and winning.

6. The following suggestions are directed to assessing the organic, spontaneous, and open-minded aspects of Renaissance intelligence which embraced, in part, the unimpeded exploration of problems and experiences: (1) The S would be asked questions of the following kind: Assuming the present economic system did not exist, what should be the ideal nature and structure of one that would be both equitable and free? If one could start de novo, what plans should be devised to build good cities, to train fine men, or to solve the problems of war? (2) The S would be presented with new types of fabrics or forms and asked how they would be used for particular purposes, e.g., for clothes, for decorative or functional uses with furniture and coverings, or for other interior design purposes. (3) A phenomenon or experience such as a unique sunset, a new space experiment, or a "new" visual or auditory sensation would be presented to the S, who would be asked to respond to it in a number of different ways: How would he explore it further? What does it signify or how is it related to other kinds of experiences he has had? What further aesthetic stimuli or experiences could it lead to? (4) A novel political process would be described and the S asked what its ramifications might be for the entire political system and for norms of political behavior. (5) He would be asked to project what kinds of adult personalities would emerge if children were raised by different specified methods which would be described to him. (6) He would be asked to imagine and describe (or otherwise demonstrate) new visual, auditory, or verbal stimuli

that would result in such experiences as serenity, abrasion, incongruity, volatility, stridence, precariousness, dissolution as well as novel or bizarre reactions.

In all this, the S's orientation to the test questions should not be directed to one solution or approach but rather to an open-minded pluralistic view. As he goes on with this "open," many-vistaed orientation, he may find new and richer facets to the problem and its solution, emerging complications, and significant levels of conception different from those that first appeared or that would emerge under present testing conditions. Hence, by encouraging the exploration of facets, levels, or side issues of the problems, by allowing its transformation into richer, multidimensional issues, and by fostering a variety of solutions to them, the reorientation of intelligence toward the Renaissance mode may be facilitated.

Renaissance Perception

1. In the Renaissance view, the character of the perceptual process was different and more varied than that typically acknowledged by contemporary American psychologists. Our hypothetical Renaissance psychologist would see the perceptual process as one marked by spontaneous transformations and constantly emerging perspectives and orientations. He would have viewed much of American studies as static, overintellectualized, narrow and, at the very least, untrue to perceptual experience as the Renaissance predominantly knew it. Renaissance perception was characterized by a revitalizing or renewing quality, a fresh "seeing" of things in the world including that of forms, perspectives, colors, and human experiences. In this view, contemporary American perceptual studies are too inadequately oriented to invention, variation, and other kinds of change and too much concerned with the engineering and mechanical aspects of perception. Because, in substantial degree, the ethos of contemporary American society is concrete, production-oriented, and materialistic and the cognitive and valuative approaches of positivistic science and engineering are the orientations best suited to perceptually dealing with such tangible objects and viewpoints, what would be more natural than to have a great deal of perceptual experience formulated and explained in terms of simple physical rules, geometric formulas, and reductionistic principles common to the physical and engineering sci-

ences? To make this an effective case, however, perceptual phenomena that are amenable to these formulations must be selected for study while those characterized by richness, inventiveness, and novelty—and not subject to such simplified or reductionistic conceptions—must be ignored. The Renaissance psychologist would contend that it is exactly these irreducible, emergent, and novel factors that are the most uniquely human and enhancing of perceptual experience. He would argue that the contemporary orientation to perception is, in goodly measure, divorced from the organic context of richness of feeling, pleasure, novelty, and other humanistic experience that, as an historical case in point, the Renaissance manifested and emphasized. If the strong current emphasis on cognitively oriented perception comes, in part, from a positivistic view of experience and from a pragmatic desire to transform perceptual meaning and experience into manipulable and concretely comprehensible data that possess the same "intelligibility," amenability to rigid conceptualization, and capacity for pragmatic use as any other materialistic or physical information, then the consequences for perceptual experience and research will be devoid of any reasonable amount of humanized feeling, sensory richness, depth of affect, and eruptive novelty.

2. The Renaissance psychologist would have affirmed that perception should be studied as it authentically exists: rich with life, complex, and affect-laden, and not, as it is largely studied now, with neat and pristine designs and laboratory stimuli. For, in the Renaissance view, this neatness is a figment of contemporary perceptual theory and, in the end, a creature of particular social and economic values and patterns of thought. It is not, except as a product of constriction and formalization, the Renaissance psychologist would hold, what perception is really like. In the train of this approach come rigid controls, the dehumanized laboratory environment, and phenomenally or conceptually abstract stimuli—all of which further limit, formalize, and intellectualize perception and perceptual sets. These conditions, and others previously discussed, combine to freeze the modalities of feeling, sensory richness, and inventiveness, which for the Renaissance were intrinsic to perception. Such modalities can only flower in an experimental or naturalistic study where there is freedom and opportunity for spontaneous vital reactions. Hence, the Renaissance psychologist would see the contemporary emphasis in perceptual research as a distortion of the organic modalities of perception and as enervating its genuine nature with concepts and procedures more appropriate to the condition of the physical sciences than to authentic perceptual experience.

The Renaissance psychologist would demand that modern perceptual research allow the S much more freedom of response to perceptual stimuli, include many more naturalistic stimuli in its studies, employ much more relaxing conditions in its actual experiments, and utilize more zestful and delight-inciting environments. He would especially insist that there must be less emphasis on the presentation of discrete, structural stimuli accompanied by requests for clear-cut categories of response from the S and more stress on the emotional context and the varied sensory modalities that are intrinsically involved with naturalistic structural stimuli. He would urge that there should be as much freedom for the response of all perceptual and sensory channels of the S and as much complexity and richness of the "test" stimulus as is, at least, usually present during the spontaneous, undeterred perceptual process as it freely and intensively occurs.

3. Related to these foregoing points is the view that contemporary perceptual research is too confining and preoccupied with structural issues. The structural dimension, the Renaissance psychologist would contend, is really only the bones of perception—not the substance, feeling, and value of the full-bodied organic perceptual experience itself. Further, it is quite possible that perception of distance, motion, size, etc. are substantially modified as value, feeling, mood, and cultural background enter as variables into the perceptual process and for every such variable interaction these "pure" laws of perception may change. In a sense, structurally dehumanized perceptions are like symbols of economic transactions (i.e., money) or engineering tables. They are to be viewed in terms of their concrete, material value in modern society and as facilitating practical actions and adjustment. Perceptual research that reflects such values is dominated by a matter-of-fact orientation, cold depersonalized percepts (without emotional complexity, sensory richness, or novelty except as these may contribute to practical advantage), perceptual abstractions far removed from a humanistically rich perceptual experience, and such principles as contribute to the active manipulation of a perceptual world that has been molded by a pragmatic, materialistic, and scientific culture. Use and productivity are salient values in such a culture and perceptual experience and experiments are reflexively fashioned to subserve these values. Thereon the important tenets of perception essentially become practical ones which devalue noneconomic, nonutilitarian, and nonconcrete components.

What regularities and principles of perception would result, however, if conventional, structural stimuli were to be presented under relaxed, humanizing conditions—conditions where efficiency and impersonality were not paramount influences—or in larger settings of richly varied "humanistic" structures, decorations, and forms such as those of Renaissance-like rooms? Would the traditional geometric and structural perceptual "laws" hold and would comparable rules of size, distance, and grouping also be sustained under such different conditions?

The Renaissance saw the relation between structural and affective, substantive, and aesthetic elements as an interweaving one. Indeed, the perception of structure was itself profoundly influenced by the nature and configuration of these latter elements so that it varied significantly as these factors shifted. The division of structural elements and their context in perceptual studies is possible, of course, but may also lead to "special" results that would not hold except under analogous perceptual conditions to those found in abstract modern art. The Renaissance orientation would simply emphasize the diversity of perceptual contexts and values that impinge on and affect the structural elements, point to the cultural conditions that produce the structural vs. emotional-valuative schism in contemporary experience, and contend that such a division is an artificial one, a reductionistic and mechanistic abstraction, and in effect, a truncation of the natural integrated perceptual process. As such, it is symptomatic of the split between feeling and thinking that characterizes so much of the experience of contemporary man. The Renaissance approach would maintain that though such "contemporary" perceptual experience may be valid for study, it must nevertheless be recognized for what it is: an artificial, abstract, or fragmented manifestation of the authentic perceptual process that excludes or distorts many of the components naturally integral to it.

What is needed then in present perceptual research, according to the Renaissance psychologist, is the integration of emotion, sensory richness, novelty, and similar factors with structural elements. This cannot be achieved unless different stimulus materials and types of Ss will be used from those presently employed and until more opportunity for the interplay of ideation, feeling, sensation, and structure is provided. Under such prospective conditions, the affective, color, form, or other elements of the stimulus would be increased or decreased in intensity or the S would be made (by selection or training) more or less "humanistic," exhilarated, fragmented, dissociated, and perceptually rich. These procedures would be extended until the stimuli or the Ss reach the stage of the cognitive-emotional schism characteristic of much contemporary perceptual research or approximate the integrated, multifaceted experience of Renaissance perception. Through the use of such methods, significant variations in the present "laws" or regularities of perceptual research may be found.

4. A critical objection to contemporary perceptual work and theory is that it does not come to grips with deep, delicate, and uniquely individual levels of perceptual experience. Because collectivity and uniformity of perception are its main concerns, it favors concrete percepts that can be explicitly and consensually identified quite easily and devalues unique, intangible, and subjective ones that cannot. Uniformity in perceptual response is abetted by the cultural norm of the "greatest common denominator" which makes for fewer individualistic perceptions and more concrete, simplistic, and conventional ones. It also influences perceptual experience toward a reductionistic, physical, biological common level. Such forms of perception coalesce nicely with positivistic science and empirical methodology and avoid the nonmaterial, individualistic, and soft-headed components—or assessments—of perceptual response. The latter are ignored in the interest of the compulsion for uniformity, scientific law, and practical, hard-headed percepts which are rigorously testable and therefore in accord with the American values of "know-how" and "show me." Such hard-headed, testable percepts are also favored because they are cognitively meaningful to the concerns of American Ss, i.e., practical issues and pragmatic modes of thought. The more individualized, deep, and intangible perceptions are less amenable to this sort of rigorous proof, have to be searched for more intensively, and are more prone to be acknowledged as odd, erratic, or predominantly emotional. Thus their investigation cannot be trusted to yield reliable data on which to establish regularities of perceptual response or from which to formulate "general laws" of perceptual experience. The thrust to ignore or eliminate these "deviant" perceptions often takes the form of channelizing all perceptual experience into cognitive, conventionalized, or concrete perceptual channels and percepts. In contrast, the Renaissance psychologists would contend that the individualized and intangible perceptions are potentially as universally prevalent as the uniform and tangible ones, have as high an incidence as the latter in certain cultural and social milieux or under given psychological circumstances, and are certainly as significant in human experience, encompassing, as they do, the richest, deepest, and most liberated dimensions of the perceptual process.

The Renaissance psychologist would call for the use of more complex patterns of stimuli in perceptual research: more richness of form, more individualized materials but of a less clinical or "unconscious" type, and more stimuli concerned with beauty, sensory richness, eruptive novelty, deep and versatile affect, zest, delight, and other humanistic properties. Such an exploration of perception would require stimuli consisting of rich and variegated textures and colors as well as those with novel, ingenious, and intricate forms or designs—all possessing, in varying degree, the capacity to evoke exhilaration, joy, wonder, or adventure in the cognitive, emotional, and kinesthetic functions and to instigate new and many-faceted forms of perceptual experience.

It is also not impossible that the same object may evoke the most varied and complex dimensions of perceptual experience provided the appropriate conditions and environment are present. Such possibilities may be explored by relevant perceptual mood inductions and proper selection of Ss by trance or drug-induced states, by appropriate physical and psychological atmospheres or environments, and by indoctrination in and empathy with Renaissance-like perceptual experience and sensibility. It should be noted that such Renaissance inductions may be effected through a variety of methods including historical, cultural, or psychological orientations and through the influence of appropriate groups, eminent persons, and respected models. An effort must also be made to involve such deeper levels of perception and feeling of the S as are associated with states of inner exhilaration and perceptual intensity, states of emotional and sensory empathy with the stimulus, states of kaleidoscopic sensitivity, states of pure sensation, and states of a full identity with the vitality of the processes of life.

5. The Renaissance-oriented psychologist would contend that the right-wrong or similar mutually exclusive responses required in much current perceptual work correspond to the right-wrong action decisions and pragmatic frames of reference required in business, positivistic science, and engineering, where correct or erroneous decisions can have the most important practical consequences and where the time factors to reach such decisions may determine success or failure. But factors that are pertinent to business, the marketplace, and engineering should not dominate the investigation of those large areas of perceptual experience that often require time for the incubation and emergence of clear phenomenal perceptions—perceptions that have no right-wrong orientation, pragmatic character, or clearly defined structure and that, for authentic assessment, require conditions in which their rich, inventive, emotionally significant, and gradually developing character can be fostered and eventually fully activated. Many different types of perception become viable and fully genuine only when certain conditions of time, relaxation, latency of response, and affective-cognitive commitment are satisfactorily fulfilled. In this class are sensory and artistic kinds of perception which require an open flow of sensation and feeling through multiple sensory and affective channels, an incubation of the perceptual experience before it reaches full authenticity and maturity, and sufficient time and relaxa-

tion to permit a natural and indigenous integration of the many-faceted elements of the emerging perception. With many types of perceptual stimuli, demands for rapidity of response and for dichotomous or other mutually exclusive choices may result in (1) freezing the S's perceptions at a very elementary or unformed level of perceptual formation; (2) a mechanization and stereotype of perceptual experience; (3) a disarray of the unintegrated perceptual components with a resulting amorphous or confused percept; (4) obstruction of the spontaneous deepening and integration of the perceptual experience that might have occurred in time as well as inhibition of the influx of impulses from other perceptual sensory channels that might have further deepened and enriched this experience. Therefore complex perceptual experience will be molded to the current dominant research methodology (1) if its rich, organic components are abstracted, fragmented, and schematized when presented as stimuli to the S; (2) by only allowing (or making available) artificial or orthodox response options and eliminating those variants and ambiguities of response that might facilitate the experiencing and reporting of rich perceptual responses; (3) by selecting only Ss with action-directed, instrumental, or concrete perceptual orientations; and (4) by the restriction or conversion of the total organic perceptual process into a simple cognitive or practical one. In effect, these conditions deny to those Ss with the requisite capacities the opportunity of demonstrating the nature of rich many-faceted perceptual processes and thereby impede the scientific collection of unbiased, comprehensive research data.

The patterns of perceptual experience and response displayed by subjects in contemporary research are derived from our contemporary society which sanctions and deems it appropriate for its members to be perceptually quick, cognitively concrete and pragmatic, and, simultaneously, disapproves of their being perceptually uninhibited, freely inventive, or richly sensitive. It is now our task to correct this contemporarily learned "scientific image" of perception and, if possible, remake it into a more authentic, richly textured model by drawing on the Renaissance perceptual experience.

RECTIFICATION

1. Much greater spontaneity of the Ss who participate in perceptual research must be encouraged. This can be done by employing a richly appointed natural-appearing setting for the experiment rather than the usual laboratory environment, by exposing the S before the experiment begins to model Renaissance-like persons and to large amounts of

racy, happy talk, by involving him in gay, uninhibited parties or Bohemian groups, by showing him movies or plays that vividly represent Renaissance-like gaiety, by having him read about such aspects of Renaissance life in detail, and by involving him in the kind of role-playing that captures this rich spontaneity of the Renaissance spirit. Any pertinent experience might be used for these orientation purposes whether it be viewing Renaissance-like paintings and drama or engaging in ebullient conversation, exhilarating interpersonal relations, and other sensory delights.

The spontaneity to be encouraged for these studies should be of all kinds: intellectual, poetic, pictorial, scientific, narrative, conversational, social, humorous, etc. Numerous figures in the arts would serve as good spontaneity models, and, in many cases, their lives could be used as examples of Renaissance-type experience and perceptual orientation. Specific anecdotes from lives of other eminent persons illustrating their perceptual openness, fluidity, richness, and spontaneity could similarly be used. By the E's permissive acceptance of the S's behavior and personality, however zany or deviant they may be, by encouragement of the S's own visions, insights, productions, and expressions, by close rapport with him to reinforce and augment any Renaissance-like orientation he initially may have and, if necessary, by counseling to encourage his perceptual freedom and spontaneity, much could be accomplished. These methods would have to be tailored to each individual S: one needing a detailed description of Renaissance models and behavior patterns, another warm acceptance in a Renaissance-type group, another encouragement and enhancement of his infrequent moments of perceptual richness or spontaneity, and still others needing to be placed in situations and rooms where such "free" perceptual conditions would regularly prevail. Whatever orientation is used, the actual experiment should follow soon or immediately thereafter and should, in its spirit and nature, be consistent with the quality of these orientations. As much perceptual freedom as possible should be encouraged in the S during the experiment proper and, to this end, the experimental atmosphere should be transformed into a milieu of cheerfulness, amiability, and freedom-enhancing relationships as well as being divested of all mechanical appurtenances or other mementos of a traditional laboratory environment. This type of perceptual experiment, then, should be made as casual, spontaneous and "unexperimental" as possible: the E might attempt to carry it out as an unexceptional event of the day that fits into the ordinary, natural round of the activity of the subject or, if it must be handled as a distinctive experience, it should be played down as not calling for special notice. Indeed, a friend with whom the S closely and regularly associates could serve in the role of the experimenter. Questionnaire forms and the like should be eliminated, if possible, or introduced in a most muted and casual connection. (The correct nondisturbing, nondefense evoking, and natural-appearing procedure for introducing questionnaires into naturalistic situations still requires extensive research.) Even "experimental" directions should be conveyed in the form of friendly conversation or as permissive suggestions. If one wants to find what happens to these "encouraged" spontaneous preexperimental orientations under subsequent, more conventional experimental conditions, some of the traditional research procedures may be retained during an actual experiment including a conventional E, characteristic apparatus, orthodox experimental directions, etc. Also, the effects of temporary exhilaration and *joie de vivre* should be compared with perceptual effects stemming from a deeper, more permanent exuberance and freedom which is derived from the character and value system of the S. Other variables that should be systematically incorporated in these studies include: the personality of the S (ranging from most to least perceptually free, inventive, and richly faceted); the value system of the S (roughly comparable to the above personality dimension); stimulus materials (from most to least structural, simplistic, cognitive, and concrete.)

2. Studies should be conducted on the differences between perceptual reactions when additional response alternatives are offered to the S than are usually provided, when free response is allowed, and when hints, suggestions, or intervening events are introduced before the response is made. Other studies would have the S delay his response to the stimulus for a substantial interval—perhaps as long as a day—while simultaneously affording him a congenial environment in which to mull over or incubate his prospective response; alternatively, he might be given the opportunity during this interval of discussing his response with another person at a cocktail lounge, a dance, an uninhibited party, or in some other zestful situation. This person should also have temperamental and perceptual qualities of a Renaissance-like nature. The longer the free, unimpeded interval directly after the stimulus presentation, i.e., the fewer practical concerns or activities the S has in this period and the greater the number of Renaissance-like facilitating conditions he is exposed to, the stronger the likelihood will be that his response will have rich, multifaceted, and emotionally fluid proportions.

3. The same perceptual studies should also be performed during different moods of the same S. Such moods may include the conventional, cognitive moods of routine life in contemporary society; the exhilarating

moods of uninhibited exceptional moments or occasions; moods of tactual, visual, or auditory preoccupation and sensitivity; moods of quiet enjoyment; moods of intense cognition and intellection; hearty, robust, pleasure-loving moods; subtle, crafty, and devious moods; clever, satiric moods; moods of great sensitivity to form, spatial, or plastic values; moods of wild, intense, hallucinatory or synesthetic responsiveness; moods of adventure and exploration; moods of vast curiosity and openness to all experience; moods of interpersonal manipulation or exploitation as well as those of genuine, empathetic, interpersonal communication; moods of geometric and structural preoccupation; moods of rich, multifaceted sensory responsiveness. The induction of such moods can be pursued by educational orientation, by example, by therapy, by role-playing, by close personal relationships with friends or prestige models who may typify or sometimes portray such moods, by extending and stabilizing irregular or exceptional moments in which such moods may naturally occur, by the use of drugs, and by sensory and perceptual awakening Esalen-type exercises, e.g., muscular, proprioceptive, tactual, visual, and other sensory-liberating and revitalizing experiences.

To take an example, let us assume that we are interested in inducing a mood of spatial empathy. Preexperimental orientation would be given in the development of sensitivity to cubist and impressionist paintings, to various types of geometrical symbols and compositions, to the paintings of Mondrian and the abstract expressionists, to studying spatial relations in nature, and to observing various types of forms and spatial relationships in Renaissance paintings, Greek temples, contemporary designs of furniture or architecture, and in the abstract structure and composition of objects, e.g., a drop of water, a glass tube, a pipe, a sphere. Practice would be given the S in sensing, feeling, and composing such spatial designs and forms. Other training procedures could be adapted from the large amount of work done in this area by the pre–World War II Bauhaus and carried on further by Moholy-Nagy [5,6] and his followers at the Chicago Institute of Design.

To completely orient the S to this type of spatial sensitivity may require suppression of conventional, concrete perceptions that could conceivably be accomplished by depriving him of conventional, tangible perceptual stimuli and by compelling him to continually orient himself to a full awareness of an empathic responsiveness to abstract space. Further, in training discussions or demonstrations, when interpretations are to be made of some perceptual stimulus, the spatial orientation should be emphasized—but without pressure and with an intangible and fluid sensitivity so that the tone and feeling of empathic spatial orientation is effectively represented and possibly implanted in the S's perceptual orientation. Further cultivation of this orientation may be achieved by constructing an environment amply furnished with pictures, designs, objects, and patterns that powerfully illustrate and emphasize empathic spatial perception. During the course of such intensive experiences and training, the empathic spatial orientation may become a prominent perceptual approach of the S, perhaps even being internalized as a basic and instantaneous reaction to the stimulus world.

The requirements for actual experiments in this area would consist of an airy, free environment and a relationship of friendly interest and cordial detachment of the E to the S. So far as actual stimuli are concerned, form and spatial relation figures might most usefully be used but it is quite possible that symbolic designs, photographs of nature, and even colored decorations will also be perceived from a spatial empathic orientation, if less frequently and powerfully. Indeed, it may be true that some perceptual moods extend their orientation and influence to the most diverse stimulus fields and do this more than other perceptual moods. Conversely, certain types of stimulus materials may be perceptually resistant to the most potent moods and will impress their own distinctive character on the mood's perceptual response, whatever it may be. Certain moods may influence only a limited range of stimulus materials and may lose this influence as these materials deviate from the spirit or substance of the mood in question while, in contrast, other moods such as deeply emotional or psychically profound ones (rapturous happiness, Zen states, rich sensory experience, etc.) may have a more potent generalized effect on all stimuli. Stimulus materials of all types, therefore, should be prepared and the influence of each designated perceptual mood on them should be determined.

The shift in perceptual orientation during the observation of each specific type of stimulus, when owing to the shift of the S's perceptual mood, is a phenomenon that should be noted though it will not be explored further here. It was, however, a characteristic experience of Renaissance men. Doubtless there are many contemporary persons who, because of this reason, have a capacity for varying their perceptual orientations while observing one set of stimulus materials. A specific research program to investigate the various dimensions of this entire phenomenon remains to be formulated in the future.

4. Much more effective use must be made in perceptual research of naturalistic environments that reflect the perceptual orientation under study and of Ss whose own personalities or perceptual viewpoints embody this orientation. Thus to facilitate spatial empathic perception, e.g., it would be useful to have such settings as rooms, buildings, foyers,

cathedrals, auditoriums, landscapes, and seascapes available for the actual experiment at different times of the day, such as daybreak, dusk, or noon. In such settings, Ss selected for their spatial sensitivity and empathy would be confronted with various relevant perceptual materials. Comparable arrangements would be made for other Renaissance perceptual orientations, e.g., sensory richness, perceptual novelty and adventurousness, versatile perceptual affect. The perceptual assessment or confrontation—be it pictorial, verbal, tactual, etc.—would emerge naturally and authentically from the setting itself and, indeed, seem to be part of it. Thus pictorial material—if these were the "test" stimuli of a study—would hang on the walls of an appropriate room in which a perfectly natural conversation would be held between the E and the S; this conversation would be artfully used to ascertain the S's responses to the pictorial stimuli around him, i.e., in effect, it would be a record or "test" of the perceptual responses of the S. To take another example, in a resplendent Renaissance room occupied by many zestful, urbane, and uninhibited persons engaging in delighted conversation or other gaieties, the S would, in the spontaneous course of these pleasures, artfully be solicited to perceptually respond to a decoration, a spatial design, a person, or whatever else might be the specific perceptual stimulus of this "naturalist experiment." Similarly, a vignette might be recounted, under similar circumstances, and the S would be spontaneously drawn into a conversation leading to his perceptual response to the "experimentally" relevant elements of it. Assessment could also be carried on in more explicit and formal ways and the different methods of appraisal of the S's responses then be compared. In general, however, the methods of assessment—as the methods of presenting the perceptual stimulus—should be consistent with the perceptual orientation being investigated. A Zen perceptual orientation, e.g., would require an oblique, ambiguous, and sensitive "presentation" of the perceptual stimulus as well as a similar method of soliciting the S's response while some components of the Renaissance perceptual orientation would require more novel, spontaneous, or exhilarating presentation and solicitation methods. Similar consistency between the "presentation" procedures and the perceptual orientation being studied should be employed in naturalistic situations for investigating the Renaissance-like perceptual moods of exhilaration, subtlety, adventurousness, etc. Stimulus materials should, in all cases, be integral to the distinctive quality of each situation and environment. Some of the "situations" could be set up in scenic backgrounds of the countryside, others in various kinds of Renaissance-type rooms, some in frantic backgrounds of city streets, and some in highly novel or adventurous mood-inducing environments.

The conditions, then, for carrying out this type of "perceptual orientation" study are that (1) the environment and the situation are as natural and "pure" as possible for the perceptual orientation being studied; (2) the subject has been trained in this perceptual orientation or has been selected because his own characteristic perceptual reactions are consistent with it; (3) the presented stimuli materials, techniques of evoking perceptual responses, and methods of appraising them are consonant with the perceptual orientation being studied; (4) other stimulus materials to be presented should vary from those less than completely consonant with the perceptual orientation and situation being studied to those most discrepant from them.

Study of naturalistic situations, without predetermined or specific stimuli, should also be carried out. Data should be collected from the conversations, monologues, gestures, motor behavior, or other nonverbal perceptual reactions of Bohemians, Renaissance afficionados, hippies, and artists in each of their own natural environments to ascertain their perceptions and perceptual orientations in regard to other people, art objects, furnishings and decorations, natural scenery, poetry, spatial designs, etc. Historical chronicles, sociological reports, literary criticisms, biographies, autobiographies, newspaper reports, literature, art criticism, and other documents would also be useful sources from which to obtain knowledge of naturalistic, ongoing perceptual orientations of various groups in contemporary and past societies. One object of such studies would be to determine which perceptual orientations are emphasized by different types of people in a broad range of naturalistic situations. Also, do their perceptual orientations vary with the time of day, number of persons in the given situation, season of the year, nature of the topic being discussed, and numerous other variables? Indeed, almost any natural situation, type of group, or environmental setting can be a source of useful data on perceptual orientation.

5. In the foregoing studies it is imperative to avoid the kinds of stimulus materials generally used in present research. Aesthetic stimuli would particularly be germane to Renaissance modes of perception and would include lush decorations, richly designed furnishings and tapestries, and art works of Titian, Cellini, Veronese, Bellini, etc. Spatial forms and earthy human materials would also be relevant stimuli. Human faces in various aspects of live, mobile expression, a broad range of different types of subtle and gross human gestures and expressions, and various kinds of conversations or other social interactions should also be presented as perceptual stimuli in the form of motion pictures, plays, skits, or as ongoing events in natural life situations.

In addition, some of the following research proposals may prove useful in the illumination of various aspects of Renaissance-like perception. For example, what are the first perceptions that the S has of an adventure, or a novel experience, or a pioneering phenomenon in art or science? To take a few possibilities, an uncharted ocean or unexplored mountain scene, or an unusually new kind of research apparatus would be presented to the S; thoroughly novel findings from a scientific study of the day would be conveyed to him, such as the discovery of quasars, anti-matter, or RNA; he would be exposed to a totally unexpected and unheard of experience such as being precipitously confronted with St. Mark's square in Venice when he had no previous hint of its existence or seeing a completely new and yet undreamed of aeroplane design, or an unexampled objet d'art or an unprecedentedly beautiful human being. Are these stimuli perceived by the S as mysterious, as scientifically mind-expanding, as exhilarating adventures, as lonely experiences, as rich delectations, or as dull, threatening and odious episodes? Similar perceptual materials might also be used in appropriate pictorial or verbal forms as backgrounds on which the S could focus and evolve whatever Renaissance-like perceptions might emerge.

Renaissance Groups

Among the characteristics of Renaissance groups were the following:

1. Intensely strong loyalties and commitments to the welfare and pre-eminence of an association (be it guild, city, neighborhood, athletic unit, etc.) and involvement in almost any sort of activity or effort to further its interest. Such loyalties absorbed a goodly amount of energy of the Renaissance citizen, and though not often demanding extreme sacrifice, nevertheless made their burden of full commitment and intense group absorption strongly felt. In these groups there truthfully was an identity between the person and the group experience and though the group was an essential medium for individualistic achievement and distinction, it was also a superordinate entity to which members gave deeply of their energies and in which they were significantly absorbed.

2. Nevertheless, there was intense competition between individual members within each of these groups for fame, power, and wealth. This competition was over relative gratification of their personal needs for recognition, splendor, and power as well as for the fulfillment of their talents or interests. Such potential gratifications, too, were facilitated by attainment of fame and by the freedom of action and expression that power or status would bring.

211

3. The forms of this competition, both within and between groups, were remarkably infused with guile, duplicity, and other varieties of deception. Ruthlessness of all sorts was practiced. Morality was used to dissimulate wickedness of the most vicious kind. Gaining preeminence in a group or advancing the interests or power of a group at the expense of other persons or groups justified, indeed, demanded the employment of any methods that would secure, most expeditiously, the ends of self-interest or group interest. Machiavellianism was, in part, the formalization of these amoral operations.

4. Another salient quality of Renaissance groups was the vigorous and violent competition between groups. This took forms as varied as rivalry in art, scientific work, accretions of power, aspirations for fame of all kinds, and desire for splendor or riches. Such rivalry, carried to extraordinary lengths, infused the relations between cities, neighborhoods, and other social units with a vigorous thrust toward power and eminence. In their behalf, no act was too perfidious, effort too great, sin too base, deception too intricate, design too complicated, artistry, achievement, or ingenuity too extraordinary, splendor too exquisite, passion too consummate, acumen or analysis too subtle, construction too noble, or art work too remarkable so long as they brought preeminence or influence to the city, faction, group or other social unit from which they emanated. Fame, power, and esteem were, in part, the ends of this mazurka of rivalry, and in their service was impressed every noble, beautiful, exquisitely expressive, enriched, ingenious, and imaginative talent as well as every wicked, base, vicious, cruel, counterfeit, and deceptive aptitude.

CRITICISM OF CONTEMPORARY STUDIES

In the light of this description of Renaissance groups, certain strictures may be leveled against contemporary small-group research. There is little grasp of the necessity of studying groups with fully authentic and deeply committed involvements. Too many studies are of the laboratory type or, if they are of naturalistic groups, are rarely of deeply committed and intensely loyal ones—the condition necessary for the genuine assessment of the role that authentic loyalty and commitment play in group life. One cannot establish authentic loyalties or cohesions in experimental groups by a few parsimonious directions, some minor interpersonal manipulations, or a few dollars compensation per subject. Such commitments must evolve, as they usually do, from some substantial tradition, a background of extended group experience, some nuclear emotional events, deep affinities and oppositions, or certain vicissitudes and experiences that seriously affect group members in the warp and woof of their lives. It is almost impossible to obtain a significant and compelling identity between group purpose and individual commitment in those studies that extend over only a limited period of time and where the group members are not involved in a mission or task that has authentic significance to the fabric of their own lives outside the "group experiment." The kind of full group commitment inherent in the flow of life of the Renaissance man together with the delight and pride he took in his group's preeminence or victories and the despair or fortitude he experienced in the wake of its failures cannot be simulated in a few group meetings that have no historical past or significant future for the individuals who participate in them nor in which they feel a significant continuity between their own life's meanings and that of the experiment in which they are being studied. This is especially true in regard to competitive zeal for fame, worldly goods and power which, in the experimental situation, can rarely have the reality or significance that it has in actual life. Can competitions in group experiments be as organically experienced and as instigatory of as many ruthless, ingenious, and deceptive acts as they were in Renaissance or even modern daily life experience? What can emulate, in these studies, the great fame, material wealth, and power that were often the rewards of Renaissance and present-day competitions? Is the recompense of a few dollars and the praises of the experimental group, or of the E himself, equivalent to the great bounties of life, the acclamation of an elite or the multitudes, and the ramifications of fame that were the incitements of great Renaissance (and modern) competitive enterprises? What can induce, in an experiment, the exercise of all the group's capacities in deadly serious ventures or in the authentic actualization of its members' artistic, imaginative, and devious abilities in a manner comparable to that exhibited during the Renaissance. The very emergence of these qualities requires not only authentic motivation and freedom for action or expression but the available realistic opportunities that only a real life situation can provide.

Beyond that, the repertory, ingenuity, and freedom for the execution of acts of artifice and ruthlessness are limited by (1) the relatively narrow range of behavior permitted in small-group studies (so narrowly channeled because of the need to rigorously "test" limited scientific hypotheses and to operationalize certain measures of behavior—as required by the model of positivistic science prevailing in many of these studies), (2) the oblique impressions conveyed by the E and by the experimental environment or by directions that only certain forms of behavior will be acceptable or acknowledged, and (3) the S's awareness of the "experiment" as a conventional and respectable "stage" or occasion where he is on exhibit before the "established" adult world.

RECTIFICATION

It must be clear that to capture the Renaissance emphasis on group competition and zealous group commitment would require extraordinary experimental concoctions. Because this is not likely, perhaps certain specific, if remote, approximations may be made to these conditions either in the laboratory or in some instances of contemporary life. To these prospects we will turn later.

The primary phenomenon for study, however, would be the nature of the Renaissance groups themselves or those group conditions, in history, that roughly approximate them. It would not be beyond possibility to survey the nature of group zeal and commitment, the mechanisms of intergroup rivalry, and the character of the intragroup competition for fame and leadership that existed in Florence, Rome, Siena, and other Italian Renaissance cities—as well as in other historical communities of the West. All such historical data would be tabulated and analyzed as would the results of any other survey or compendium. Issues such as the following might be studied: the relation between the intensity of intergroup and intragroup competition; the relation between intensity of commitment to a group and, when expedient, participation in ruthless and devious practices; the relation between the amount of affluence, power, or fame that can be obtained by successful intergroup competition and the nature and degree of the duplicity or ruthlessness that is practiced to this end. Among historical groups and issues that might be studied in reference to these problems would be competitive business groups at the onset of the Industrial Revolution and the various competing religious sects, literary groups, schools of music, and intellectual movements of nineteenth-century Europe. In contemporary society, groups that approximate the Renaissance type that might be studied include the following: athletic teams, some academic departments of universities, business enterprises skilled in the uses of deception and viciousness, the behavior of adversary national states, and the rivalries between certain elites, i.e., intellectual, academic, or artistic. Included in the latter would be the competition between scientific centers for research grants and recognition (including those "groups" concerned with research on group competition), conflicting schools of scientific or scholarly thought, rival artistic movements, and academic or ideological factions.

In respect to naturalistic studies the following proposals may be useful: in contemporary naturalistic groups of Renaissance-like dimensions it is not impossible that special sorts of high acclaim or reward can be "authentically" introduced into an ongoing intragroup process or into intergroup rivalry situations and their effects on competitive behavior observed in both instances. Similar assessments can also be made when these rewards and plaudits are genuinely bestowed on groups in the above situations in the natural course of their activities. The latter might be an intergroup literary competition or the efforts of rival groups to obtain funds for a project, to win a prize for an athletic victory, or to achieve academic superiority. When such contests do not occur in the normal course of events, it may be possible to induce or escalate rivalry between groups by providing special prizes of high acclaim for the victor. Such opportunities may occur in college group competitions, in artistic or dramatic group competitions, in athletic events, etc. Through the introduction of a very large reward (a new trophy, large sums of money, acclaim by prominent persons), through the deliberate instigation of rivalry (rumors of enmity, incitement of bad feeling, and invidious comparisons), through permitting wide latitude for excellence, guile, and ruthlessness of group behavior, a very crude approximation to some of the conditions determining Renaissance group process may be reached.

In regard to experimental group studies, the difficulties are enormous, as previously indicated. One remote remedy would be to have natural groups (Renaissance-like, if possible) taken out of their normal, everyday context and gradually be acclimated to a Renaissance laboratory environment and orientation. Perhaps small groups, in time, nurtured in Renaissance settings and exposed to much Renaissance-type training, experience, and practice could approach, if remotely, the spirit of some Renaissance-like groups. Try as one can, however, the result would probably be a simulated one. If, of course, the laboratory can be made into a Renaissance-infused real life situation with its own authentic purposes and commitments, its own cohesiveness and significant rewards, and its own flow of serious, meaningful-for-the future experiences (all of the foregoing permeated with a Renaissance-like spirit though employing appropriate contemporary cultural forms and content as the media for achieving these conditions), then it could be a viable locus for the study of these Renaissance-type group experiences. But to have this happen means the transposition to the laboratory of the flow of fully absorbing and fully compelling organic life experience. Is this possible? Only by sensitively and comprehensively carrying these proposals through will we be able to tell.

If one is determined to carry on laboratory studies of this nature, they should be done in Renaissance-type milieux. After long periods of ac-climitization to Renaissance-type group behavior (through role-playing, experience in inter- and intragroup competition, historical readings, etc.) the experimental groups would be given various kinds of rewards and acclaim—substantial amounts of money, vast praise by the laboratory personnel and fellow group members, recognition in the "laboratory newspaper," and admiration by others—provided they were successful in achieving a competitive success over similar laboratory groups in the arts, construction work, problem-solving activity, maneuvering for power, and other relevant contests. Intensity of competition could be variously instigated by the amount of the reward or acclaim conferred, and by the degree of rivalry induced between one group and another through in-citing desires for revenge, victory, achievement, etc. The groups would be given the widest latitude in the techniques and tactics they could employ to achieve these ends. Thus, if it were to suit their purposes, they might subvert rectitude and employ subterfuge and dissimulation. Such behavior could be executed under the cloak of propriety and probity. CIA-type, conspiratorial-like, and "bugging" operations might also be used. In other situations there would be the opportunity to make use of more ruthless and vicious practices. Thus, between groups in competition for an important goal, false rumors might be spread, fifth-column tactics used, leaders "bought off," harassment of adversaries arranged by "minorities and saboteurs" in the group, and false "laboratory news-paper" reports circulated. Vicious personal attacks could be arranged against an antagonist, confidential and personal information used for purposes of blackmail, crookedness employed in competitive situations, members "detained" or "diverted" from coming to important meetings, and materials for group projects sabotaged or stolen.

Through proper orientation of the group, by establishing the necessary competitive atmosphere, through appropriate use of rewards and praise, by cultivating a zeal for group commitment in members as well as by inciting their passion for victory, and by practice in the behavioral tech-niques and machinations required for success in competition, intriguing group processes could be generated. Though simulated and circum-scribed, it is nevertheless not impossible that some suggestive informa-tion may be obtained from these studies on competitive group behavior. Comparable orientation and experiences could be developed for the instigation and investigation of group activities having to do with excel-lence, expressiveness, etc. in connection with intergroup competition.

The Renaissance Ego

1. The Renaissance ego was highly individualistic, immoral, and self-confident and, in addition, was characterized by strong, pleasure-loving, aesthetic, sensual, and self-indulgent tendencies. It was rich and complex in its diversity of talents, feelings, and executive capacities. It was also preoccupied with self-expression and self-enhancement, concerned with titillation of the mind and senses as conducive to intellectual and emotional pleasure and capable of violence though not encumbered with guilt about it.

One expression of such an ego structure was the great flood of energy poured into all types of actions and expressions of feeling. Large segments of such feeling were directed to art, especially the visual arts: architecture, sculpture, painting, and design. The sustained emphasis on action, expression, and energy had important implications for the strength, independence, confidence, tonus, and vitality of the ego. Daring, dash, enterprise, adventurousness, exhilaration, risk-taking, the literal gulping up and reveling in life, and the vital pursuit of whatever pleasure, challenge, and excitement it could yield were among the fundamental qualities of this highly expansive, energetic, and richly invigorated ego.

2. There was a minimum of repression in that impulses, energy, fantasies, and ideas, though being continually generated, were continually discharged and directed into some form of executive or expressive action. As a result, there were considerable consequences for the prevention of neurosis, for the development of an active, vigorous society, for minimal arousal of autistic and similar "unrealistic" mechanisms, for the blooming of personal happiness and confidence, and for a spontaneous and richer life. Other consequences were evidenced in a high degree of violence, diminished consideration of others, low fear and anxiety for the future, and minimal personal conformity and subordination of oneself to others. Consequently there was more candor and less hypocritical "niceness" in general. There was more conviction, directness, vigor, and unambivalent aggression in the expression of opinion and action among men as well as more unimpaired loyalty and affection toward them; this in contrast to a tepid, conforming loyalty and expedient conviction that were neither deeply nor genuinely felt.

3. There was much immediate impulse gratification by word and action in the Renaissance ego. Characteristically, beauty was unashamedly and immediately sought after and experienced, and appreciation of it was

spontaneously and lavishly expressed. Sex impulses were acted on vigorously and dramatically as well as being spontaneously expressed in ebullient, rapturous, or earthy speech. Except for reasons of tactically deliberate deviousness, personal convictions were not mitigated or discouraged in expression and whenever possible were strongly stated. There were other Italian cities to which men could go if they did not find life congenial in the one where they resided. Similarly, verbal and physical anger and resentment were immediately expressed except, again, for tactical or strategic reasons. Personal murder and physical attack were common during the Renaissance and such violence was committed as much for violation of personal honor, vanity, and self-interest as for reasons of state, factional struggle, or on behalf of one's local neighborhood. Inevitably, this "license" and lack of repression ensured more vigor, confidence, readily available resources of energy, and richness of personality.

Pleasure in sensory experience was also expected and sought after; thus touching was a great delight and much time was spent in handling fabrics, furniture, or clothes and in touching people or objects. Similarly, mouthing and composing the beauty of words and phrases was a source of enormous kinesthetic, vocal, auditory, and aesthetic delight. All sorts of visual and auditory sensations, natural or artificial, were delighted in. Eating and drinking were pursued with great zest as were the multitude of sensory and emotional pleasures that came from social contact and good talk. It goes without saying that sexual pleasure was a primary goal, pursued constantly and without inhibition or compunction. All these pleasures were regularly indulged in, giving delight, adding energy, innervating courses of action that may have suffered setbacks, and providing the personal fulfillments that prevented any overcommitment to work from reducing zest, vitality, and robust interest in the enterprise of life. In addition, such activistic gratifications led to a sense of expansive well-being and an ardent eagerness for adventure and exploration.

4. Because of all this, there was less psychic pressure toward subordination and conformity to others. There was more ego strength, more faith in life, and more confidence for obtaining its pleasures and gratifications. Thus, there was less necessity to compensate for deficiencies of self-actualization by compulsive seeking after love and popularity, by "niceness," by "not rocking the boat," and by similar devices designed to mitigate personal frustration and anxiety.

5. For Renaissance man, the love of the arts provided much sensory pleasure as well as a diversionary release for other unfulfilled feelings. It

provided a happy balance to the essential and serious enterprises of life, excited the imagination to new visions, experiences, and ideas, and aroused new depths and dimensions of emotion and sensitivity. The realm of art could make a man happy and fulfilled, though he might have neither power nor money. It was a way of life and needed no other justification or practical reason for its indulgence.

6. Thus the Renaissance ego was marked by an individualism that was based on courage, *élan*, independence, and artistic or intellectual expression. As indicated, the inevitable correlate of this was less dependence on the group and on social approval. However much personal satisfaction or material reward such compliance might bring, it would often be turned aside if it meant the abdication of personal goals, freedom of self-expression, or self-determined use of talents. More vital was the consideration that denial of the prospect of one's self-fulfillment or personal happiness would have been an injury of such seriousness that even the rewards that compliance might bring could not compensate for it. Moreover, it was the Renaissance view that acclaim and material reward would be forthcoming to those who fully developed their individuality and talent and exercised it with freedom and lavishness. And even if such rewards did not materialize, the happy use of one's energies and faculties and the personal delights and stimulations that one obtained by following his own conceptions or fulfilling his own talents had sufficiently great power to prevent him from easily relinquishing his particular identity or artistic uniqueness.

7. The fact that these individualistic and artistic values were sustained in the Renaissance ego is attributable, in no small measure, to a dedicated, self-conscious elite of nobility and taste that governed the great Italian cities during this period. This elite maintained their high values of discriminating taste and cultivated intelligence through the standards they set for members of their own class, through the education of their young, and through recruitment or support of others who exemplified exceptional intellectual, artistic, or cultural talent. There was no inclination to popularize or produce for mass taste and, hence, no need to sustain mediocrity in artistic or intellectual areas. Further, the congruence of the artist's or intellectual's values with those of the governing elite brought the former a sense of identity with society and thus enhanced their pride in unadulterated artistic and intellectual expression rather than leading to the debasement of their work for the purpose of quick sales on the mass marketplace. Such orientations further strengthened the ego's sense of well-being, pride, zest, and self-fulfillment.

From this elite orientation came an aristocratic contempt of poorer tastes, a self-appointed superiority, and the conviction that there was no need to make oneself hypocritically agreeable to vulgar groundlings in order to win favor. Though shallow humility, sycophancy, and bland niceness were all selectively practiced for purposes of expediency during the Renaissance, they never became preeminent behavior patterns. Naturally there was some degree of adjustment to the Renaissance patron, but the arrogance and pride to withstand strong pressures from "above" or "below" and to have confidence in one's self-fulfilling, individualistic mission were salient components of the Renaissance ego.

IMPLICATIONS FOR RESEARCH

1. Individuals with Renaissance-like egos, as previously defined, should be studied with regard to confidence, independence, courageous sustaining of their convictions, forthrightness, unwillingness to compromise the integrity or expression of their talent, openness to new ideas or experiences, adventurousness, zest, capacity for sensory delight, and spontaneity. Contemporary Renaissance-like types might be found among certain poets, artists, humanistic historians or avant-garde writers, among emancipated and uninhibited literary or artistic members of college communities, and among those who attract others to themselves by reasons of the unconventionality of their ideas, expressiveness, richness and versatility of their talent, and rich spontaneity. Other Renaissance types may be found among beatnik or hippie poets, men with original and unorthodox ideas who have not yet communicated them, among not yet fully realized artists who are on the way up, among musicians of various kinds, among certain dissenters, and among art groups such as the former Chicago School. Some prospective American subjects of this type also may be found living as expatriates in various European cultural centers, in foreign art colonies, or in such unspoiled areas of the world as Crete, Rhodes, Elba, and Minorca. Other persons who have been oriented and trained in Renaissance-like ego functions and attitudes, as previously described, might also serve as prospective Ss in these studies.

2. Because an important factor in sustaining the viability of the self-actualizing Renaissance man was the support of his patron, studies should be carried out on historical and contemporary persons and in experimentally or naturalistically devised situations on the effects of patron support and its withdrawal on Renaissance-type ego qualities. Comparative historical studies should be made of both Renaissance and non-Renaissance artists and scientists with and without patrons (Donne,

Chopin, Michaelangelo, Swift, Rembrandt, Raphael, Pasteur, Copernicus, etc.) and of Renaissance artists or scientists who suffered the loss of patron support (Galileo, Dante, Raleigh, Michaelangelo, etc.) in relation to their possession of Renaissance ego traits. Studies should be made of those contemporary Renaissance-like artists, scientists, or scholars who, after being abandoned by their patrons, have been able to "go it" or not "go it" alone in contrast to others who have never had such patronage and have struggled by themselves. Those of the latter type have once been and might still be found in New York's Greenwich or East Village, in San Francisco's North Beach, and in small coteries and islands of artists in other large cities or in such scenic retreats as Big Sur, certain regions of Cape Cod, and some mountainous or wooded areas in New England and the West.

3. Another useful research direction would be to study such Renaissance-type persons with regard to the influence that fame, fortune, and status may have on the tendency for them to become more conventional, lose *élan*, reduce individuality or adventurousness, and compromise freedom and authenticity of expression. These processes may be naturalistically studied but also may be observed in the course of deliberate study designs in which money, rewards, and praise would be conferred on the S, access to esteemed, delightful, or powerful persons would be secured for him, invitations to splendid dinners, good restaurants, chic parties, and exclusive clubs would be tendered to him, and attractive women (or men) would make evident their interest in him (or her). All this would be done to impair the standards of excellence, crush the individualism, and undermine the expressiveness, freedom, or adventurousness of the S's Renaissance-type ego orientation.

In studies of this type, material and status rewards or praise can be discreetly introduced into various natural situations and their effects noted on specified ego characteristics. It is also possible to conceive of an experimentally contrived milieu that approximates the atmosphere of an authentic Renaissance-like environment. All the previously described methods for achieving this milieu should be employed. When this environment—be it in a laboratory, a home, or some other setting—is so natural and congenial for the subjects that, hopefully, a symbiotic interweaving occurs between it and them, a favorable time would have arrived for introducing the various "experimental conditions" described above.

The effects of these "conditions" would be determined by observation of the S's natural behavior, by situational tests, by choices he would have to make involving Renaissance or non-Renaissance-like behaviors and attitudes available to him, by his responses to various social or aesthetic stimuli, and by the quality of his expressiveness and spontaneity. In addition to those already described, other tests designed to evaluate the S's ego reactions in these studies would include opportunities for engaging in uninhibited fantasy, fun, dancing, and in bold or zany displays of imagination; opportunities for initiating and following through on the novel, complex, and ingenious in a number of areas rather than on the sure, the obvious, and the conventional; chances for selecting the more complex, challenging, and potentially significant scheme, adventure, or strategy rather than the easier, more orthodox, or more efficient one; opportunities for preferring situations and persons with *élan,* warmth, and intensity rather than those of stability, coldness, and predictability; opportunities for choosing solutions to problems that involve the most imaginative and unorthodox conceptions in contrast to those of an ordered, programmed or pedestrian kind; opportunities for preferring richness, inspiration, novelty, and fluidity of feelings in the choice of a work of art or literature to a solid, conventional, and uncomplicated work; opportunities for preferring risk to security in enterprise and adventure, the risk involving the prospect of despair or self-fulfillment, defeat or delight, disaster or fame, fascination or dullness, and fortune or loss. Such risk vs. security options would be presented as hazardous, bold, and novel decisions and actions vs. safe, compliant, and conventional ones in the areas of art, selection of clothes, uninhibited behavior, offbeat development of a business or intellectual idea, rebellion against authority, expressive freedom, etc.

The S should also be confronted with a choice between pleasurable or ego-delighting activities that are not rewarded or approved and conventional activities or work that are given praise and remuneration. On the one hand, choices would be made of such ego exhilarations as indulging one's artistic fancies, going to a marvelous party, traveling to unusual places, indulging in uninhibited freedom of expression, or otherwise being exclusively concerned with what fulfills and gives one pleasure; none of these would bring rewards, compensation, praise, or social acceptance. The alternatives would consist of engaging in one of the following: conventional work that is well paid; dull parties with important people; prudent, stuffy behavior which, however, is rewarded by social acceptability; respectable joke-making with no genuine hilarity or delight but which brings social acknowledgment; a status project or activity involving important people but with no personal fulfillment or adventure; elaborate recreations with wealthy companions in opulent surroundings but with no expressive freedom or personal delight. The

S would have to choose in each "test" one of two alternatives (one from each of the foregoing optional groups of activities) that would be presented to him and in which he would, afterwards, be required to participate. Comparison of these choices would be made between those possessing and not possessing Renaissance-like egos. These alternatives would also be presented when the S would be in different social or psychological states: deprivation, affluence, ego strength or weakness, happiness or depression, supported by friends or in isolation, and exhilarated or bored.

4. Studies should also be carried out on persons with Renaissance and non-Renaissance-like egos in their own natural groups and settings, e.g., homes, hangouts, clubs, schools, or places of work. In these natural situations, how do such egos react to threats, frustrations, rewards, praise, conventionality, novelty, openness and adventurousness of thought, and spontaneity of behavior and expression? Discreet and careful observations would be made of these reactions in such a way as not to influence the ongoing natural behavior being studied. In addition, observations should be made of the S's tendency to notice or enjoy beauty during his ongoing, routine activity, to engage in spontaneous fun and high-spirited humor whenever possible, and to either appreciate or practice artistry of speech and language. If it is possible for the observer or a confederate to quite naturally introduce into this flow of behavioral interaction ploys, stimuli, and other devices—such as had not spontaneously appeared until then—that would further prove capable of gauging S's Renaissance-like ego capacity, this should be done provided it can be managed as an authentic, normal, and continuous part of the ongoing interaction.

5. The general nature and prevalence of zest, exhilaration, and exuberance should also be assessed. Constant indulgence in these feelings and experiences at the expense of material reward or the acquisition of high status was not incompatible with the spirit of the Renaissance ego. They represented an expression of its capacity for joy and for rich, bountiful response to sensory, aesthetic, and other humanistic stimuli. The type and degree of these reactions to different classes of such "humanistic" stimuli should be determined (in natural or experimental situations) and then compared with responses to stimuli of a "nonhumanistic" variety. In addition, responses of persons with Renaissance-like and non-Renaissance-like egos should be compared. A determination should also be made as to whether the Ss exhibit more *élan*, exhilaration, and vitality in Renaissance-like settings and atmospheres (rooms and buildings) than in those of a non-Renaissance type. Finally, it would be useful to survey the frequency with which Renaissance-type ego attitudes and behaviors

occur naturally in various social classes, groups, occupations, or educational backgrounds and in various social situations and relationships such as work, home, casual contacts, crisis situations, relationships of close friends, recreational situations, vacations, and social conversations.

6. A salient feature of the Renaissance ego was its generous superintending of impulse activity, sensory indulgence, and mood transition—all of which redounded to increased ego vitality and strength. Such indulgent custody made not only for the diminution of tension, restraint, and repression but also for greater self-confidence and the capacity to adopt resilient, bold, and adventurous means to attain one's ends. Accompanying these dynamics was the reduction of anxiety related to aggression, sexuality, and comparable drives, the liberation of increased psychic energy for extended aesthetic interest and commitment, and the enhancement of the feeling of well-being, *élan*, and zest.

These and allied phenomena can be studied by comparing the behavioral responses of Renaissance with non-Renaissance type egos to various frustrations, censures, or defeats and their respective capacities to recover from them through participation in self-actualizing tasks and instinctually satisfying pleasurable activities. Other behavioral indices of this form of ego stewardship would include the capacity to effectively and resiliently respond to personal opposition or attack; the ability to employ any required technique to achieve one's goals, including those of ruthlessness, deviousness, deceit, etc.; and the capacity to express hostility or exuberance when moved to or when expedient.

It is presumed here that as impulse indulgence, personal pleasure, and self-fulfillment diminish so will the viability and degree of the aforementioned ego qualities. Studies can be devised in which the S is deprived of these ego gratifications through a variety of methods: denial of pleasurable experience, deprivation of free expression, diminution of delightful interpersonal interactions, and reduction or elimination of other self-actualizing experiences or sensual and aesthetic stimulations. These deprivations should be effectuated in as authentic and natural a way as possible. It is important that the S does not feel that they are contrived and artificial and that they do, in fact, have some genuine meaning for his ongoing activities or bear on some vital issue or interest in his own life. They should be executed in naturalistic situations or ongoing projects, fitting into his daily activities as realistically and normally as possible. For all this, comparisons should be made of the previously enumerated behavioral variables between persons with Renaissance and non-Renaissance-like egos both in and out of Renaissance-like settings.

If it is predicated that deprivation of these impulse indulgences and other pleasures has a specified debilitating effect on the ego, then enhancement of them should have a facilitating and fortifying effect on it. Hence, studies should be carried out in which actualization and satisfaction of these same impulses and pleasures are brought to an optimal level. Techniques for achieving this goal would include a vast array of aesthetic and sensory delights including the visual, auditory, tactual, and kinesthetic (psychedelic scenes and Esalen-type activities should also be utilized); exuberant conversation and enriched and stimulating interpersonal relations; liberation and indulgence of numerous feelings; authentic and candid expression of affection, intimacy, robustness, and hostility; spontaneity in bodily movement, dance, muscular activity, and sexual contact. Such practices could be encouraged through orientation and induction procedures such as those previously described. The effect of these pleasures and indulgences on the aforementioned behavioral qualities should then be determined.

Each one of the designated impulse or sensory modalities can be denied or enhanced independently of the others and the effects ascertained on the previously specified ego qualities. What would be the effects, e.g., when indulgence is restricted to one pleasure alone—say eating marvelous food, drinking wonderful wine, having an exhilarating conversation, or experiencing an inspiring work of art—as opposed to having several such delightful experiences preparatory to the time the "test" events or stimuli are introduced. Thus, the gradation in the number, the variety, and the duration of such pleasures or denials would be important to explore.

It is also not impossible that in certain naturalistic situations there will be found to be an authentic embodiment of many of these conditions of deprivation or fulfillment together with corresponding effects on their related ego functions. Studies of such situations would represent authentic testing points of the psychological parameters and issues previously discussed. In these naturalistic situations lies a vast body of evidence which can, with judicious analysis, be distilled in the form of findings bearing on the foregoing research issues. Indeed, both a historical and contemporary statistical survey can be carried out on all pertinent data from biographies, histories, chronicles of the times, autobiographies, letters, newspaper accounts, sociological studies, participant observations, etc. that are available about such situations.

7. Aside from the broad grouping of subjects in these studies as Renaissance and non-Renaissance types, it would be useful to employ specific subdivisions or variants of these types in order to determine more

precisely how the foregoing proposed Renaissance-like conditions would affect particular personality traits, behaviors, and attitudes. Included among the Renaissance-like subtypes would be very independent individuals who no longer have the need to obtain love, impress others, or win recognition; adventurous, individualistic, and courageous persons of all types including buccaneering, free-swinging entrepreneurs with great originating capacity and vision—the pioneers, discoverers, and tycoons of another age who forged new frontiers in commerce, science, art, or geographical exploration and who, despite great obstacles, carried through their convictions and purposes. These would include such persons as Pasteur, Lister, Freud, Gauguin, Rembrandt, Beethoven, Columbus, Balboa, James Hill, and J. P. Morgan, Sr. Other subgroups would include (1) those who have rebelled against strict controls or tenacious conformity and now want to find personal fulfillment, freedom, or pleasure; (2) free-lance writers, journalists, lecturers, or theater people; and (3) still other types of "liberated" or emancipated individuals in the arts, sciences, professions, and auxiliary fields.

Some of these ego subgroups may resist the influence of material reward and praise in changing their behavior and attitudes, but a given subgroup may be unable to resist the adverse effects of the denial of certain sensory pleasures (e.g., music or visual beauty) while another will experience detrimental effects as a result of denial of the delights of good conversation. Because each such subgroup of subjects has a different focus of ego strength, each should have experiments specifically designed to assess its unique Renaissance-like ego resources as well as the specific pleasures or self-fulfillments necessary to foster them.

8. In naturalistic or experimental stress and frustration studies, various types of Renaissance-like "tension releasers," sensory delights, and other gratifications should be investigated for their effectiveness in sustaining the S's zest and revitalizing his resourcefulness, adventurousness, and inventiveness. Art objects, liquor, good food, vigorous exercises, persons or things on which resentment and ridicule can be discharged, materials available for artistic activity (paints, brushes, music paper, musical instruments, pencils, etc.), poetry readings, and opportunities for exhilarating conversations should be provided, singly or collectively, in these research situations when they are not discordant with the design, procedure, or atmospheric setting of the specific experiment. Similarly, various "tension releasers" and pleasures of a non-Renaissance type should be available for the utilization of those Ss who may want to take advantage of them. Examples of these would be: make-work activities,

watching television, listening to the radio, ritualistic party games, conventional conversations, and similar formal or semiformal activities.

The procedure for appraising these variables in experimental or laboratory situations would be roughly as follows: after the Ss (those with and without Renaissance-like egos) have experienced frustrations and defeat in various discussions, tasks, and other enterprises, the Renaissance-like and non-Renaissance-like stimuli would be introduced. These may be presented for varying intervals of time in the experimental room and, for comparison, in another room immersed in the spirit and appointments of the Renaissance period. The effects of these enhancing interludes on the above ego responses and experiences of the S would then be assessed.

Such "releasers" and pleasures would be studied with regard to the optimal revitalizing effect they would have on the S after he had experienced specific types of frustration, denials, and defeats. Thus, in the case of a Renaissance-like ego one kind of pleasure or "releaser" might be most effective for one kind of frustration while quite another pleasure or "releaser" would be most reinvigorating for another kind of frustration. Quite a different order might hold, however, for non-Renaissance-like egos. Also, friends and acquaintances of the S could be strategically placed in these research situations to serve as objects of release or as sources of delight and pleasure, depending on their particular personalities and the nature of their relationships to him. Among the roles they could play in these situations would be that of one who would vigorously engage the S in an exhilarating discussion of vital interest, one who would be sensual and seductive, one who would be spontaneous and fully tolerant of all the S's impulse expressions, one who would be aesthetic in every perception and attitude, and one who would be a receptive target for the S's resentments.

REFERENCES

1. Kelman, Herbert C. "Human Use of Human Subjects: The Problem of Deception in Social Psychological Experiments," Psychological Bulletin, LXVII (1967), pp. 1–11.
2. Rosenthal, Robert. Experimental Effects in Behavioral Research. New York: Appleton-Century-Crofts, 1966.
3. Cartwright, D., and Zander, A., eds. Group Dynamics, 2d ed. New York: Harper & Row, 1960.

4. Hare, Alexander P. *Handbook of Small Group Research*. New York: Free Press of Glencoe, 1962.
5. Moholy-Nagy, Lazlo. *The New Vision*, 3d rev. ed. New York: Wittenborn, 1946.
6. Moholy-Nagy, Lazlo. *Vision in Motion*. Chicago: Theobald, 1947.

GENERAL REFERENCES

Barnes, Harry Elmer, with David, Henry. *The History of Western Civilization*. New York: Harcourt, Brace, 1935.

Boccacio, Giovanni. *Decameron*. New York: Modern Library, 1930.

Boring, E. G. *A History of Experimental Psychology*, rev. ed. New York: Appleton-Century, 1950.

Burckhardt, Jacob. *The Civilization of the Renaissance in Italy*, tr. by S. G. C. Middlemore, 2d ed. New York: Oxford University Press, 1945.

Castiglione, Baldesar. *The Book of the Courtier*. Garden City, N.Y.: Doubleday, 1959.

Cellini, Benvenuto. *The Autobiography of Benvenuto Cellini*. Garden City, N.Y.: Garden City, 1927.

Cheyney, E. P. *The Dawn of a New Era, 1250–1436*. New York: Harper, 1936.

Descartes. *Discourse on Method* (1857), pt. 2, 3d ed. Strasbourg: Heitz, 1905.

Fahie, John Joseph. *Galileo: His Life and Work*. London: Murray, 1903.

Faure, Elie. *History of Art*. New York: Harper & Row, 1921–1930.

Ferguson, Wallace. *The Renaissance*. New York: Holt, Rinehart & Winston, 1969.

Gardner, Helen. *Art Through the Ages*. New York: Harcourt, Brace, 1926.

Gellespie, James Edward. *A History of Geographical Discovery*. New York: Holt, 1933.

Goodman, Paul. *Growing Up Absurd*. New York: Random House, 1960.

Hayes, C. J. H. *Political and Cultural History of Europe*. New York: Macmillan, 1932–1936.

Heaton, Herbert. *Economic History of Europe*. New York: Harper, 1936.

Hobbes, Thomas. *The Leviathan*. New York: Dutton, 1914.

Hobson, James A. *Evolution of Modern Capitalism*. New York: Macmillan, 1954.

Hulme, Edward Maslin. *The Renaissance and Reformation*, rev. ed. New York: Century, 1915.

Krutch, Joseph. *Human Nature and the Human Condition*. New York: Random House, 1959.

Leonardo. *Frammenti Letteri e Filosofic*, tr. by Edmondo Solmi. Firenze: Barbera, 1913.

Leonardo da Vinci. *Notebooks*, tr. by Edward MacCurdy. New York: Scribner's, 1908.

Lucas, H. S. *The Renaissance and the Reformation*, 2d ed. New York: Harper & Row, 1960.

McCurdy, Edward. *The Mind of Leonardo da Vinci*. New York: Dodd, Mead, 1928.

Machiavelli, W. *The Prince*. New York: Mentor Books, 1952.

Marcuse, Herbert. *One Dimensional Man*. Boston: Beacon Press, 1964.

Mather, Frank Jewett. *A History of Italian Painting*. New York: Holt, 1923.

Mumford, Lewis. *The Condition of Man*. New York: Harcourt, Brace, 1944.

Murphy, Gardner. *Historical Introduction to Modern Psychology*, rev. ed. New York: Harcourt, Brace, 1949.

Orwell, George. *Nineteen Eighty-Four*. New York: Harcourt, 1949.

Randall, John Herman. *The Making of the Modern Mind*. Boston: Houghton Mifflin, 1940.

Robinson, James Harvey. *The Mind in the Making*. New York: Harper, 1921.

Roeder, Ralph. *Men of the Renaissance*. New York: Viking Press, 1933.

Russell, Bertrand. *A History of Western Philosophy*. New York: Simon & Schuster, 1945.

Smith, Preserved. *The Age of the Reformation*. New York: Holt, 1920.

Smith, Preserved. *A History of Modern Culture*. 1930. Reprint (2 vols). New York: Macmillan Company, Collier Books, 1962.

Stimson, Dorothy. *The Gradual Acceptance of the Copernican Theory of the Universe*. New York: Baker & Taylor, 1917.

Tawney, Richard Henry. *Religion and the Rise of Capitalism*. New York: Harcourt, Brace, 1926.

EPILOGUE

What, then, is the upshot of this exploration into the past, or more accurately, of the past as it lies latent in the present. It is that the images of man—of which three have been presented here—will profoundly influence the conception of the nature of man and of his related capacities and resources. In so doing, they will shape a particular view of what the salient characteristics of men are and, equally important, of what they are not.

Each image of man, including those discussed in this study, reflects the ethos, spirit, or aspirations of an age or of the vested values and orientation of an eminent class or group in it. Thus, in a sense, the images of man and the specific analytic and investigative orientations that flow from them are a reflection of the spirit of an historical period and of the qualities and capacities that eminently characterized it as well as of the features that it excluded or deemphasized. Thus, if the age is of an empirical or practical character, the image of man flowing from it will surely be marked by these features, and its conception of man's nature, stemming from this image, will have strong components of pragmatic and materialistic qualities. In addition, the theories, essays, clinical studies, experimental researches, and other forms of evidence flowing from this image will be substantially directed to such pragmatic and empirical emphases, not only in the explanations of behavior put forth and in the orientation of investigations carried out, but also in the particular capacities and resources of men that are the subject of study. Simultaneously, those qualities of men, together with related methods of investigation, that are not compatible with this conception of human nature will be deemphasized or ignored.

These images of man often serve the historical and ideological function of justifying the attained or aspired-to power of a class or elite group, may serve as a rationalization for an already established way of life, or may constitute a coordinate particularized system of behavior necessary for the operation of a given society and of the values it aspires to establish. In effect, the image of man may be a device to win power, an ideal for man to achieve, a glorified view of the men of an age for purposes of their self-enhancement and egotism, or a detailed picture of congruent psychological systems essential to implement a particular societal or ideological orientation.

In the large array of images of man, this study has considered three notable ones: images that have informed and directed the course of Western history, led to vast accretions of behavior and traits which have been among the most sterling acquisitions of modern man, and which, by virtue of their resemblance but yet dissimilarity to the contemporary image of man, deserve the greatest interest for the capacities and resources they have emphasized insofar as these have been depreciated or ignored in the image of man reflected by modern psychology. Thus, the images of man discussed in these pages—though among numerable others that might be described—have at least one thing in common beside their role in the evolution of modern man: their distinctly different orientation to human potentiality and capacity from that of the latter. And the nature of the dissimilarity they share is in their emphasis on a more humanistic perspective of man's capacities and on his uniquely human qualities and aspirations, however much these views may vary among themselves in detail. It is the aspiration for a particular integral human dimension and for a uniquely human excellence of mind, spirit, and temper that endows these images with a transcendant, spiritual, or richly tapestried quality in contrast with the animal-like or machine-like quality that marks the images of man in contemporary theory and research.

It is particularly pertinent that these images be revived today—in the ethos of a world that is moving ever more inexorably on a path of mechanization and dehumanization. Indeed, there are many signs that an effort is being made by contemporary man to break away from his cultural and psychological limitations, whether these breakthroughs take the form of the creation of youth cultures, communes, drug cultures, or in the generalized efforts of young people to find a new refreshing humanism. Thus, these past images of man are particularly useful to study now, not only because they are in resonance with the contemporary humanistic revival but also because they point to aspirations and models that have, at particular times in the past, possessed extraordinary richness and reached glittering heights of human splendor, bringing forth a heritage that has enriched the Western world thereafter, however much its living spirit and fire may be banked at the present time. In these past images we can see elements of the present humanistic renaissance, though more clearly, more purely, and with a confirmed certainty of their importance and viability. Perhaps their activation, now, authentically merging with the present, will present realistic and proven models and aspirations for the new humanism as well as guidelines for it to achieve the largest possible fulfillment of its potential.

What, briefly then, was the nature of these past "humanistic" images? They included the Greek qualities of intellectual excellence and speculative freedom, artistic purity and synthesis of feeling and idea, courageous independence, and deep-rooted integrity. The medieval image comprised symbolic cognitive orientation, inner spiritual and mystic perception, group altruism and benevolent collective love, and an ego oriented to benign feelings, tacit resignation, and compassion. The humanistic qualities of the Renaissance, which, in principle, were those most fully represented in the contemporary Western world, were those of robust extrovertive energy, earthy exhilaration, an empirical hearty intelligence, a realistic and concretely oriented perception, a vigorous and mundane delight in the material, instinctive aspects of human life, a keen and often ruthless competition between individuals and groups, and an ego that was vastly courageous, extroverted, exuberant, practical, self-aggrandizing, and toughly individualistic.

These images represent what may be called the humanistic dimensions of man's potential and may, as a class, be contrasted with the mechanistic, collective, materialistic, and instinct-ridden approaches that characterize the psychological orientations of the present day. There are other humanistic images embodying quite different dimensions of man's resources which have not been considered here and still others which may yet emerge in the future. Indeed, the entire spectra of the Eastern images of man, the Enlightenment, the romantic age, and the contemporary humanistic revival have not been touched on and promise still further varieties of nonmechanistic, spiritual, and other eminently unique human qualities. All these images could and will yet produce still different varieties of theories of behavior, conceptions of man's capacities, and research orientations than are now accepted. What has been done in these pages is to show how three of these humanistic images may be empirically studied in terms of specific psychological processes and the effect that such an investigation might have on enlarging vistas, concepts, and research orientations of contemporary psychological science.

Related to these considerations, particularly in such areas as cross-cultural psychological research and the bearing of one psychological orientation on another, is the concern that the research methods compatible with one image may be transferred without further qualification to a quite dissimilar one. Thus the mechanistic image of man, so popular in the recent past, often had its research procedures unwarrantedly transferred to varieties of behavior falling into more humanistic categories. Hence the irony of aesthetic or spiritual qualities being assessed by standardized paper and pencil test or by conventional physiological measures and the absurdity of speculative intelligence being evaluated by tests suited to practical problems. The lesson of this is that research methods and designs should flow from the image of man germane to the psychological processes or attributes studied and not from a previously established but alien image in association with its congruent methodology. Otherwise there is the danger of fitting previously unexplored human potentialities and capacities into old preconceived categories with no further resulting knowledge or understanding. What this means is that for each particular humanistic image or, indeed, for any image of man, the research procedures applied to the human attributes it embraces must authentically derive from its correlated image, though these procedures may violate the spirit or conventions of the then prevailing image and its related methodology, which at the time may appear to possess exclusive legitimacy. Thus research orientations, which, because of their deviation from established, prevailing approaches, can appear to be unscientific and capricious, may, in time, if carried out carefully, repeatedly, and with appropriate quantitative developments—but always as an authentic expression of the image of man in question—become fully accepted as standard scientific approaches, particularly as reliable funds of knowledge accumulate as a result of their application.

That these "images" of man are "thrown up" by distinct cultures, each placing certain of man's potentials in psychological prominence, has already been made clear. That each culture uses its mechanisms of thought and techniques of proof to justify or sustain the image of the man that is prevalent in its particular society has also been made evident. To achieve this legitimization, it uses the prevailing thought processes of the day and the accepted techniques of proof or advocacy of the times. In one culture this may be essays and logical argument, in another philosophical analysis, in a third clinical study, and in a fourth rigorous empirical investigation. Thus, the qualities comprising the Renaissance image, to be genuinely clarified and investigated, must, as a first approximation, be reached, understood, and possibly evaluated by the congruent cognitive processes associated with the Renaissance image. The same is true of the Greek, the medieval, and the contemporary images of man.

233

With the revival of humanism in contemporary life and, most recently, in psychology, the question is how these past images—hypothetically latent in modern man—can be made persuasively evident without exclusively drawing on the cognitive processes and verifying methods that distinctively marked the historical periods that spawned them. Is it possible to perform a transhistorical act—taking these images as starting points for a humanistic, though scientific, exploration into man's potentialities—by utilizing some of the methods indigenous to the historical period corresponding to these images but adding to or integrating them with whatever approaches appear to be fairly compatible with modern cognitive processes and procedures so that these past images can be shown to be more abundantly viable in contemporary experience as well as credible to contemporary scientific images of evidence and verification? At times, this may mean transforming present research designs to effectively deal with the verification of these past images and, in general, changing the orientation and methods of psychological proof, even if they were then to deviate from presently established scientific procedure. Such a prospectus would entail—as set forth in this book— the modification of current research orientations to fit the nature of these latent images by transforming experimental environments, changing the traditional role of the experimenter, and revising the nature of the stimulus material presented to the subject. When the body of past documenting methods is accumulated and integrated with contemporary ones and a wide variety of individuals and groups are studied by the resulting procedures, what may be revealed is that certain of these latent images are more salient than others in modern man, some exist minimally or not at all, and some may be more prevalent in certain groups than others. Beyond this, it may be found that present methods (even when derived from the past and adjusted to the present) are not yet good enough to appropriately assess these dormant potentials or that the art and sensitivity of authentically understanding the historic cognitive processes and methods that were once used to justify or document these images as well as of adapting them to present human and scientific conditions are in rare supply. It may also mean, however, that it is incorrect to fully or exactly apply these past images to modern man—that though some of their components may still be latent in him, their total pattern must be somewhat restructured, for they no longer exist in the exact symmetries of the past but have been modified with only certain aspects of their original historic form remaining. If so, this would require the development of still other research methods or the modification of those described in this book to uncover those components of historic images that still remain in modern man either in addition to or integrated with more contemporary behavioral systems.

What is the structure of these images? They consist of particular organizations of human resources and capacities, sometimes oriented mechanistically, sometimes humanistically, in some cases emphasizing spirituality, in others animal energies. They are analogous, in the case of individual human beings, to particular ego organizations of human potentiality and capacity that in one person would emphasize certain qualities and subordinate others and in another would radically change this order. In a more general way, these images may be compared to cultural hierarchies of the basic psychological resources of man which are oriented, in the case of each image, to a particular social value or ideology that marked a particular historical era. If one is driven to make dubious analogies with physical science, these potential resources may be very tenuously compared with the uniform constituents of matter, i.e., electrons, protons, neutrons, etc., which are organized in various hierarchies and patterns to produce, in each case, quite different types of physical behavior. These images—or organizations of cultural-psychological potential—emphasize as well certain ideological and valuative orientations and deemphasize still others. The reason may have something to do with the adjustment and survival of societies in the particular historical period considered but, in any case, the value-ideological system is carried through as a psychological way of life or as a patterning, of human potential that is embodied in the various images described in this study. Thus these images become internalized as counterpart psychological systems and have two complementary faces: the social, ideological, valuative side and the psychological, human behavioral side.

Just as these images require particular orientations of thought and methodology to be reached and appraised, so the psychologist who wishes to understand and investigate them must find the openness of mind and feeling to be responsive to the nature and spirit of the qualities that make them up. To reach this end, he must either himself possess some of these relevant qualities in a reasonably developed form, have the prospect of actualizing them if they are but rudimentary in him, or have the emotional expansiveness and cognitive resiliency to appreciate and respond to them in others. Surely, if he attempts to impose a narrowed and ethnocentric orientation, native to the habits of mind associated with another image of man, if he lacks the generosity of intelligence and feeling to try new directions, if he is confined either ideationally, educationally, or spiritually, or if he has but one paramount—and often rigid—scientific orientation, then he will be little persuaded by the prospect that these images may be present in contemporary man. For he will then fit all these different and "new" phenomena into the old preconceived, established "scientific" formulations and their related methodologies. The Renaissance, the Greek, and the medieval images will then become the contemporary image with a few adornments, decorative motifs, variations, and—if the psychologist is an imaginative one—autonomous dimensions.

It is true that such an imaginative scientist, working within this established framework, may forge a research procedure that touches on a genuine dimension of an alien, humanistic image, illuminates some of its facets, or shows its connection with diverse or dissimilar psychological processes. But for a psychologist to see that a significant research orientation for investigating the scope of an alien humanistic image must be predicated on a full vision and understanding of that image would mean that he would be prepared to dethrone—or at least have substantial questions about—the sovereignty of the prevailing image of man and its associated methodology. Only by grasping that the orthodox methodology that he characteristically practices in his daily research activities is a function of a particular value orientation and reflects an ideological position concerning the nature of man and society will he understand that, however sophisticated it may be, such a methodology cannot speak to the total configuration of a dissimilar image or to the hierarchy of qualities that make it up.

Thus, those who cry for a "real science" in the emerging humanistic psychology are often calling for a particular image of science which they wish to impose on a dissimilar image of man and, in so doing, may have the effect of distorting or destroying the nature of this image along with its constituent patterning of qualities. In this way the outlook for scientific advance will be dimmed, for it demands fresh eyes to see the rich prospects ahead and intellectual courage to admit that the nature of present knowledge and the methods for obtaining it should not constitute the ultimate guidelines of future psychological science. But to do this requires the intellectual vision and independence (Greek image traits) to give up the emotional and cognitive security (contemporary middle-class image traits) of the established orientations of science for the unsure but vastly challenging vision of a humanistic-scientific future of psychology and, indeed, of man himself. Whether the contemporary image of man, both in psychology and modern life, based largely on a middle-class value system can be dethroned by middle-class psychologists who have sustained it and who, in their own behavior, scientific orientation, and topics of research, embody so evidently the prevailing, established image is, itself, a most important ideological and research issue of psychology today.

How can the psychologist overcome these orthodoxies of imagination and thought and become more accessible to the different images of man which either have originated in the past or which involve patterns of behavior not yet clearly actualized?

To accomplish this, he must apply to himself those orientations and experiences that, it has been proposed in this study, he employs with his own subjects in order that their own latent images and resources become more viable. Initially, then, he must find these potential or actualized qualities in himself or respond to their germination as inchoate concepts, visions, or feelings before he can hope to genuinely understand their nature and dimension. If he is not endowed innately or by cultivation with these resources or does not have the openness of mind to be responsive to them when possessed by others, then sensitive introspective analysis, meditation, or deep and informed search may, in time, induce a sympathetic appreciation of their nature. He may also follow the path of reading about the history and literature of these past images, observation of the distinctive nature of their art and architecture, and study of the temper and form of their constituent features. He may travel to places that embody and invoke their spirit or that, in general, induce an appreciation of humanistic sentiments. By intensive contact with others who have abundant supplies of these "humanistic" characteristics and the power to make them personally significant to him, some comparable qualities or, at least, empathic responses to them may be fostered. In this way, constant absorption in "humanistic" experience, provided it occurs with an open-minded sensitivity and porous receptivity of feeling and thought, could facilitate the sympathetic understanding and possible evocation of these responses. Thus the searching out in oneself of these latent resources, i.e., their recognition, sensitivitization, and activation, is an essential step in the process of achieving genuine and deep awareness of the nature of these images and their related attributes. Such an opening and broadening of mind and feeling may possibly also be accomplished through the modern-day "liberating" procedures of sensitivity training, Esalen-type experiences, and participation in Zen Buddhism, inner meditation, or other mystical practices.

What is required, then, is to have a sort of cultural psychoanalysis—not one involving the reawakening of intimate childhood experience but one of acute awareness of contemporary cultural values and ideologies, of the prevailing personal and social characteristics of men and their society, of the historical ideas that are influential in present human experience, and, in general, of the texture of present-day consciousness that is both evident and that lies latent or repressed. In so doing, we will have performed the necessary historic-cultural analysis of those latent images and qualities that the present culture and its counterpart psychology have ignored, shunted aside, or repressed, whether unwittingly or because of incompatibility with the prevailing middle-class, mechanistic, organization-bound images of man.

This, then, is the proposed remedy for the current cultural ethnocentrism in psychological science. By recognizing, experiencing, and investigating dimensions of behavior not fully acknowledged or studied at present, such an approach would uncover resources of mind that were once viable but now, for ideological and methodological reasons, have lost prominence and scientific credibility. In this way, the exploration of the historic and latent images of man will become both a rediscovery of the humanistic past as it bears on his present psychological condition and a reacknowledgment of the rich and significant resources of mind and spirit that must be illuminated if psychological science is ever to achieve a fully proportioned and authentic picture of man's diverse nature.

INDEX

THE
IMAGES OF
MAN